The Dutchman's Suitcase

THE DUTCHMAN'S SUITCASE

A Young Man's Story of Forced Labour in Nazi Germany

~ Based on True Events ~

Brad & Elisabeth Seltzer

Cover Art by Sheila Rae Van Delft

Cover Design by Cass Van Delft

Published by Mokeham Publishing Inc.
Oakville, Ontario, Canada

ISBN 978-1-7390232-1-8

**To Abbey, Jill, Adam,
and our grandchildren**

because your Opa would want you to know.

And to Dad

for trusting us with his story.

Table of Contents

Prologue 9

1. Innocence 15
2. The Message 21
3. Ausländer 28
4. Change of Pace 37
5. Karl 43
6. #128 49
7. How It Is Now 57
8. The Cavalry Pants 67
9. Trust and Betrayal 75
10. Razzia 83
11. Foxholes 91
12. Consequences 100
13. Survival Skills 111
14. No Overtime Allowed 118
15. The Flying Dutchman 124
16. Resistance 133
17. No Choice 137
18. Hände Hoch 143
19. The Red Tie 149
20. Midnight Run 156
21. Too Much Death 164
22. The Retaliation 176
23. Letters 183
24. Worse than Hell 195
25. Demons at Play 207
26. Doing Without 214

27. A Stranger Waits 220
28. We Go Mobile 229
29. Deutschland Kaput 237
30. The Hunger Winter 246
31. On the Move 251
32. Vengeance 257
33. Interrogation 266
34. Fragile Trust 273
35. The BBQ 278
36. Stay in Touch 287

Epilogue 299

Acknowledgements 309

About the Authors 313

Appendices
Map of the Netherlands 316
Map of Germany 317
The Fürstenmoor Compound 318

Whether nations live in prosperity or starve to death interests me only in so far as we need them for slaves for our culture; otherwise, it is of no interest to me.

- Speech delivered to senior ranks of the SS in Poland
October 4, 1943
Heinrich Himmler

Prologue

Ontario, 1965

"What did you do in the war, Dad?"

Growing up, that was the question that I often asked my father. I wanted to know, but regardless of the many times I asked, he never wanted to talk about it. My father, Peter Manshande, was born in the Netherlands in 1923. I knew he was in Europe during the Second World War and did not move to Canada until the early 1950s. I knew he had a story to tell but he kept it to himself.

~

When I was a teenager, he and my mother had visitors from the Netherlands. It was not the first time that Dutch friends or relatives had come to stay with us. I had not met the man and his wife before, and this visit was one I would not forget. On a warm summer afternoon, I joined Mom and Dad at the backyard picnic table for an iced tea with their guests. I understood Dutch and I was thrilled to be listening to the four of them in animated conversation. I watched my Dad's face as he and his friend laughed together sharing stories. It was obvious that they were renewing a strong friendship from years ago. A low-flying airplane flew over the house and nobody paid it any attention. We lived close to the airport and small private planes frequently flew over our neighbourhood. But this plane was different and the mood at the table suddenly changed.

My mother and the other woman continued with their discussion, but the two men stopped. This was a bigger plane, and it was louder. Both men stood up and without saying a word, stepped away from the table walking in different directions. As the plane flew over the house and out of sight, my Dad and his friend returned to the table, looked at each other and shaking their heads at the same time, both said, *ja*. That was the only word they spoke, just *ja*.

In that instant, I knew they were reliving something they had shared in another place and another time. Nothing else was said as they sat down and continued their visit, but I knew something had just happened. That single word between them had spoken volumes, and I was curious to know why. It was never talked about but I always wondered if it had any connection to the war. In time, I forgot the man's name but it was an event that I would remember.

~

Years later, while standing in my father's garage during a visit, once again something intrigued me. I wasn't looking for it but suddenly it was there. Teetering on a step-ladder Dad was doing some cleaning and re-arranging. He moved some boards and an old window frame in the rafters and there it was.

"What's that old box?" I asked.

"It's not a box," he said, "it's a suitcase." He carefully removed it from the loft. I could see that it was an old, rectangular wooden box with a hinged lid and a steel handle. Gently, as if it would break, Dad used a cloth to wipe away the dust that had gathered on it. It had been abandoned for a long time. "It was my suitcase. I used it when they sent me to Germany during the war."

Carefully, he opened it. The box smelled stale and I could see that it was empty except for a few cobwebs.

"It's empty," I said.

"It is not empty," he responded, staring at it. "It is full of memories."

"I'm confused," I said. "You weren't a soldier, why did they send you to Germany?"

"When the Germans occupied Holland, most of their young men were in the army. The German economy was flourishing but they did not have enough men left at home to keep it going. They needed workers and many of us in Holland, who were between 18 and 40 years old got letters. The letter told us that we would be sent to Germany to work. The only ones excused were farmers, businessmen, or other essential workers - doctors and such."

"What if you refused?"

"You couldn't refuse. It was a small town and the German army had access to all the records in the local municipal office. They knew where we lived. If you tried hiding, they threatened your family and hunted you down. Many became Onderduikers."

"They became what?"

"Onderduikers - *divers*. They disappeared by hiding out in the marshes or under the floorboards in barns and houses. They were simply called divers and, like the Jews, they went into hiding to avoid deportation. Others joined the resistance and went underground. That was dangerous too. I was afraid to go but the safety of my family was more important than what I was afraid of. I remember the day that my letter came. That was the day that changed my life. I was 19 and working as a truck driver. When I got home from work that day, my mother was crying as she handed me the envelope. The instructions were very clear. I had to go to Alkmaar for a physical exam and then to the town hall in Wognum for a train ticket. I would be in Germany within a week."

"How long were you there?"

"Two and a half years, until the war ended."

"Doing what?" I asked.

"I was a mechanic. I repaired vehicles and worked in a scrap yard. I worked for the German army wherever they sent me."

"The army… did that make you a collaborator?"

"Hell no, collaborators willingly volunteered. I didn't want to go. I had to go. It was forced labour. We didn't even want to be there. There were other men there, forced labourers from all the occupied countries, who all had to work together."

He stopped talking. I could see that he was uncomfortable. "It was a horrible, scary time," he said. "I don't like to talk about it. When I came home from Germany, people asked me about what I did. When I told them, they didn't believe me, so I stopped talking about it. The memories have been locked away for years but I know that they happened. The suitcase stores them for me, that's why I keep it."

He gently closed the lid. The conversation was over.

"That old suitcase was with you all through the war. You brought it with you to Canada and now you keep it here in the garage. I've never seen that suitcase before but if the memories are that painful, maybe you should talk about them. Tell me what happened. I'd like to know."

"It's been forty years. It's not something that's easy to talk about. Why do you want to know?" he asked.

"So many people tell me that their fathers were in the war, but they don't know about their experiences. When people die, those memories are gone. The only way memories are kept alive is by talking about them. If you can't do that, maybe you could write them down?"

"I don't know. I'm not a writer, but I'll try," he said.

~

Several months went by and I was home alone when the doorbell rang. I found Dad standing alone on the porch with a small book in his hand.

"I'm trying my best but I can't do what you ask," he said. "I wrote some stories down but they are just random. I didn't know where to start."

He handed me his journal, and said, "I can't finish it. When I write I have to remember things exactly as they happened. When the memories return, so do the fears and the nightmares. I wake up in the middle of the night; I'm back there again and I'm scared. I can't do it."

I made us a pot of tea and he told me about Germany. He told me about being in Braunschweig. When he talked, I listened without interruption. "It's easier when I'm not alone," he said.

"Go back and tell me again about getting the letter." I said, "tell me what happened next. Tell me as much as you want; just start at the beginning. Who took you to the train station?"

"My father took me to the train station. It was a hard day for him. The weather didn't help, it was overcast, windy and rainy. As he shook my hand, he didn't say anything. We could hear the train in the distance and I knew we wouldn't have much time. He stood looking at me as if he was memorizing my face. He gave me a hug with a nod of reassurance and turned away. Without looking back, he walked slowly to his truck and I remember the impact that moment had on me. I was alone and scared stiff of what the future would bring."

~

And so, it began. It took over 25 years for Dad to share his experiences with me. He visited me often and we talked. Almost every time we were together, he told me something. Sometimes it was a lengthy story and other times it was just a quick memory. They were often painful and occasionally humorous, but he allowed me to record them all – and this is what he told me.

Elisabeth Seltzer
February 2023

Chapter 1
Innocence

Hoorn, North Holland, April 1943

The rain beat against my face as I turned up my collar against the cold April wind. Standing on the platform, even the wind and the rain reminded me that I was powerless and had to submit.

My wooden suitcase felt awkward, knocking against my knee as I walked, and its large steel handle - from a barn door - felt cold in my hand as I waited to board the train. The suitcase was the only thing I was taking with me. It was a simple, wooden rectangular box made by a neighbour: an undertaker. He usually made coffins.

Listening to the pounding rain on the tin roof, I felt my pulse race. Was it fear, or excitement? Maybe it was a bit of both. Had I made the right choice, or would it have been better to have gone into hiding like some of the others? I, like the many young men who were gathering at the station, did not think we had much choice. Ever since the Germans had occupied Holland, we no longer had control over our own lives. Soldiers had occupied our land, taken our food, our horses, our bicycles, and anything else useful. Most of all, they had taken away our dignity and our freedom. The life I had known was gone. At 19, I had become a prisoner, and as such, I would be given roles that I, and others like me, would never have anticipated. Young men and their families stood about crying while saying their goodbyes. The station platform was swarming with

German soldiers. Their uniformed presence alone was enough to keep control.

A few hours before, I had been home with my parents, brothers, sisters, and my girlfriend. Now I was being watched by armed soldiers, and I would soon be on my way to Germany. I wasn't alone. There were other young men, waiting like me; and like me, they all looked nervous and afraid.

The loud shrill of a powerful steam whistle warned me of the approaching train.

"Kommen Sie in der Linie," barked one of the soldiers. *Get in line.*

Though I didn't understand German, his voice and his actions made it clear that he expected immediate obedience. His uniform was different from the others. The shine of his boots, the insignia on his hat and his official demeanour left no confusion, he was in charge. We were told to take one step forward when our name was called. Reading from a paper, the officer started calling names and I watched as other boys stepped forward in a new line. Then, I heard my name. "Peter Manshande," said the officer, and I reluctantly joined the others.

As the train approached, the soldiers formed a line behind us and we were blocked in. There was no place else for us to go but to wait for the arriving train. The soldiers stood there with their rifles ready.

I had never been afraid of locomotives. I had seen them before but had never been so close to one. This one was frightful. Belching steam as it rolled past me like some black prehistoric monster, it slowed with a deafening rumble and came to a stop just past the station. Once again, the senior officer yelled an order and the soldiers immediately moved towards us, forcing us to climb aboard. I hesitated momentarily, and felt a hammering blow between my shoulder blades. It caused me to stumble slightly and as I recovered my balance, I looked back quickly enough to see a soldier standing behind me with a stern look on his face. He had used the butt of his rifle to coax me along. My shuffled movement was apparently not fast enough and it cost me my first injury in the war. The pain in my back was excruciating. I needed no more encouragement. I fell obediently into line and quickly followed the others as we climbed aboard the train. The first car was already full and I walked past other men who had been picked up from neighbouring towns. Everyone sat staring forward, wide eyed and fearful. Some seats were occupied by soldiers, monitoring our movements. I moved along into the second car and was relieved to see an empty window seat near the back and I quickly sat down before it was taken. I waited while the last of the men and the soldiers took their seats. Within minutes the train jolted and started to move. I watched out the window as the train gathered speed and the familiar landscape of Hoorn shrunk behind me. So much had happened in just three years.

In 1940, I was living with my parents and making a good wage driving trucks. I had a girlfriend and lots of friends around town. Like most of the Dutch locals whom I knew, I was a happy man. Then came the German occupation and we lost everything. Now, I was on my way to work somewhere in Germany because of "Arbeitseinsatz" - *mandatory labour conscription.* I turned to the young man sitting beside me with his lunch on his knee and alone with his thoughts. He was about my age and looked quite business-like, wearing a dress shirt, a dark tie and a brown suit. He looked as if he were going to church.

"Any idea where we are going?" I asked.

"Not a clue," he replied, without looking at me. "All I know is that I am going to work in Germany. I got a letter telling me that I had to report to the station, prepared to go to Germany. How about you? Did you get a letter or did you volunteer?"

"I got a letter, just like you did. I'm Pete."

"Hi Pete. I'm Hank. Where are you from?"

"I'm from Wognum. What about you?"

"I live near Enkhuizen on our family farm."

"Are you a farmer?" I asked.

"I help my family on the farm," said Hank.

"Why did you get a letter? I thought farmers were essential and exempt."

"So did I, but I have three older brothers, and they are more involved with Dad's farm than I am. My brothers didn't get letters. I'm the only one who got one. Maybe it's my age. What do you do, Pete?"

"I'm an apprentice mechanic. I used to work driving trucks for my dad. Before the war he had a small trucking business. I drove for him and helped maintain the trucks, but not long after the occupation, the Germans confiscated them. Now he runs the business with a horse and wagon. I drive trucks for my uncle. He owns Roemer Trucking and lives close by."

"They just took them?"

"Yes, Dad got a letter explaining that the army needed trucks and he should be proud to contribute to the great nation of Germany. He was ordered to deliver his truck to a depot near Amsterdam. When he got there, he was told to leave the truck and without compensation, he was left to find his own way back to Wognum. When Dad questioned the lack of compensation with one of the soldiers, the soldier drew a pistol and pointed it right in Dad's face. That was the end of the negotiations."

"I wonder what we'll be doing in Germany?" asked Hank, redirecting our conversation.

"I have no idea," I replied. "The letter just said to be here and take this train."

"I can't believe some guys volunteered for this? Did you ever think about not showing up and taking your chances hiding out instead, Pete?"

"I did, yes, until I heard stories about other guys who tried to hide out in the marshes." As the kilometres rolled by, the train made its way towards Germany. "After receiving letters ordering them to report for forced labour, a couple of local men ran away with a few Jewish guys who needed to stay out of sight as well. The only reason the *divers* came out of hiding was to visit their parents, where they thought they would be safe for a few hours. The German soldiers somehow learned about the visits, from a neighbour; or a *collaborator*," I said, emphatically.

"The soldiers came and raided the parents' home in broad daylight. When the men saw the army truck, they ran out the back door and tried to escape into the fields behind the house. Without hesitation or warning, the soldiers just opened fire and shot them. They left the bodies where they fell and went back into the house to make sure no one else was still hiding. When they were satisfied that they had killed them all, they forced the parents into their truck and they were never seen again. The whole family was just gone. The men were my age," I continued, "that scared me enough. I figured I better show up or my whole family would be killed."

"Those Nazi bastards," said Hank tightening his face so hard his cheeks became flushed, "they're heartless. They couldn't care less about the hardship they cause." He went on to tell me a story that happened to a woman in Enkhuizen. "She was riding her bike home, carrying a few groceries that she managed to get with her ration coupons. Coming around a corner, she almost ran into a German soldier. She couldn't avoid him. The soldier pushed her off her bike and simply took it - and he took the groceries too. Without any concern for her he just rode away, as if to say, I want what you have, so I'm taking it. You mean nothing to me."

I shook my head in disgust, then turned back to the window to watch the familiar Dutch countryside slide away.

Young Peter with his Dad, around 1940

Chapter 2
The Message

Dutch/German border, later that day, April 1943

As we travelled across Holland, we made frequent stops to pick up other men who were going to Germany with us. I tried to relax and focus on the scenery rather than dwell on my fears about the destination. The Dutch countryside was flat and the pasture fields were starting to turn a deep green with the spring weather. Cattle were grazing peacefully, without any concern for the war. The train sped through the traffic controls at intermittent roadways and crossed bridges over the canals, normally busy with boats and vehicles moving people and products, but now quiet and nearly empty.

After several hours of travel, we left Holland behind and crossed the border. By evening, the train eventually slowed and stopped. With loud shouts and pushing by the soldiers, the cars were emptied and we were shuffled off into the darkness alongside the railroad tracks. The lights from the train gave us just enough vision to recognize a few structures, newly constructed in the adjacent field. Together, we were jammed towards a small building. It was a foreboding building without any windows. The poor lighting and overpowering stench identified it as a latrine. We stumbled in the darkness and were pushed inward by the shouting and impatient soldiers. The interior was without privacy walls or doors and, barely visible, were several rows of wooden benches with holes cut to accommodate as many as possible at a time. With the soldiers watching, we had to quickly empty our bladders and bowels before being hurried out the back door. That lack of privacy and respect for personal dignity was humiliating; I no longer felt like an individual. The soldiers treated us as they would a herd of sheep.

We were separated into groups and each group was assigned to a small building. As I joined my group and scrambled inside, the doors were closed behind us. Again, we were forced to line up and a soldier took a head count, so each small group was accounted for. The buildings were simple structures with wooden clapboard walls, exposed framing and wooden floors covered in straw. The interior was lit by a few lanterns precariously hung from the frame; I could smell the coal oil. The guards opened the doors and six or so poorly dressed civilian workers sheepishly set up makeshift tables, then left. The way they looked and behaved made it seem clear they, too, were forced labourers. They returned quickly with several pots and pails, setting them on the tables. By hand gestures and verbal commands, the soldiers ordered us to move in single file, to receive some food, and just sit down anywhere on the straw to eat. The meal consisted of watery cabbage soup and a chunk of black bread. Hank and I sat together and as we ate in silence, the German officer in charge spoke to us. A soldier interpreted the speech in Dutch. The message was very intimidating and threatening, every word was read out emphatically:

> *You are now employed by the greatest nation in the world and great things are awaiting you. You must do as you are told. If you disobey, you will be punished. If you escape, because you think Germany can do without you, you will be found and you will not live to talk about it.*

I didn't know it at the time, but it was a script that I would hear repeatedly in the months to come. Nothing was ever added to the message or left out – there was to be no misunderstanding. When he finished, the officer turned sharply and walked out. We returned our bowls to the food tables and the workers folded up their equipment and left directly behind him. We could see soldiers being posted outside the door as guards and we were directed to lie down and sleep. The lanterns were carefully extinguished by the guards and the doors shut. The sound of the locking bolts on the outside was unexpected and gave me an ominous feeling. As Hank and I struggled to find comfort and tried to sleep, I could hear men talking in hushed whispers. Somewhere in the darkness, I heard a man crying.

~

Morning came abruptly. With loud shouting and commotion, the doors were opened and the guards invaded our sleep, as they brought the building to life. The inside of the building was foul with stale air and the nauseating smell of sweat and body odour. I thought that if I couldn't get outside and breathe fresh air soon, I was going to vomit. They shouted commands in German, and we were made to get up, and form in line as a head count was taken. When all were accounted for, we were led back through the latrines and then onto the train. When all were seated, several moments dragged by while the train puffed loudly but remained motionless. I could see soldiers coming towards us in the forward car and I was concerned as to why we were waiting. They entered our car and stopped, looking at papers in their hands. Then, loudly shouting names and pointing – expecting immediate compliance – they selected some of us to join them at the front of the car.

"You," said a soldier, pointing at Hank. My new friend got up as ordered and turned to say goodbye to me. The soldier impatiently pushed him forward and without a word, Hank was gone. Where he went and what job he had been selected for, I never knew. I never saw Hank again.

The train rumbled onwards into the morning, and I watched the flatlands turning to rolling hills as we travelled further and further into Germany. Around mid-day, while still on the train, we were provided with a simple lunch of a chunk of bread, some cheese and a warm drink that they called coffee. It had been brewed from something, but it certainly didn't taste like coffee. Food was not abundant. The soldiers were fed first, and we were forced to share what was left. I was observing them and learning that the German army was responsible for us and we had to be kept alive in order to work, but proper nourishment was not going to be a priority.

I tried to distract myself for the next few hours by studying the passing scenery. We crossed wide, fast-flowing rivers as they tumbled downward from green hillsides and passed through kilometres of coniferous forest. It was spring and the weather was beautiful. It did not look or feel like the world was at war when nature through the window seemed so peaceful. I tried to relax but I was nervous and, with Hank gone, I was alone with my fears of the unknown. Suddenly, I was jolted out of my trance by the sound of the train whistle. The train was coming to a stop. I grabbed my suitcase as a soldier pulled me out of my seat. He pushed me forward and down the aisle towards the doors.

"Raus, Raus," he yelled in German. *Out, Out.*

On the platform, I could see other men having arrived on earlier trains, lined up and under the command of other soldiers. The soldier pushing me stepped off the train and motioned for me to follow and join the group of other workers. I was reluctant to step forward, but scared not to. My back was still hurting from the jab I had received the day before, and I was not eager to repeat that experience.

"Hier," he said, as he pointed to an open spot in one of the lines. *Here.*

I stepped into an empty space in the formed ranks and from there, I could clearly see the station sign. We were in Braunschweig.

The train stood motionless as the platform became a hive of activity. Groups of men were taken off, made to stand together in military formations and sorted out by the soldiers. It was organized confusion. Soldiers were talking amongst themselves as men were pulled out and shoved systematically into smaller groups. A soldier approached our group and stood before us. From his tunic pocket, he pulled out a paper and in German, he addressed the group as he read from it. I did not understand his language but despite his mispronunciation, I distinctly heard my name.

"Peter Manshande," he said, then again, louder… "Peter Manshande."

It was only the second time that I had heard my name spoken by a German and I didn't understand the rest of his message. Another name was called and the guy next to me stepped forward. I did the same, thinking there was likely a reason why they made me stand next to him in the first place. The soldier pointed at us and, by gesturing, ordered us to follow him to a waiting army truck. He pushed us to climb up and into the back of the truck. The soldier climbed into the front cab of the truck as the driver revved the engine and engaged the clutch to put the truck in motion. Surprisingly, we were the only two passengers. We had to struggle to remain seated on the wooden benches in the back of the truck as we drove off, leaving the groups of others at the platform. Where were they going, we did not know? But then, we did not know where we were going either. I did not know whether to be relieved or scared. Had we done something wrong? Things had changed. Suddenly I found myself alone with another worker and our actions and conversations were no longer being guarded. In the noisy cargo area of the back of the truck, we could speak freely and I offered my hand as I looked at my new companion. "Pete," I said. He seemed about my age, although maybe a bit younger, with a slight build, dark blue eyes and blond hair. He introduced himself in a quiet voice. "I'm Jack," he said, "Where are you from?" he asked and I was glad that he spoke Dutch.

"Wognum, a small village in North Holland," I said, "it's north of Amsterdam, near Hoorn."

"I know where Wognum is," said Jack, "I'm from Ursem, only 15 kilometres away from Wognum."

"Out of everyone, why would they just call us?" I asked, "do you think they put us together so we'll be more comfortable; you know, coming from the same area?"

"No, it's not," said Jack moving closer so I could hear clearly. "They don't care about our feelings. I think we have something they need? Do you have any special training?"

"I have a driver's licence?" I offered questioningly, "and I have training as a mechanic."

"I think that's it," said Jack, "cause I'm a registered motorcycle mechanic." We agreed. We were being sent to do a special job. Not a factory job or a farm job, our job would be different: and whatever that was, wherever that was, we were on our way. We sat back quietly as the truck lumbered through the busy side streets of Braunschweig.

Jack

Chapter 3
AUSLÄNDER

Braunschweig, Germany, April 1943

I knew that Braunschweig was an industrial city in central Germany and, as the truck entered the city, I became increasingly apprehensive. Wherever you looked there were German army trucks and equipment of all description; I had never been surrounded by such a strong military presence. Uniformed soldiers were everywhere: some marching in order, some climbing in or out of vehicles while others just seemed to be milling about. Our truck came to a stop at the gate of a fenced compound. The soldier escorting us talked to the guards as one of them checked the back of the truck. Saying nothing to Jack and me, he then yelled something to the other soldiers, and the gate swung open with the screech of rusty hinges as the truck moved forward.

I had never seen anything like it. I felt overwhelmed by the sight confronting us. The compound was similar to a parking lot, packed with passenger cars, trucks, tracked vehicles, armoured and transport vehicles. But it wasn't just their presence that was so astonishing, it was the fact that most of the vehicles were damaged. The effects of war were obvious. Some vehicles were little more than a pile of dented and twisted steel. Many had been bombed and burned, some had doors missing and some had front ends blown off. Some did not appear to be damaged at all and just needed mechanical repair, but all of them sat motionless and seeing them made the war shockingly real to me.

We were taken to a barracks to stow our belongings. The barracks were old and the monochrome of gray paint was everywhere. At least it was neat and clean. I couldn't help but notice that in every room, as though watching over everyone, was a framed picture of Adolf Hitler.

Our quarters had two bedrooms with three cots in each. Jack and I were to share one room and the other room was already occupied by three men from Belgium. There was a common area, with a wood or coal burning stove, six lockers, a table, and six chairs. There was a long hallway leading off to a bathroom and, opposite the bathroom, was a shower room. The soldier left us in the care of one of the Belgian men who took us off to get our bedding. We were introduced to a short, sturdy woman, looking severe and stern.

"This is Frau Schmidt," said the Dutch-speaking Belgian, "she is in charge of the bed linen for the compound. She will get you what you need to be comfortable."

From her we each received a pillow, two sheets, a blanket and a large flat canvas bag with a flap closure on one end. We were told this would be our mattress. She took us to a nearby truck that had fresh straw in the box and we were shown how to fill the bag with enough straw to make a reasonable bed. Once settled in, we were given a light supper of bread and cold meat and told by the Belgian that we would be left on our own in the barracks until morning. Compared to my first night in German custody, my situation appeared to be improving. We had some time to get to know the other men who shared our barracks. The Belgians could communicate with us because Flemish and Dutch are quite similar. We were happy to be able to ask questions and learn about our new and strange environment. Each of our three new companions identified himself in turn.

"I'm Lowie," said the first one, the one who introduced

us to Frau Schmidt. "I'm from Antwerp and I've been here the longest," he said proudly.

"Yah, but only by about two weeks," said another laughingly. "I'm Frans. I'm from Kortrijk. We all came about the same time, really."

"And I'm Rik," said the third. "I'm from Brussels."

In conversation, Jack and I got to know our new friends. I learned that all were older than we were. Frans, the oldest, was 37. He was tall and slender; wore glasses and always had a smile when he talked. The youngest of them was Rik. He was 25, slim, dark haired and quiet. Lowie was around 30, a chubby friendly person. He seemed to laugh and joke a lot. All three of the men had been in Braunschweig for several months. Lowie was a welder, Frans an electrician and Rik was a mechanic like me. Jack and I were very curious about where we were and what we would be doing but the guys were quick to let us know that we had to be careful about asking a lot of questions. They seemed to understand our curiosity, but they warned us.

Pointing his finger at us, Lowie glanced back over his shoulder, leaned towards Jack and me, and said, "Don't ever forget that you are now at the mercy of the enemy. Braunschweig isn't just a German city, it is a Nazi city, there's a training school for the Hitler Youth near here," he said.

"Lowie is right," said Rik, jumping in, with further warnings: "The young people here are more fanatical than their parents so stay away from them."

"Yup, for sure," said Frans, stepping away from the table, "people here don't like us, they don't want us here because we are foreigners. Forced labourers are treated with contempt and we're often harassed and ridiculed."

"When dealing with the Nazis it is best to stay out of their way. Don't ask questions, and speak only when you are spoken to," said Lowie.

"Do the job requested of you," said Frans stretching his hands forward in physical expression, "and mind your own business. People who ask questions are taken away and never seen again."

The Belgians explained the day-to-day aspects of our new situation. We learned that our workday started at 8 a.m. and ended sometime in the evening whenever the job was done. Our supper and breakfast rations would be delivered to our barracks during the afternoon, so we would eat supper later, and then save enough for the next morning's breakfast. The compound had a large military kitchen. The staff prepared a hot meal at noon for the soldiers, and we would eat with them, in the same building. They also fed local people who were hired to work in the yard. The Belgians told us that although we would get fed every day, the rations were small. I knew that was going to be difficult for me because, although I was not a big man, I had a hearty appetite.

"Get used to being hungry," said Frans.

"That's enough for now," said Lowie with a yawn. "It's time for us to get some sleep. Tomorrow could be a difficult day for you. The first day always is, for everyone."

I had had a tiring day and even though I was exhausted, I didn't sleep well in my straw bed. *What will tomorrow bring?* I wondered as I lay there in the darkness.

~

The next morning started early. We were awakened by uniformed guards as they came through the barracks yelling for us to get up, get dressed quickly, and get outside. When Frau Schmidt had issued our bedding she also gave us our work clothes. We fumbled about in the predawn darkness with our heavy cotton coveralls and poorly fitted boots. I was beginning to understand the routine, as we were once again made to form up in five ranks for a head count and to listen as an interpreter reminded us of the rules of conduct.

> *You are now employed by the greatest nation in the world and great things are awaiting you. You must do as you are told. If you disobey, you will be punished. If you escape, because you think Germany can do without you, you will be found and you will not live to talk about it.*

The hair stood up on the back of my neck as I listened to those threatening words again. After his speech, the senior officer, who made the delivery, introduced another who was to be our boss. The officer was middle aged, in his late forties or early fifties, tall, trim and very authoritative, in his well-pressed uniform. Within the German military, he held a high rank and I felt intimidated just being in his presence. His name was Hermann Harms.

Harms called us together as a group and tried, with the help of the Belgians (who by now understood basic German), to communicate the job to Jack and me. We were part of a Mobile Vehicle Repair Unit, and the unit included Jack and me, along with Lowie, Frans, and Rik.

Damaged or broken military vehicles would be brought to our compound for repair. Our job would be to return the vehicles to operable condition so they could be returned to their units. Vehicles that could not be repaired would be dismantled for parts and scrapped. I was also told that because I had been a registered truck driver in Holland, I would be called upon to make deliveries when needed. The actual job as a driver and mechanic did not sound difficult for me, but like it or not, I had become a part of the German war machine.

After Harms' briefing, our workday began. Harms directed me to a panel truck that had served as an ambulance for soldiers and showed me that it had a broken spring. My first job was to replace the spring with a new one, and I was relieved because I felt quite comfortable with the task. My brother Tinus and I had lots of practice replacing springs on my Dad's trucks that were used to build the dikes and repair the roads in Holland. The task was not a difficult one and, when I had finished, I could tell that the boss was pleased with what I had done. Rik, or another mechanic, would work with me on bigger jobs and I learned a lot from the more experienced men. If I was given a job that was just mine to do, it usually involved a mechanical breakdown and, as an apprentice mechanic, I was left on my own to repair it. Lowie was a welder and he replaced battle-damaged doors, fenders and body parts. Often, it took all of us to tear the vehicle down completely before it could be repaired, or parts could be replaced. The work in the vehicle repair shop was heavy work and usually required long hours to complete.

I liked working with Lowie. His sense of humour was helpful in such a strict and disciplined place. But even Lowie's jokes and fooling around could not fully change the mood of our situation. We regularly worked with soldiers who were also mechanics or welders. One morning as we were taking a break together, one of the soldiers, a well-known motorcycle mechanic, pulled everyone together and in a whispered voice, told a little joke. My German was far from fluent but Rik, was close enough to hear and understood enough German to know that the joke was about Hitler. Though some laughed, the others seemed to be uncomfortable, and no one said anything as we went back to work. Later that day, the soldier who had dared to make fun of Hitler was escorted out of the compound by the Gestapo, the Nazi secret police. They were seldom seen but I learned that they could be anywhere, and always eager to pick up anyone who dared to speak against the regime. Someone who had heard the joke had reported the incident to them. We all were nervous now. Was it somebody in the forced labour group trying to gain favour with the Germans, or maybe a fanatical soldier who took offence at any slight to his Führer? How could we feel safe working together knowing that someone was spying on us and that they could destroy us?

~

The next morning, Frau Schmidt, the woman in charge of the linen in the compound was also taken away by the Gestapo. She was married to the soldier who had told the joke. The Gestapo reported the couple to the Schutzstaffel (SS) and they were never seen again. An incident like this was enough to make me constantly wary; nervous about trusting anyone. If they did this to one of their own, what would they do to an "Ausländer" – *foreigner,* like me?

While we were in Braunschweig, we were issued ration cards that allowed us to buy food, tobacco, a razor, or other personal items at local stores. There was a store close enough that it was a short walk from the compound but far enough to be an uncomfortable walk. The locals knew that we were foreigners and as we walked down the street we were often yelled at and called *Ausländer.* Even children would boldly yell at us, calling us "Schweinischer Hund" – *filthy dog,* while spitting or throwing stones in our direction. Insults from children were difficult to accept. Even though we were furious we didn't dare say or do anything about this abuse. We had been warned that, young or old, they were all Germans and we, the foreigners, were at their mercy.

On one occasion I went to the local store to get a ration of tobacco. As I greeted the owner in the best German words that I knew (after a few weeks, my German was getting better), he looked at me with a scowl and totally ignored me. I wanted my tobacco, so I waited and watched as he helped all his customers. When new shoppers came in after me, they were greeted with an enthusiastic "Heil Hitler," and he looked after their purchases, continuing to ignore me. Finally, when there was no one in the store I politely said to the owner in my most practiced German, "Darf ich etwas Tabak haben?" *May I have some tobacco?* The storeowner reluctantly gave me my tobacco, took my ration card, then without a smile or a word of acknowledgement, he pointed me to the door. That kind of treatment was common in Braunschweig.

Foreigners were treated like scum and constantly reminded that we were not wanted. As bad as it was for us, it was much worse for workers from other countries such as Poland. The Poles, like the Jews, were forced to wear identification patches on their clothing. All Jews had to wear a yellow Star of David and the Poles were forced to wear a diamond-shaped purple patch with a yellow border and a yellow P in the center of the diamond. Like the Jews, they were required to wear the patch everywhere they went and were subjected to more restrictions and more abuse from the locals than we were. The Poles were banned from restaurants, cinemas or libraries, and forbidden to use public transit. Like us they were paid for their work but their monthly salary was much less and they received even smaller rations than we did. I was often hungry but the Poles were starved. They were considered to be an inferior race and were often called "Untermenschen," *subhuman*.

Hermann Harms at his Desk

Inside the barracks – Pete (centre) and friends

Chapter 4
Change of Pace

Braunschweig, July 1943

By July 1943, I had been in Braunschweig for about three months. I was called into the office, late one day, after my shift as Harms wanted to see me. This was not a common occurrence. Had I done something wrong? Was it something I'd done or something I'd said? How would I be punished? I had never been singled out and called to Harms' office alone before. My hands were shaking, and I had dry heaves as I crossed the compound to report to the office. I was scared beyond anything I had ever experienced. I remembered what happened to the soldier who had simply made a joke about Hitler. What could I have done? To my surprise and relief, I was not in trouble at all. The sole reason for my attendance was so that Harms could provide me with a German driving permit. He invited me to sit down while he explained to me - in words that I could almost understand by now - that I was to report to the Transport Office first thing the next morning. I had become a driver for our unit and would now be driving to destinations outside of our compound, with cargo and supplies when required. I was so busy learning my new job in the yard as a mechanic that I had forgotten about the possibility of transport duties.

~

Over supper in the barracks that night, we all discussed my new assignment.

"Why did you have to go see Harms?" asked Lowie, who instead of telling his usual jokes was now quite serious. "Are you in trouble? What are they going to do with you?"

I was still shaking and scared despite my relief. "He gave me a German driver's licence and told me to report to the Transport Office first thing in the morning." I said.

"Where are you going?" asked Frans in a whisper, as he bent closer as if the others were not supposed to hear.

"I don't know," I said. "All I know is that I am driving something: somewhere other than here. Has anyone else ever done that?" Lowie, Frans and Rik were not drivers and all shook their heads, without expression.

"I am the only other man in our barracks that has a driver's licence," Rik said, "but I don't think the Germans are aware of it because I have never been put on transport duty. And I don't want to, so don't be telling them."

We were all very curious about what would be expected of me. I always enjoyed driving and I was looking forward to the change in routine even though I was nervous about the new and unknown task. Before I went to bed that night, Lowie reminded me that even though I was curious and a little excited, I needed to pay attention. "Listen and learn," he said. "But do not ask questions. Remember, people who ask questions disappear."

~

Early the next morning, I reported to the Transport Office as directed. I was introduced to the soldier who was to accompany me on the trip. I politely wished him "Guten Morgen," – *Good Morning*, and he snapped to attention and responded with a reflexive, fervent "Heil Hitler." He directed me to a large and cumbersome army truck. It was a Krupp truck: a big dark gray, double-axle truck with a huge protruding front end. To me it looked big, awkward, and intimidating. Behind the truck was hitched a large cargo trailer with side racks covered by a tarp. I knew by its appearance that I would be responsible for a load of significant size, but was never told what was on board. I remembered Lowie's advice, and didn't ask. We left the compound and I was relieved to be on the open road. I may as well have been alone as the soldier guarding the load only spoke when giving directions to me. His tone was never friendly; never polite or cooperative. It was very clear to me that we both just had a job to do. My job was to drive and his job was to ensure that the load got to where it was intended. If we were met with local interference, he would handle it.

~

After a couple of hours driving in silence, he directed me to stop at a camp in the country. It was surrounded by a high fence and there was a huge iron gate at the entrance. A couple of other trucks, without trailers but of the same type, were lined up to enter at the gate and I pulled in behind the last one. I was instructed to stay in the cab. The soldier with me got out and spoke to other soldiers guarding the gate. When the gates opened, I was told to drive through. I was barely clear of the posts, when the gates were slammed shut behind me. I had never been to such a place before and was nervous as I pulled up beside the other trucks. About half a dozen dirty human beings were herded towards my truck and it became clear that they were to unload it. They too were under guard and moved painfully, yet methodically, to remove the boxes from the trailer and pile them aside. I was told to remain in the cab and was happy to do so. The camp was fairly large and resembled a small town, made up of roads and buildings. Soldiers and civilians alike were busily moving about but I paid no attention. Lowie's warnings echoed in my head and I sat in the truck without appearing to be inquisitive. I felt sorry for these poor workers as they were beaten at random with rubber truncheons carried by the guards. It angered me to see such tyrants being allowed to make life miserable for the men. They were thin, sickly looking workers, poorly dressed in ragged clothes and visibly famished. I appreciated that although I disliked being here, I was better off than these poor wretches - whoever they were.

~

When the delivery was completed at the camp, the guard directed me to drive back through the gates. I was glad to hear them slam shut behind me and I soon was on the road again. We drove on to deliver supplies to a couple of remote military outposts. When my load was gone and the truck and trailer were empty, the soldier left me. It was awkward to be alone, but I was to learn with future trips, that this was the routine. When I had a full load, I would be accompanied by one, sometimes two, armed soldiers. Once the truck was empty, I was on my own to find my way back to the compound as best I could. The German countryside was beautiful with large expanses of green fields dotted with grazing cattle. What I had seen had been upsetting and I was glad to have some time alone on the drive back to try to process the day. After a bit of repeated and unintentional meandering on the back roads, I eventually found my way back to Braunschweig. Though I never felt really secure there, I was glad to be going back to my friends and the nearest thing I had to a family, after this miserable day. How odd to feel safe in a place I feared so much but for now, it was home. It was all I had. Jack and my new Belgian friends were waiting for me. "Where did you go today? What did you do?" asked Jack.

"I had to deliver supplies to soldiers in a rural area. But I also went to a horrible camp. I have never seen anything like it. The people there looked starved and beaten. I don't know who they were but I'll tell you, they looked a hell of a lot worse off than us."

"There used to be another driver here," said Frans. "He is gone now, and nobody talks about him. We don't know where he went. Anyway, he told us that he went to such camps as well."

"What did he say about them?"

"That they are camps for political prisoners of different nationalities including some German nationals. Anyone who shows any dissent against the Nazi regime is arrested and taken to camps such as these to remove any threat they might pose."

"Do you mean that Frau Schmidt and her husband could have been sent to a place like that? She didn't do anything and all he did was tell a Hitler joke," I said. "Who knows," said Frans, "but that other driver said it was the type of camp they send their own people to. You either agree and support the Nazi regime, or you are taken away. One of the guards told me that there are many of these camps scattered across Germany." That night, as I laid on my bunk, trying to get some sleep, my mind wandered fretfully over the events of the day. Every minute I had been guarded by an armed soldier and every place I went was surrounded by barbed wire. The prison camp I had visited was cruel and inhumane.

I had never minded driving trucks for my dad but the truck I drove today was as unfriendly as everything else in this godforsaken country. It was big, and I had to fight with it to keep it on the road. I knew how to drive but had never driven a truck like that one. It was a monster that needed to be controlled.

I hoped that I had not said too much to my new friends. Trust was something that needed to be earned here. It bothered me to think that Frau Schmidt, a German, might have been taken to such a place because her husband had said something forbidden. But most of all, I thought about the other driver. The one that was here before that nobody talks about anymore and nobody knows where he went. Maybe he had been sent there, just like me. Maybe he was Dutch or Belgian like us. Maybe he had seen too much. Maybe he was dead.

Chapter 5
Karl

Braunschweig, late Summer 1943

The weeks passed without incident as August slipped into September. I worked long hours in the garage, ate tasteless meals as provided, but tried to stay focused on what I had to do to stay alive. I frequently made trips, as required, driving to scattered military posts around the Braunschweig area to deliver supplies. As usual, I was accompanied one way by a soldier to guard the load. The soldier was usually cold and indifferent. To him, I was only a civilian labourer, and was just to be tolerated. I was frequently surrounded by German discussions when we passed through checkpoints or gates. However, and on occasion, I was expected to be a part of brief conversations with them as to where I needed to take my load. My German began to improve on these trips.

The rest of my days I repaired military vehicles at the compound, and I started to feel less anxious in my daily work in the garage. I could communicate well enough that I could follow orders and stay out of trouble. My job as a mechanic was easy enough but I still could not relax. I was constantly reminded by unfamiliar language and different customs, that I was forced to work for the German military. They were the same people who had invaded my home in Holland, terrified my family, and sent me here against my will. I was always guarded by armed soldiers and I knew better than to trust any of them. Most were older, career soldiers having spent time on active tours of duty in battle, and who were now relieved to be at home in Germany, with a relatively easy policing role at our compound. They were less aggressive and talked with me about home and life before the war. All were very careful to avoid any political discussions or give any opinions about the Nazi regime. While they were polite, they were not allowed to be overly friendly. They too had rules restricting friendship with us. Though we ate in the same kitchen, the soldiers were directed to avoid sitting at our table and to keep social contact to a minimum.

There was one exception. A soldier, whom we all just knew to be Karl, worked in the office of the compound. Although small in stature his personality was larger than life. Having served on a battle front, Karl had been wounded several times and the army brass had determined that a more administrative role suited his diminished physical capabilities. Karl only had one arm, having lost the other in an explosion, and a piece of shrapnel embedded in his right leg caused him to limp noticeably. His frontline battle experience had left him with a nasty scar under his right eye, but Karl was very friendly to everyone and we all liked him. It was through Karl, that I met Arie.

"This is Arie," said Karl, one morning as he accompanied a new arrival to our team. "Arie is a mechanic and like you Pete, Arie is also a driver." I took an immediate liking to Arie. He was my age, clean-shaven and had thick, curly hair. He seemed eager to be one of us. He loved to laugh and like Lowie, was always joking around. He was Dutch but his German was better than mine. Arie had been a part of the forced labour group for over a year but had been assigned to another team in Braunschweig. I was eager to know why Arie had been moved. Had his team been punished and disbanded? Had he been transferred to our team because more work was coming for drivers? But I was not about to start asking questions. We got along well, and I was just glad to have another driver to share my role.

~

Jack and I were in the barracks one evening playing cards. It had been a wet day and we were both just tired. We often worked in the same area and we had become good friends. Jack was a quiet man, always cautious. Generally, he kept his opinions to himself. He surprised me when he asked, "What do you think about the new guy, Arie?"

"He seems like a good guy to me. I'm glad he's here. It's nice to have someone share the driving. Some of those camps I have to go to are pretty brutal. Besides, he seems like a lot of fun. Why do you ask?"

Jack frowned as he said, "Arie seems kind of reckless, like he would take chances that could get him or anyone around him in trouble. He leaves sometimes and goes out for a beer."

I laughed. "But Jack, that is what I like about him. I'm getting tired of being scared all the time. I want to go out too and have a laugh if I get the chance. Come on, we are allowed to leave the compound and we just need a break from working here all the time."

"I agree, but Pete, you read those posters around town nailed onto posts or buildings forbidding foreigners to fraternize with the locals. You have to be careful. You can hate this war all you like, and I do, but I plan to go home in one piece. I'm not giving the Germans an easy excuse to make my life more miserable than it already is."

Just then, there was a knock on the door. It was Arie.

He joined us at the table and the conversation turned to the day-to-day happenings at the compound. Before long Arie was talking about going into town for a beer. He wanted us to join him some night. At this point Jack excused himself and said he was tired and ready for bed. Arie and I talked for a while and I learned all about the Bruchstrasse, the entertainment district in Braunschweig. I had heard about it, but I was nervous about actually going there. On my driving trips I had read, with my basic familiarity of German, the signs that Jack had mentioned, posted all over the town and countryside. The posters were a warning to the locals, as well as the foreigners, that fraternizing was not allowed and offenders would be punished. I had avoided going there because the locals were so often hostile to foreigners. Arie, however, tried to persuade me otherwise: "This place can make you sick," said Arie. "The food is bad and you work too hard. Sometimes you need a break from war to keep your sanity. On the Bruchstrasse, you get a chance to have a beer and relax a little: buy some decent food. The girls are eager to join you; so, you buy them a drink and they will be your friend; make you laugh. Having a few laughs reminds you that you are human. We don't have to work at night unless we get yard duty, and Karl will take us just for the company. In civilian clothes, we fit in. Just don't talk a lot and you won't attract any attention with your accent. Besides, we will be with Karl. We will be fine," he said, "as long as we stay with Karl."

Arie had accompanied Karl a couple of times, but I was still not sure that Karl could be trusted. Was it really a mutual companionship, or was it a ruse by a German soldier to test our obedience to the rules?

~

Next morning, Karl was in the yard where Arie and I were working on repairing a German staff car. "Hey Karl," Arie said, as Karl came close to us. "Pete says he's a little nervous coming with us to the Bruchstrasse. He's worried that we could get into trouble."

"No worries," said Karl looking at me. "I'll take the lead if we are challenged and as far as I'm concerned," he said with a grin, "I was on the Eastern Front and have these wounds to prove it. What more can they do to me?"

"I'm not worried about what they will do to you, I'm more concerned about what they might do to me," I said with a smile, although my concern was real.

"Don't worry," said Karl, "sit quietly, drink a beer and don't draw attention to yourself. Nobody will even care." After a lot of prodding from Karl and Arie, I agreed to go. We were off on Sundays to rest, and were allowed to leave camp on Saturday night for supplies. We had a 10 p.m. curfew and we agreed to leave after work. Saturday evening, we skipped dinner, cleaned up, shaved and left the camp as soon as we were able. The Bruchstrasse was in the center of the red-light district and we took a streetcar from the compound to the entertainment district. The Bruchstrasse was a short street with iron gates at each end. These gates were not at all threatening, like the other iron gates I had often seen in Germany. These were smaller, hung partly open, almost luring, inviting us in, if we dared. Stepping inside was like entering a world that had forgotten there was a war. The party atmosphere was exciting and contagious. People were drinking beer, laughing and enjoying themselves. There didn't seem to be any rationing or restrictions here. There were hookers seductively inviting us to join them. Even the German soldiers seemed to relax their vigilance. Arie laughed when he saw my expression of disbelief, as we made our way down the street.

"Well, what do you think Pete? Are you glad you came?" asked Arie as we entered a bar through a front door off the busy street.

"Yeah, I'm not sure whether to be scared or excited, but I'm glad to be here."

Karl snickered as he led us to a table at his favourite bar and bought the first round. "Don't speak," said Karl as if he was creating a game plan. "You look like anyone else in civilian clothes and nobody will notice you unless you speak. Your accent will give you away so I'll do the talking."

I looked around the small bar and noticed some local girls enjoying a beer. They waved at Karl, and smiling at us, waved us over to join them. Karl acknowledged them with a friendly smile but did not leave our table. I think he was being more considerate of our situation than he was of the girls' intentions. Maybe I could trust him after all.

Karl leaned in and spoke in a quiet voice to Arie and me. "It is great to come here and relax, but you guys have to be careful. Remember, you are foreigners. Hookers are one thing, but be careful around the other local girls. You are a novelty to them. Most of the German guys their age, are off fighting a war. If their parents find out that you have been messing around with them, or even if soldiers notice you, and suspect that you are too friendly, they will report you and you'll be punished. You have seen the posters around town. Take them seriously. Now... whose turn is it to buy a round, I'm thirsty."

Chapter 6
#128

Wognum, North Holland, Summer 1943

By 1943, the Dutch were surviving in fear of the German army and the restrictions they imposed. Some of the locals had joined the Dutch Nazi Party – the Nationaal-Socialistische Beweging in Nederland (NSB) – and they received extra rations or other favours for being informants to the Germans about any resistance activities. With neighbours reporting on neighbours, we lived in a world of resentment and suspicion.

I lived close to Peter's family and often spent time at their home. His parents Jan and Elisabeth, treated me like one of their own. His sister Marta was my best friend and his brothers frequently teased me about being his girlfriend. I knew he was initially sent to Braunschweig, but I had only received one letter from him and the mail stopped. We all wondered where he was in Germany and were always fearful for him. We could only hope that he was alive and well.

Elisabeth was kind and would often invite me for a family meal. "Stay for dinner, Corrie," she would say. "We feel close to Peter when you are here." Food was rationed but Peter's family shared with me what little they had. One evening, after dinner, I was having tea chatting with Marta when Elisabeth joined us.

"Tell me more about yourself," she asked.

I was reluctant, at first, to share the secrets that I had

never before told anyone, except Peter. But the kitchen was warm and as I sat there with her at the big wooden table, I remember her touching my hand with kind curiosity. I told her the very personal, sometimes painful but unvarnished facts of my life's story.

"I was born in the town of Bovenkarspel. My birth mother died soon after I was born and my father remarried when I was five. My stepmother despised me, she called me unmanageable; she was always cruel and abusive towards me. I believe she was jealous of my father's love for me. In November 1935, when I was 14 years old, she sent me away to a home for wayward girls, run by the Sisters of The Good Shepherd in Zoeterwoude, near Rotterdam. I did not know why I was being forced to live there. I was being punished, apparently, as an unruly child. My stepmother did not love me and invented stories so that they would keep me there."

"What about your Dad?" asked Elisabeth, with compassion.

"He was there," I said, "and I believe it was difficult

Klooster de Goede Herder

for him. I remember him kissing me goodbye and walking away without looking back. I think he thought I would be safer if I weren't living with my stepmother. He knew that she often beat me."

"That's heartbreaking," said Elisabeth, as she poured more tea. "How many girls would have been at Zoeterwoude?"

"About 150, I think. They were all young Dutch girls. We each were given an administration number. Contact with our families was discouraged and we were not allowed to leave the home. We were forbidden to talk about our lives before arriving there and we never knew each other's proper given names The Mother Superior assigned us all with new names and Willie was the name that I was given. For five years, I was only known to the other girls as Willie," I said. "The nuns also called me Willie or just referred to me as #128."

"Living with the nuns at Zoeterwoude was both hard work and isolating. We spent our days cleaning the buildings, then cooking or doing laundry for local businesses in the area. It was slave labour really and we worked 60 hours a week. We were often punished if we failed to work hard enough or disobeyed."

"But you were so young. What kind of punishment?"

"You could be strapped, denied recreation time or sometimes locked in a dark closet for hours, kneeling on dried peas."

"That must have been a very scary time for you. How did you cope?"

"There was a lot of religious ritual and we went to church every morning. We were awakened early by a bell summoning us to get up, get dressed, make our beds, and proceed to the chapel as a group before breakfast. The service started with prayer and contemplation, followed by Mass with ritual and song. I was born into a Catholic family but my parents were not practising. In my younger years, I didn't attend Mass, but in Zoeterwoude, I bought into it. I was taught to believe that my life was shared by something greater than myself. I was taught to believe in an all-loving, all-powerful God, and a commitment of my faith in God would provide me a life of happiness. At the time, I didn't know why I had been forced to live there working for the Zoeterwoude nuns, but when I turned 19, I became old enough to leave. I left there afraid of being alone but at least I could be me again. I left Willie behind and no longer had to be #128. I had my name back. I again became Corrie de Jong. With nowhere to go, I went back to my parents' home in Bovenkarspel, but life there was no different than when I left five years earlier. My stepmother remained cruel to me and when my father died a few months later, I had to leave once more."

"Is that when you came to Wognum?" asked Elisabeth.

"Yes," I said. "My step-grandmother lived here. She was not like her daughter. She was kind to me and let me live with her. After a few months, she helped me to get the job as a live-in maid for the Roemer family. They had several children and a large house. I felt quite fortunate to have a job and a new place to live. But most of all, I felt valued."

"What a sad story Corrie, I never knew," said Elisabeth. "But, where were you when the war started?"

"When the war started, I was still in Zoeterwoude. Early in May 1940, we all had been frightened by the sounds of the bombing of Rotterdam. The nuns had told us of German troops invading Holland a few days earlier, but we didn't understand what that meant. We had heard some explosions and seen a few airplanes heading towards Rotterdam for a few days, but we were never allowed beyond the front gate, so happenings elsewhere meant very little to us. But just after lunch on that day in May, wave after wave of airplanes passed over the convent. You could see them extending to the horizon. There was so many of them and they all were so loud. Rotterdam was less than 40 kilometres away and so we could hear the bombs. The relentless and destructive bombs killed hundreds of civilians and almost flattened the city.

We were used to solitude and quiet. We lived in a private world, separate from the rest of the city. The harsh *ka-boom, ka-boom, ka-boom* was a terrifying experience. We had nowhere to hide for safety and the nuns hustled us into the basements of the church and the convent. They were the sturdiest buildings there and they had solid basement walls. We huddled there in fear, trembling throughout the afternoon. At night, you could see the fires and the smoke in the air on the horizon towards Rotterdam.

Within days, German soldiers had occupied the main buildings in Zoeterwoude. Not only were we afraid of them because they were soldiers, but afraid of them because they were men. Until the German army came in, the only men in our isolated lives had been priests and the old men who tended the property gardens. Now soldiers entered the convent buildings freely and the nuns were even forced to feed them. The Catholic church was attached to the home and the convent – *Klooster De Goede Herder.* The soldiers climbed the stairs up to the bell tower of the church. It became a vantage point for observers and snipers. They used it to watch for any signs of resistance. I lived that way for almost six months: soldiers eating and sleeping at the convent, showering and using our bathrooms, using our laundry facilities daily, army trucks on the grounds, and everyone was terrified as to what would happen next. We were displaced from our beds, our kitchens and all of our old spaces. All we had left was the sanctuary of the church.

I was on my way back from Mass to our residence on the church grounds one morning and a soldier yelled at me. 'Raus hier' – *Get out of here.* I didn't understand what he said. I didn't know German. I recognized his gesture that meant I was to leave, but I was so confused. Leave to go where? I did not know where I could go; I did not know what was beyond the walls. I was scared.

I ran to my room in the dormitory and hid under my bed, out of sight. It became incredibly frightful with the German troops around Zoeterwoude, and I was so pleased when six months later, I was able to leave the convent. The world had changed and I was nervous and unsure of my new-found freedom. Going back to Bovenkarspel was the only option I knew."

"How terrible for you, Corrie," said Elisabeth. "So, being at the Roemers is how you met Peter?" she asked. She knew that part of my story, but I think she liked hearing it again.

"Yes," I continued. "After driving all day, Peter would return to the yard at Roemers to do truck maintenance and I was often in the yard with laundry or the children. Over time, we got to know each other, and we would chat about the weather and the local news around Wognum. He was 19 and we knew that the Germans were gathering young men to work in Germany. We knew that he would soon be selected to go and this was not the time to plan our future. Until then, Peter and I were content to just spend time together in the evenings. When he had to go, we exchanged pictures and he promised to write as soon as he was able. We want to be together again someday but I know it is dangerous for him working in Germany. But when he left, he told me not to worry, and that he would come back to me. I live for that day."

#128

Elisabeth reached out to take my hand. "You have had an unfortunate past. We know that Peter loves you and I hope you know that we love you too. You deserve the warmth and the love of family. Unfortunately, with the war and the German troops here, we all have to struggle for now."

It was frustrating but I understood. For years, I had lived under someone else's strict control. First, it was my stepmother, then the nuns, and now the Germans. Was I ever going to be free?

Pete and Corrie exchanged photos

Corrie and Marta as friends

Chapter 7

How It Is Now

Braunschweig, Fall 1943

It was late in the day in early October. The trees were coloured by their autumn leaves against the blue sky. They rustled in the breeze, lending a false sense of peace. Arie and I had worked together all afternoon. We had replaced the axle and the front wheels on a Krupp truck. It had been a challenging job and we were glad to be done for the day. We cleaned up our tools and were headed across the compound to the barracks when we saw Harms walking across the yard. He moved like a man on a mission and, when he had seen us, he called us over. His demeanour was abrupt and he frowned as he pointed his finger at us, "I want to see you both in my office in fifteen minutes. Don't be late," he snapped.

"Yes sir," was all I could manage to respond.

Harms stomped away and just left us standing there. Arie looked at me and I could see that he was as baffled and as scared as I was.

"What the hell did we do to piss him off?" Arie asked.

"I don't know. I think we did a pretty good job on that truck today. When Rik checked our work, he seemed to be satisfied."

"I agree," said Arie. "But Harms looked pretty upset."

"Arie, do you suppose he heard about us going to the Bruchstrasse?"

"Oh no, well maybe. But we didn't do anything wrong.

Surely, smiling or talking to a German girl isn't against the rules."

"Remember, there were soldiers there. Maybe some of them recognized us. Who knows what kind of story they might have told Harms?"

"You're right. What do you think might happen to us?" he asked, as we walked together towards Harms' office.

"Right now, Arie, I'm too scared to think about that."

"Well, we're here now. Let's go in and find out what he wants."

The door to Harms' office was open and I was surprised to see that our entire unit was waiting inside. Maybe we all were in trouble. When Arie and I walked in, Harms looked up from his paperwork. Without any preamble, he made an announcement.

"Good, everybody's here. We have orders. We are all moving. Clean out your lockers and pack up your possessions. Be ready to go first thing in the morning. There has been a lot of bombing in Hannover, and the unit is needed there. Pack everything you have, we won't be coming back to Braunschweig."

Then we were dismissed. I had not seen Harms upset before. He was generally pretty even tempered but was obviously annoyed by the orders to move. If he was worried maybe I should be as well. Hannover? I was just getting familiar with Braunschweig. As Arie and I walked out in silence, I had to take a breath to calm myself and adjust to the fact that I was not in trouble. Shaking my head in relief, I nodded to a grinning Arie, as we headed to our barracks.

"Wow," said Lowie. "I didn't expect this. I wonder what Hannover is like. I don't know how you guys feel, but I'm nervous about moving closer to any bombing. I hate it here in Braunschweig, with all these Nazi fanatics everywhere, but what if where we're going is even worse?"

"I was thinking the same thing," said Jack, "here, we understand the rules, we know who we can trust. If they are bombing Hannover, shit, we could get killed."

For the second time in five months, I took everything I owned and packed it away in my suitcase. That night we again discussed our misgivings about the move. None of us had ever been to Hannover and were not sure where it was in relation to Braunschweig, but by morning, we would have to be ready.

None of us slept well. I think we all had similar fears. I could hear the other men tossing around on their straw mattresses, each preoccupied with his own apprehensions about what lay ahead. From Braunschweig I had sent a letter to Corrie, and now my thoughts kept drifting back to Holland. I hoped that they were all safe in Wognum. By now, Corrie and my parents knew where I was, but if I was not able to send another letter soon, they would have no idea that I had been moved or, how I was.

~

The next morning, we woke early to a lot of activity and commotion in the compound. We wolfed down our meagre breakfast of stale bread, jam and coffee on the run, and joined the soldiers outside by a row of trucks. Those in charge were screaming orders at the soldiers loading military supplies and we soon understood that it was our job to load our own tools and the equipment, which would be needed in Hannover. Although we were all busy, we were all quiet. Even Lowie refrained from his usual jokes and antics. Nobody was in the mood that day. I remember that the day was dismal; cloudy and overcast, which did nothing to help lift our hopes or spirits about the journey ahead.

Harms told me to get in and drive the second truck as we started off in a convoy of four vehicles. Other drivers joined us. I did not know who they were, but they wore civilian clothes. They may have been from another labour unit, as they were not in uniform and did not act like soldiers. The first truck was driven by one of them and it was full of machinery. I followed driving the second vehicle with more tools and equipment. Arie had been directed to drive the third vehicle and the fourth truck was, driven by another, unknown driver. Jack, Lowie, Frans, and Rik were in Arie's truck, along with some soldiers. The fourth truck was full of soldiers as well. Each truck had a soldier up front with the driver. We travelled in a line, maintaining a safe distance between each truck as directed by the soldier. It seemed to be his role to tell us where we would go. By now, I understood German well enough to understand his basic commands. Driving was a welcome distraction from my own thoughts and concerns for Corrie and my family in Wognum.

We drove for about 65 kilometres, until we reached Hannover. It was larger than Braunschweig and the surroundings were more industrialized. There was a railway junction situated near many large industrial plants and an oil refinery, so it had often become a target of British bombing.

As we entered the city, we could see a lot of evidence of recent heavy bombing and many areas appeared to be completely demolished. Fires caused by the incendiary bombs were still smoldering, and destroyed buildings stood out as burned-out shells, hollow against the open sky behind them. It made me think about the devastating bombing of Rotterdam by German bombers three years ago. While safe in Wognum, I could only see newspaper photos and imagine what Rotterdam was like. But being here and seeing the reality was damn scary.

I just followed the truck in front of me, but I had trouble keeping mine on the road. The heavily loaded truck was big and cumbersome to handle, and the road itself had been damaged by bombing. It took a great deal of concentration to steer clear of deep craters and drive safely through the piles of brick, broken glass, and destruction. I had the eerie feeling of being in a city that was normally bustling with activity, but which was now quiet and empty. People had gone, or at least, had been prohibited from entering the area and it was uncanny for us. As we cautiously bumped along, I caught a single movement out of the corner of my eye, as a lone gray cat slipped between the buildings in front of me, like a ghostly thief scrambling to avoid detection.

We left the area and drove to one of the suburbs. Our new compound was set up much like the one in Braunschweig, although it was larger. There was a small comfort in knowing that our work and our daily routine here would be similar to what we had experienced in Braunschweig. I had always been scared in Braunschweig but now I almost missed it. There, I had been afraid of the German fanatics but now I was facing a whole new set of fears. My greatest fear now was the possibility of dying in a bombing raid. I was scared in Braunschweig but death was further away, here I was surrounded by it and it rattled my sense of hope for the future.

We were directed by the soldiers to our new barracks. A senior soldier, apparently in charge, sternly told us to choose which bunk we wanted, get settled in, and make our way to the kitchen to be fed. The barracks was more like a small garage, just wooden planks on wood framing.

The one thing that was familiar to us was the picture of Hitler hanging on the far wall. It was the first thing one saw upon entering. The door was at the opposite end and each side had two windows. The back of the room opened to side rooms. One side room was for showers and the other room had toilets and small sinks for shaving. At least we had running water as we did in Braunschweig. Our bunks were against the outside wall arranged so that the foot of our bunks all met in the middle of the room. Each bunk had the same canvas bag full of straw as a mattress. In the middle space at the foot of the beds, a small stove sat on a concrete pad near a table with six chairs. Beside each bed was an open wooden closet without a door. My suitcase fit nicely in the bottom of my closet. A shelf for personal items was on the wall above the headboards; I had a razor, soap, and some tobacco. The only other personal item that I had was a picture of Corrie, but I kept that with me in the pocket of my work jacket. Jack and I took bunks along one wall, with Arie taking the third. The other three bunks on the opposite wall were taken by Frans, Lowie, and Rik.

Once we had settled in and had tested our straw beds only to be disappointed by their lack of comfort, we all walked to the building that housed the kitchen. It was a busy dining room area full of soldiers laughing and carrying trays. Those who had finished were enjoying a second coffee or tea and relaxing with conversation and a smoke. All eyes were on us as we entered, as unlike the uniformed soldiers, we were dressed in work clothes. Harms was among the soldiers and said nothing but, with his nod of approval, we took off our hats and lined up with other soldiers for our meal. Our hot lunch was watery stew, black bread and strong tea. It was a welcome break but the food was still rationed. During the meal, Harms left his seat at another table with the soldiers and came to us. "Stay in your barracks," he said sternly. "For the remainder of today, rest, shower, and get settled in. Your work will begin in the morning. Any questions?" We knew better than to actually ask any questions, but we all appreciated the gesture.

~

Next morning, and before we started work, we were once again forced to stand in lines and listen to the rules. The commanders were new, but the message was the same.

> *You are now employed by the greatest nation in the world and great things are awaiting you. You must do as you are told. If you disobey, you will be punished. If you escape, because you think Germany can do without you, you will be found and you will not live to talk about it.*

The word *employed* was a disturbing euphemism, as if I had a choice to be here. The entire message sounded more threatening every time I heard it, and we were forced to hear it frequently.

Work in Hannover was much the same as before but here I spent more time working with Lowie. Arie took over the main job of driving when required, leaving Lowie and me to dismantle vehicles that could not be repaired. Lowie was a welder and was quite skilled with a cutting torch. Together we would cut up the battered vehicles and load the scrap onto the truck to be delivered by rail to smelters, where they would be melted down for reuse.

Braunschweig had its problems and now Hannover would take a while to get settled into. After having been in Germany for six months now, a new problem began to gnaw at me. The small amount of rations provided by the army was becoming a hardship. I had never before experienced hunger. At home as a boy with my brothers and sisters we were poor, but my parents made sure that we always had enough to eat. The orchards and gardens on our property provided plenty of fruit and vegetables. My father's network of friends and neighbours meant we always had some kind of meat or fish for the table, bartered or traded, as was his habit, when money was scarce. But here in Germany, I was always hungry. It was a new experience to be always looking for more to eat, and the constant wanting and search for more food changes you. It becomes an effort and in this bizarre world of war, the unnecessary distraction of hunger could be dangerous. I knew that I had to stay focused on the dangers around me to survive, and yet, when one is always hungry, that becomes difficult.

Sometimes, our unit was given the job of delivering rations and supplies to other camps and compounds around the area and, if it was a heavy day's work, Harms told me to assist Arie with the driving. I hated making deliveries to the camps, but these trips often allowed for me to have something extra to eat. As I drove along country roads, unguarded and on my way back to the compound, I could discreetly find some reward. But this was, however, stealing. I was not raised to be a thief. I was taught not to steal and my parents raised us to respect the property of others. But here, life was different. Here, life was a daily struggle to survive. It was the fall, and apples were ripe in the orchards bordering the roads. I sometimes parked my truck on a quiet back road and quickly helped myself to as many apples as I could carry. Fruit was a real luxury that I had not enjoyed since I left Holland. I was self-conscious of my efforts at first, knowing full well that the orchard crops belonged to a German farmer and his family. For me to take apples was to steal his property and I knew that if caught stealing property from a German, I would be severely punished. But desperate times lead to desperate ways. Anything I could steal I would hide under my coat in the cab of the truck and enjoy later, with my friends, back in the barracks. When I returned from my delivery trips, my friends were always eager to greet me and grateful to share my supplies. They did not want to know where the bounty came from, and never asked. Such knowledge could be dangerous for me and for them.

~

A soldier approached me in the yard one morning, while I was changing the tires on a staff car. He told me to meet Harms at the transport office for instructions - I had to make another delivery. As usual I was introduced to a soldier that would be my guard and then Harms dismissed us both. I was pleased to see that he was an older soldier. Young soldiers were often more fanatical, which often made the trip uncomfortable. The older soldiers were usually more relaxed and this one was no different. Except to give me directions, he rode along quietly. We had been travelling for a short time when we had to slow down because there was a work crew blocking the road ahead. "Stay back," said my escort, as he moved uneasily in his seat. "This could be dangerous, and we do not want to get caught up in it."

Political prisoners were often seen repairing the roads after a bomb attack, and we sometimes had to wait at a safe distance until they were done. They also had to clean up the debris in the area and search for any unexploded bombs. The bombs were reported and later defused by German soldiers. On occasion, upon finding a live bomb, a desperate prisoner would intentionally strike the bomb with their shovel to escape the drudgery. The resulting explosion was not just a suicide, but an end to the hopeless misery. I never saw it happen, but I had heard that it did, and knew why the old soldier wanted me to stay back.

As we sat in silence for several minutes, a group of about a dozen men walked past our truck. What a deplorable sight. They were dressed in the gray and blue striped clothing, the uniform of political prisoners, and were guarded by soldiers armed with rifles. The overseer had a rubber baton and whipped the prisoners as they stumbled past him. The men closest to me were walking three abreast but the two on the outside seemed to be holding up the weaker man in the middle. They looked dirty, emaciated, and were shivering. I tried to look away but could not as the men stopped for a second beside the window of my truck. The weakest one, the one in the middle, looked at me and as my eyes met his, I realized he was absolutely wretched. I saw such despair on his face and, overcome by sympathy, I struggled to swallow the lump I felt in my throat. I wanted to help him, but I could not. In the area where prisoners were working there were usually signs posted directing anyone passing by to avoid any contact with the prisoners. The signs also warned that anyone caught helping these prisoners would be punished. Even throwing them a cigarette, could result in the offender being taken into custody and forced to join their ranks.

Once the road had been cleared, my escort and I drove on in silence. We continued on our journey - each one of us lost in our own thoughts. Mine were filled with empathy for the lives I had just observed. Sitting beside me but staring blankly ahead, the old soldier seemed to read my mind and said quietly, "I'm afraid that's just how it is now."

I don't think he expected a response.

Chapter 8
The Cavalry Pants

Hannover, Fall 1943

Our meals were delivered with the same routine as in Braunschweig. Lunch was a hot meal, eaten with the soldiers. The food was edible but there was never enough. At least the coffee was decent as it was the same coffee that the soldiers received. Our lunch time conversation usually centered around the food, the work, or the bosses.

"Our boss seems to be a fair man," said Arie one day, as we all sat together.

"Seems to be," I answered, as I sipped my tea, "but don't forget, he is a German officer." I did agree that compared to some of the Nazis I had met, Harms did not seem to be a fanatic. He could be strict, but he seemed to believe that every man just needed to do his job and not attract any negative attention.

"I heard that Harms did a tour on the front," added Lowie quietly so as not to be heard by the soldiers. "He was badly wounded and hospitalized. His recovery was lengthy, and now he has a steel plate in his head."

"No wonder his attitude is less aggressive," said Rik joining the conversation. "He probably figures he has done his time for the Führer."

"Yup. He had me welding a truck fender the other day and caught me sitting on the running board having a smoke," said Lowie with a grin. "He didn't even get mad. I expected him to yell at me like other soldiers do, but he just walked by and looked at me. But the stern look on his face was enough to get me back to work. I don't want to find out how brutal the boss can be … if he wants to be."

Harms had made it quite clear that we were expected to be at work on time and put in a satisfactory effort during the working day. He was usually reasonable and fair, so we tried to comply with Harms' orders. Unfortunately, there were others working in the factories nearby who were not as lucky as we were, as not all bosses were alike. We heard horror stories of the treatment that other forced labourers had experienced at the hands of their bosses.

"Remember the guy we met at lunch that day," said Jack, jumping in on the conversation. "He had been in this camp for a couple of months?"

"Oh yeah, that Polish guy from Barrack 12," said Arie. "I think his name was Alex."

"Yes, remember," said Jack. "He was a forced labourer who worked in a local factory. He felt sick one morning and refused to go to work. Complaining of being very tired and having sore feet, he refused to leave his bed at roll call. It was not long before armed guards came to his barracks, dragged him out of bed and took him away."

Three weeks later we were shocked to see Alex when he was returned to his barracks. It was a woeful sight. The man was near death; he was a moving skeleton. He could barely walk, and he was so thin his skin seemed to be the only thing that was holding his bones together. He was covered in ugly purple bruises and his eyes were sunken in his face. He looked totally broken. Once again, we were reminded that we all were at the mercy of the Nazis.

"He got sent to Lager 21," I said. "Alex told us that he would never again miss even an hour of work," I continued. "He said he would crawl there if he had to, because he would rather die than go back to Lager 21."

Lager 21 was a prison work camp run by the Gestapo to "re-educate" forced labourers like us, who had disobeyed the rules or refused to go to work. Depending on the severity of the offence, workers could be sentenced to 21, 42- or 63-days' punishment. The working and living conditions there were often worse than those in the concentration camps. The Gestapo regularly tortured and starved the inmates. I prayed that I would never be too sick to work or get into enough trouble to be sent away to such a horrible place.

~

As the days of autumn became colder, Arie and I shared the driving jobs while Rik, Lowie, and Jack continued to work in the compound fixing trucks and other damaged vehicles. Occasionally, I had to stop at railway crossings, and I waited and watched as large locomotives rolled through pulling several enclosed box cars. I was always curious as to what cargo they carried. It appeared to be of value because each car had an armed soldier positioned in a small guard house atop of it. I thought that perhaps the cars contained ammunition, supplies or something else which was valuable to the war effort.

Arie said that he had seen them too, but it wasn't until much later in the war that we both learned the truth of what was being transported. The trains were carrying Jews, political prisoners, and various other people from across Europe who did not meet the Aryan ideals of the Nazi party. They were being systematically transported to camps to hold them until they could be exterminated. The trains made me curious, but I never asked questions. In Germany, people who asked questions were responded to in the same way - "why do you want to know?" - then they disappeared.

~

As the next few months passed, the colder weather presented new problems for us. Though our work coveralls were supplied by the Germans, socks were not. Maybe the socks went to the soldiers. Mine were worn out and I had no way to replace them. Luxuries such as these were no longer available even if you had the money. We were forced to wrap our feet in old rags, just to keep them warm in our work boots.

Occasionally, we had a day off. We kept the same schedule as the soldiers because we worked under their guard. We had skills that they needed and I was thankful that I had those skills. Compared to the stories we heard about other forced labourers in the factories, working as prisoners with long hours and often seven days a week, our world was different. They were dispensable, but our abilities were unique, that's the only reason they ensured we were kept alive.

They were not being kind – they were being efficient. We had to be able to perform. On our off days, we were allowed out to buy personal items. We received a pittance for our labours and it was intended to be spent on such things. I found a used clothing store and went there hoping to find something to keep me warm in the cold winter ahead. I found quite a prize, a pair of old gray cavalry pants. They were awkwardly shaped, short but made of heavy wool material and they fit under my coveralls. When I showed them to my friends, they were quite amused and made fun of me.

"Where did you find them?" asked Lowie, laughing. "You look ridiculous."

"Laugh if you like," I said, "but when the temperature drops, I'll be warm."

And I was. In fact, I became the envy of the group. And the temperature did drop, and as I had predicted, they all wished they had a pair. I was so proud of my find. An old, well-worn pair of military issue cavalry pants, discarded by the original owner, became my most treasured possession. The big garage we worked in had a stove at either end for heat. Coal was in short supply so we often used wood instead. The building was usually free of frost but never comfortably warm. Often, I was grateful to be working with Lowie to be near the torch for a little heat in that huge cold garage. Our barracks was a little more comfortable because we could scrounge wood from around the compound to put in the stove. The combination of hunger, cold and the ever-present concern for safety were continuous reminders of the deprivations of war. I just longed to go home.

~

The months passed and we continued to struggle with the cold and the hunger which were taking their toll on all of us. But on Christmas Eve, we were told that we would not have to work the next day. I was looking forward to a good day of rest. The only place to stay really warm was in bed, so as I often did, I was in bed early. We were awakened shortly after midnight on Christmas morning. Two soldiers came into the barracks and woke us up.

"Euch anziehen: es gibt Arbeit," they yelled repeatedly. *Get dressed: there is work to do.*

Along with half a dozen other drivers from elsewhere in the compound, we all were ordered outside and told to climb into the back of a large cargo truck. It was a miserable night, it was dark, and it was snowing. The wind was filled with swirling specks of ice that stung like barbs when they hit my skin. It was so very cold, and we had dressed in a hurry. In the rush, I hadn't time to put on my cavalry pants and I was freezing. The floor of the cargo truck had a light covering of snow that turned quickly to ice upon which our leather boots slipped at every turn. We were taken to a railway yard and spent the next several hours removing disabled vehicles from flatbed railway cars. Most were just trucks, military cars, and light vehicles. We never had dealings with tanks or armoured vehicles. It seemed to me that the vehicles we were to collect were not a priority and could easily have waited until morning. But I was not in charge.

We chained all the vehicles together and with the large delivery truck leading, all were pulled in convoy back to the compound for repair. The other drivers, along with Arie and me, were each given a vehicle to steer and in the cold of night, without lights and most without functioning motors, it was a difficult task. The ground was frozen hard and the puddles on the roadways were iced over and slippery. One or two of the trucks were without brakes and had to be placed near the front of the chain, where spacing was controlled by the braking of the last vehicles in the convoy. Had a chain broken, in the darkness, without lights and controls, it would have been disastrous. Without incident however, we returned to the compound where the vehicles were stored and, at last, we were allowed to return to our beds. I was cold, hungry and tired, but glad to be able to get warm again. After a few hours on Christmas morning, we were awakened, and provided with a simple breakfast. Surprisingly, we were each given a bottle of wine to celebrate. We spent the day quietly, each man thinking of home and of Christmases past. As we enjoyed our special treat, Frans began to sing. He had an amazing voice and we all enjoyed listening to him. Before long, warmed and mellowed by the wine we were all singing along together and, for a while, we felt a little less homesick.

~

It was a long and very cold winter in Hannover, but, at last we started to see signs of spring. After being cooped up in our barracks or the cold garage for most of the harsh season, we were glad to be able to get out of the compound when we were allowed to leave. Our barracks was not far from Hannover and so, Jack and I, decided to spend our day off to visit the town. After a short walk on a country road that took us through some woods, we could catch the streetcar. It was crowded that day and we were seated close to a couple of young German girls. They were friendly and flirted with us. I'm sure that they were as lonely as we were, as all the healthy German men their age were off fighting somewhere. They just wanted some company. I had not thought much of it before, but the only young German men we saw here were maimed in some way. Many were in wheelchairs or on crutches.

As much as we enjoyed the attention of the girls, I reminded myself of what Karl had told Arie and me in Braunschweig about being careful around the local girls. We knew that we were not supposed to be friendly with them. We knew that as foreigners, we would be punished. I was unsure as to the overall reasoning at the time, but I was fluent enough in German to read the billboards:

> *Foreigners are not allowed any contact or fraternization with local girls. Disobedience will result in severe punishment.*

The warning boards were worded strongly enough, and could be seen often enough, that we knew the rules were important. In spite of the warnings, the girls did not seem to be concerned and invited us to go for a drink. We were all living in such bizarre circumstances each day that we longed to just relax and spend time with others our own age. We agreed, and we went with them then and a couple of times after. Jack and I were the youngest men in the compound and, sometimes, we just wanted to get away from the war, and to laugh and to try and feel normal for a while. Being young and naive, we thought we were being discreet, and it worked, for a while. But as with many things, the only time that counts, is the time you get caught.

Her name was Elfrieda.

Chapter 9
Trust and Betrayal

Hannover, Spring 1944

We met her on the streetcar on a Sunday morning. Jack and I were going into town for our usual tobacco run. She said her name was Elfrieda, sat down beside us and started a conversation.

"Guten tag," she said opening a conversation with a pleasant smile and she told us her name. "Mein name ist Elfrieda."

I was sure that she, initially, thought we were German and not wanting to discourage her from conversing, we spoke as little as possible. It was April and, by now, we had been in Germany a full year. Our ability to speak the language was improving but our accent may have revealed more than we wanted to at first. She was a pretty girl about our age, tall with long flaxen hair tied back in meticulous braids. We both responded in German to say, "Good morning," and to our surprise, she continued to talk. When we reached our stop and stood up to get off, she did as well, and she walked with us while we bought our tobacco. Elfrieda had other places to be and we had to get back to the barracks as well. It was a quick but memorable introduction.

~

Back at the barracks and after dinner, Jack, Arie and I sat outside on the step rolling and smoking cigarettes charged with new tobacco. We told Arie about the girl named Elfrieda.

"It was refreshing," said Jack. "Working, eating and sleeping with you guys gets pretty boring. I miss female company."

"True," said Arie, standing to stretch his legs as he touched a match to a fresh cigarette, "the women here don't work in the garage, so other than meals, we don't have any contact with them. Besides, most of them speak Polish, Russian or French," he laughed. "I'm having enough trouble speaking German."

"Yes, and it was nice to listen to the friendly softness of her voice," I added. "Maybe we should take another trip to town next Sunday morning on the same streetcar," I said, and we all laughed - as if I was joking.

The following Sunday, Jack and I were on that same streetcar and we saw Elfrieda again. We talked about why we were in Germany and she revealed to us the difficulty of domestic life for her and her mother. "It is difficult to get anyone in the area to do odd jobs at our house," she said with a sad smile. "With our men gone, routine repairs are left undone. I told my mother that I met you. She said that if you wanted a home cooked meal, you could help with a few chores. For example, the garden needs planting."

She was very convincing and against my better judgement I said I would help. Jack did not. "Remember the billboards," he said after she left us, and we were walking together back to the barracks. "I disagree Pete. Like most of these German girls, Elfrieda is friendly, kind and good looking. It's tempting, but you and I both know that fraternizing with local girls could mean serious - and I mean serious - punishment. A home cooked dinner would be great, but it's not worth the risk." Jack tried to talk me out of it.

"I do remember the billboards, but I'm always hungry and the possibility of a good meal on a Sunday makes me think the risk might be worth it. Besides," I said, trying to convince him, and maybe even myself, "I'm working, I'm not there socially."

"The sign says fraternizing," said Jack, bluntly. I heard him, but thought differently.

~

I promised to meet Elfrieda on my next day off. I had looked forward to it all week. Although I was nervous about the warnings against fraternizing, I thought it would be worth the risk to see her. She was beautiful: tall and slender with blonde hair and blue eyes. But, I also knew that I needed to be careful. I went to her house and did the repairs asked of me. It was spring and the garden was totally weeded over with neglect.

I spent the whole day digging, raking, and pulling weeds and by the end of the day, I had a garden waiting to be planted. Her mother was not overly friendly, but I thought she was just the typical stoic German type. She kept her part of the bargain, however, and cooked a delicious meal, the most enjoyable dinner I had eaten in a long time. I declined the invitation to come into her kitchen and was happy to eat on the back porch. Elfrieda joined me after dinner, and we had a short conversation over coffee.

"The garden looks good," she said, complimenting me on my work. "Can you return next Sunday and plant it?" I agreed and in total surprise, Elfrieda reached out, took my face in her hands and gave me a kiss. For that brief moment, the fact that she was German didn't matter. I was twenty, it felt wonderful and I impulsively returned the kiss.

~

The following Sunday I did just that. I planted potatoes, carrots, radishes, and some green onions. Over the next couple of visits, I completed other chores as requested and was always rewarded with a hot meal. I fixed the porch railing, painted some window frames and swept the floor of an old barn. While Elfrieda was always friendly her mother remained aloof. Elfrieda told me that her dad and two brothers were in the army, but I figured, like most German men, they were away fighting as I never saw them at home. I enjoyed my times with Elfrieda, but I was always reminded of the warning from Jack. I needed to be careful, and I thought that I was.

~

On one visit in May, Elfrieda came to me outside, after dinner, as I was getting ready to leave. Unlike previous conversations, her tone was now different. "This will be your last visit and I am saying goodbye to you," she said without her usual flirty banter. She was quite abrupt, almost cold. "You are going to be moved very soon." I froze, anticipating what was to follow.

"How do you know this?" I asked.

She smiled and, almost proudly, responded "My father told me." She never talked about her father. I had never met him and had foolishly assumed that he was away from home and no threat to me. I could feel a sharp pain in the pit of my stomach.

"Who is your father?" I asked.

She smiled proudly and said, "He is an officer in the army." She seemed to enjoy my discomfort. In that moment I felt a cold chill pass through my body. I started to tremble. "You are also going to be punished because he knows you were here, with me." After the delivery of that shocking news, she turned away and quickly walked back into the house.

I left without saying goodbye and headed back to the compound. I was in shock. How could I have been so stupid? I didn't want to believe that Elfrieda had intentionally set me up, but why had her personality completely changed? Why was she so uncaring? She seemed to be so proud of her father's position; I didn't know what to think. She had always been nice to me, but today she was a proud German. She seemed to enjoy taunting me and letting me know that I was powerless. I was just a labourer: someone she could use and discard. Jack had told me that being in her company was dangerous. He often referred to her as a "loose cannon."

As I sat on the streetcar, I could feel my heart pounding in my chest. The ride was taking too long. I just wanted to return to the barracks as quickly as I could. It was the only safety I knew. As I watched the telegraph poles slip by and familiar corners vanish behind me, it seemed that the billboards appeared more frequently, just to remind me ...

Foreigners are not allowed any contact or fraternization with the local girls. Disobedience will result in severe punishment.

Once off the streetcar and leaving the lights of the city behind, I still had to walk through the woods towards the compound. My mind was racing as I stumbled in the darkness and the underbrush. What would happen to me? Would I be sent to one of those horrible camps that I had so often been forced to go to earlier? I remembered Alex who had been sent to Lager 21. He barely survived the punishment for being sick and unable to work. In the minds of the German soldiers, my behaviour was much more severe than Alex's. On arrival at the barracks, I was met with a barrage of questions from my friends.

"Where have you been?"

"Why are you getting back so late?"

"You look pale, did something happen?"

"Pale? He looks like shit," said Arie.

"It was my day off today and I went out. We are allowed to do that," I reminded them. I wasn't trying to be hostile or defensive, although I must have sounded that way. I wasn't being surly, I was scared, very scared. My guts felt like water.

"We had a meeting with Harms this afternoon," said Arie, "and he was wondering where you were. He wants to see you first thing in the morning: before roll call. We are getting moved again."

As I laid on my bunk trying to calm down to sleep, Jack whispered to me in the darkness. "Were you with that girl? Were you with Elfrieda?" he asked.

Again, I was so scared I could hardly speak. My voice trembled as I answered softly, "I was with her, yes, but I was also with her mother. I was at their house to do the jobs they wanted done. You know, doing work for a meal. What's wrong with that, I wasn't carrying on socially."

"Fraternizing has a broad definition," said Jack, warning me once again. "If Harms wants to see you, now you might be in trouble." Nothing else needed to be said. He was right and I knew it. There were going to be consequences, and I knew that too. I was worried as to what they would be. In my experiences with the occupation troops in Holland, the Germans were not in the habit of issuing warnings.

~

Morning was slow in coming as I spent the night in fear and restless sleep. The following morning, I washed up quickly. I did not stop to eat breakfast but produced myself at Harms' office, as requested. He was at his desk waiting for me.

"I understand that we are moving," I opened.

"Yes," he said, "and I will deal with that later. But first: Where were you yesterday?" he asked.

"It was my day off and I went into town. Was that wrong?" I asked, in a quavering voice. "We are allowed to do that, aren't we?"

"Yes," he replied, standing and moving around his desk to be closer, "but your activity in town has been reported to my superiors, and damn it Pete, you have all been warned not to socialize with the local girls. You know that your visits with that family were not appropriate. You were not allowed any contact with that woman and especially her daughter Elfrieda, and for that, I have to be on record as having told you… that you will be punished. For now, know that yes, we are moving. Pack up your stuff and help the unit to get ready. We are moving within the next 24 hours. Understand, that the move has nothing to do with you. We are moving the unit because we are needed in the Hamburg area." He said, "I don't know exactly what your punishment will be for being at that house, and spending time with the girl Elfrieda, but you are going to be disciplined for that, sometime later."

"Allow me to explain. She and her mother appreciated the work that I did and I appreciated a good meal. That's all it was."

After listening to my side of the story, Harms said that he understood my reasons, I could see an empathy in his face, as he accepted that I was there to do odd jobs for a hot meal. "But you and I both know, regardless of your intentions, a 20-year-old foreigner has no business consorting with an 18-year-old German girl," he said. "It doesn't matter what you did, it's what they think you did. That's all that matters," he said. "Especially when her father is an officer in the German army. I am sure she was quite persuasive but that is of no consequence. You had plenty of warnings: you saw the signs."

I said, as though surprised, "I didn't know that her father was an officer in the army. She just told me that yesterday."

"Doesn't matter," said Harms. "And, as I said, her role in your visits is of no interest to us, you knew better than to be involved with her." He took a deep drag on a freshly lit cheroot and looked down examining the papers on his desk. There was nothing I could do to change the situation; our discussion was obviously over and I was being silently dismissed.

Without a word, I turned and left his office. Harms did not look up as I gently closed his door and headed to the yard to get to work. We had a few things to clean up in our workshop before I could again pack my suitcase to prepare for the move to Fürstenmoor.

Chapter 10
Razzia

Wognum, Spring 1944

It was a bright sunny morning in early May. Green leaves were starting to show on the tree branches and spring usually helped to renew my hopes. But not that year. That year was different. With a chill in the air, I was hoping it would be warm enough to hang the laundry in the Roemers' back yard. The slight breeze was the kind of gentle wind needed to dry the clothes quickly.

As I started my work, I looked around the yard and immediately felt the familiar and lonely ache and a sense of loss. The garage door where Peter used to park his truck was closed. It used to be opened every day when Peter was here, but seldom was open these days since many of the Roemers' trucks had been confiscated by the Germans. Peter had been gone for over a year and I had received just one letter. I knew from the letter that he was in Braunschweig, but that had been last year. It terrified me to think about the reasons why he'd only just sent one letter. Was the mail now forbidden in Germany? Was Peter still alive? I didn't want to think about the alternatives. I had to shake it off and get back to work.

I knew that I was always welcome to visit Peter's family down the road and I was looking forward to going over that night. By 1944, we were all struggling with the lack of fuel, services, and supplies. Food was rationed, personal property had been confiscated and the constant checkpoints had become so inconvenient that daily life itself had become a struggle. Our mail deliveries had been stopped, fuel for cooking and lighting was unavailable and everyone had to be indoors by curfew at 8 p.m. The power was cut off and all lights had to be extinguished. Any light from local residences would have revealed the landscape of the German occupation to Allied bombers and so we were ordered to stay indoors, with the windows shrouded by blackout curtains. People were forced to spend lonely evenings inside their homes in total darkness.

Jan - Peter's dad, was adept at finding creative solutions for difficult situations, and he came up with an idea for our lighting problem. A bicycle frame with a wheel attached was mounted onto a portable wooden rack in the corner, and a small generator was attached to the bicycle wheel. Wires were attached to a lamp and after curfew, the family collected themselves in one room. Ordinary household tasks were accomplished in the dim but helpful light created by the tiny home-made generator. Elisabeth could do some mending and others could read or do other jobs while the boys had fun riding the bike. The rigging was very basic and, once the novelty wore off, it became burdensome, but thanks to their dad's ingenuity, the family was able to overcome the darkness. But even with low illumination and blackout curtains, the light was sometimes still visible and the soldiers were vigilant, patrolling to check for infractions.

~

One evening, I was lying in bed with one of the Roemer children, quietly reading her a story as I usually did before she went to sleep. Tina was only four and went to bed early. I remember that it was just around dusk. The calm was shattered by soldiers outside. Loud voices shouted in a language I did not understand. Fists pounded on the side door of our house and I cringed in fear. The soldiers wanted something from us. It was the first time that I was personally involved in something the German soldiers wanted. I was terrified and taking little Tina with me, I crawled under the bed. Tina took her favourite doll with her. Dolly had rosy freckles on her cheeks, big black eyes, and a fixed happy smile.

Tina held her close as we huddled together in fright. Her father, Tinus, opened the side door to them and was immediately pushed to the floor. One angry soldier stomped on his chest, while other soldiers yelled at him to comply.

"Keine lichter," they yelled, *No lights*. "Keine lichter!"

Not understanding German, Tinus was slow to react as they picked him up, pushed and half dragged him up the stairs to my room. He did not understand what they wanted and he tried to determine why they were there. They kicked open the bedroom door, exploded into the room and dragged little Tina and me out from under the bed by our arms. One of the soldiers put his face to mine and was screaming at me. He was so close that I could feel the spit off his lips striking my face. I could feel Tina cringe close to me like a tiny, frightened bird.

Still aggressive and angry, the soldier pointed at the reading lamp, and pulled the blackout curtain further across the window. When satisfied that the light was no longer visible from outside, the soldiers turned and without further comment or apology for the intrusion, bolted down the stairs. They slammed the side door behind them and disappeared down the road into the darkness of the night. I lay on the bed with a crying little Tina, and Dolly. We were shaken by the presence of angry soldiers with guns. This was an exposed light. I couldn't help but wonder, how would I have been treated had it been a more serious matter?

~

The next morning, I was still shaken by the events of the previous evening. I left Tina asleep in her bed, and I hurried down the road to see my best friend Marta. I could hardly wait to tell her about the soldiers and the terror we had experienced the night before at the Roemers. Before I even had a chance to knock, Marta met me at the door.

"Oh Corrie, I am so glad to see that you are all right," she said giving me a hug. "We were so afraid for you. We could hear the soldiers noisily making a commotion on the road, but we were too far away to hear what they wanted. What was going on?"

"I didn't understand what they wanted," I said looking for a chair to sit down. I told her the whole story, how angry and loud the soldiers were because the blackout curtain wasn't closed tightly enough and they could see a light. "It was terrifying," I said.

"Yes," she said sitting down beside me. "They made quite a commotion all along the street last night. Soldiers were going door to door hunting for bicycles," she said. "They interrupted Dad working in the back yard and pointed at his bicycle. With angry hand gestures, they confiscated all his bikes and took them to a truck. When he tried to tell a soldier that we needed to keep at least one bicycle for the family to use, the soldier moved away allowing the other soldiers to shoulder their rifles and point them at him. Nothing else could be said or done as he stepped back in resignation. He could only stand there alone and watch the Germans load his family bicycles onto their truck and drive away".

"Did they take your bicycle?" asked Marta.

"No. I had it hidden in the barn," I said. "If they had searched the barn, I'm sure they would have taken it. But they saw the light from my window first."

Peter had made me a bicycle, constructed from parts of other old bikes when we were first dating. I was so pleased to have it. Not just because it was transportation for me, but Peter had made it, just for me. I had been a little embarrassed when he presented me with it. I had never had a bike before, and I was awkward riding one. But Peter helped me and over time I learned. I cherished having that bike and I was proud to be able to ride it like other girls my age.

I felt sorry for Marta and her family. Peter had seven brothers and sisters, and bicycles were their only means of transportation. It was such a huge loss for the family to have had all their bicycles taken away, and according to Marta, her Dad was totally enraged by the whole matter. The family would have used them to go shopping and carry supplies home. Earlier in the occupation, the Germans had taken away his trucks, and now they took his bicycles too.

"Did they take all your bicycles?" I asked.

With a loving smile, Marta went on, "Except for one," she said proudly.

"The only bike they didn't take was the one that Dad had fixed a few weeks ago. He modified it just for that reason," she said with a laugh. "He took a hack saw and cut off one of the handle bars." We both started to laugh. "Not even a desperate German soldier wants a bicycle with only one handlebar," she said, and we both were laughing so hard that the emotions from the night before were quickly erased. "That's Dad," she whispered lovingly.

~

As spring slipped into summer, the shortage of supplies became more widespread and more serious; not just for the residents of Wognum, but the German occupiers as well. Anywhere we went during the day, we were required to have photo-identification, and soldiers patrolled the streets doing random checks for ID. We had to have it with us at all times. When using our ration cards, we had to be prepared to prove our identity. The locals were expected to adapt and do without, and when the Germans were in need, they expected the local people to share what little they had.

The German military devised a scheme called a "razzia" - *roundup.* The soldiers would cordon off streets in town and then systematically search each building on the street checking for the supplies they needed. They would just show up and demand food, bicycles, horses, and even blankets: whatever they needed for the military. When they found what they wanted they took it, and the owner was left without. Whatever the soldiers needed, they took from Dutch citizens. They were always prowling the neighbourhoods for food or supplies, but sometimes, the raids were far more horrific. Sometimes the soldiers hunted for men.

They searched for Jews in hiding, members of the resistance, or any able young men. The soldiers would go from house to house arresting young men in their twenties and thirties and force them from their homes to work in Germany and become a part of the labour force. If Peter had not gone in response to his letter a year ago, I was sure a *razzia* would have picked him up.

After one such *razzia,* a neighbour came to Roemer's house knocking on the door. She was asking for me. My friend Eva and her two small children were visibly upset as she stood in the doorway.

"Come in, come in," I said. "What has happened?"

"I need your help," she said. "My husband has been taken in a roundup. He will be sent to Germany to work. He and the others are being held at the square, but only for a few hours. I have to bring him a suitcase with clothing and provisions for the journey."

Eva and her children were understandably frightened. I could understand her being distraught as I had heard how aggressive the roundups were from other women in town. Brothers, husbands, sons or fathers were quickly picked up and taken away from their families.

"Can you watch my children for a few hours while I go to say goodbye to Victor?" she asked.

As I took the children and brought them into the house, she said sheepishly, "I have another favour to ask of you, one that is even more imposing." Time was of the essence and she had no other option but to ask, "Can I borrow your bicycle?"

Wognum is a small town, and neighbours help each other in a crisis. But to borrow another's bicycle at this time was a significant request. It was common knowledge that many bicycles had been taken by the Germans, but a few people still had one. Eva somehow knew that I was one such person. What option did she have? What option did I have? I thought I should help a friend and a neighbour, and even though I knew the risk, I reluctantly agreed.

~

Several hours passed before she returned. There was a knock at the door and I was glad Eva had returned. Her children were anxious and looking forward to seeing her. Eva was in tears.

"Oh Corrie, it was terrible," she cried. "The men were being herded onto the square like cattle when I arrived," she said. "I couldn't find Victor anywhere. The crowd was so big, there must have been two hundred or more. Everyone was pushing others around trying to find their men before they were to be taken away. It was hard to move with both a suitcase and a bicycle and I realized that I was one of the few people there with a bike. I quickly tried to find a spot behind a building to hide it. As I did so, a soldier approached me in curiosity, as if I was doing something wrong. I was scared. He was about my age and looked too young to be in such a position of authority. He looked at me with a boyish kindness, and I thought for a minute that he would let me go. But then, his superior came over to check.

The young soldier's face and his demeanour quickly changed. His need to obey was obvious. His response was abrupt and he took your bicycle from me. He left me standing there, as the officer looked at me with a smirk of superiority.

I ran into the square but there were so many men and they were being pushed onto trucks. I heard my husband Vic call out to me and I ran to him with his suitcase. We had only a moment to say goodbye: and then he was pulled away in the crowd."

She finished her story and fell to her knees sobbing in the kitchen. Her children came into the kitchen when they heard her. They were too young to understand, but seeing their mother distraught and crying uncontrollably, they too began to cry.

"It is ok, Eva," I said. "You're with friends: you're safe." She looked at me tearfully - her face distorted in pain. I would never forget it.

"Oh Corrie," she cried, "they are gone. My husband and your bicycle… they're both gone."

Chapter 11
FOXHOLES

Fürstenmoor, June 1944

As I crossed the yard from Harms' office, I could see that tools and equipment were being packed into two trucks by Jack and the men of my work gang. They were obviously preparing to move and when I came nearer, they stopped their work.

"What did Harms say?" asked Jack.

"Was he pissed because you were away yesterday?" asked Rik.

"Are you getting punished?" asked Lowie. Jack just rolled his eyes, looked at him with surprise and shook his head.

"Yah, you look like hell, Pete. But that's at times normal for you," said Arie laughing to lighten the mood.

"What did he say? Why did he need to see you? Did he tell you where we are going?" asked the others.

"Harms told me we are going to Fürstenmoor tomorrow morning. Let's just get our work done and get packed up to go," I said, "I don't want to talk about it." We worked all day loading the trucks and when the work in the yard was finished, we went to the barracks for our supper. As usual, it was waiting for us on the table. The portions were small but at least it was nourishment.

After eating, we sat around the table talking about Fürstenmoor. During the day, in the yard, Rik and Frans had heard the soldiers talking.

"The soldiers didn't know that we could hear them. They forget that we can understand a fair bit of German," said Rik. "They seem to be afraid about the constant and heavy bombing in Hamburg. The bombing is frequent, day or night."

"All we know is that Fürstenmoor is close to Hamburg," said Frans. "It does sound pretty damn scary. Now we have something more to worry about."

"Right," said Rik, "we could get killed there."

We all agreed that worrying about the future was useless as the future was not within our control. We agreed to just go to bed for a good rest before heading out in the morning. When the lights were turned off and we all got into our bunks, Jack put his hand down between our bunks, leaned over to me and whispered in the dark.

"You looked pretty scared this morning when you came out of Harm's office," he said. "Did he want to know where you were yesterday?"

"He knew where I was. He knew I was at Elfrieda's."

"How did he know?" said Jack quietly. "I was the only one who knew where you were going. You know I wouldn't say anything to him."

"I know it wasn't you Jack, you are a good friend. It was Elfrieda. Harms told me that punishment was coming but he doesn't know yet what it will be. You told me to stay away from her. I was stupid. Of all the girls we could have met, it had to be Elfrieda. Her Dad is an army officer… and she told her Dad."

"Holy shit," said Jack stunned by the news. "You could be in big trouble now."

Thanks Jack, that's all I needed to hear, I thought, lying there alone in the dark.

~

The next morning, with the trucks all packed and ready to go, Harms gathered us in the yard and we were on our way to Fürstenmoor. We were a Mobile Vehicle Repair Unit and the two trucks with a small trailer suited our needs; there was space for the six of us and our equipment. Harms and the soldiers travelled separately. When I had been making deliveries, a soldier was always detailed to travel with me, but this time, the soldiers moved in their own transport.

An army scout car with Harms and a couple of soldiers in it pulled out leading the way with our two trucks following. I drove one truck with Jack and Lowie. Arie drove the other one with Frans and Rik. A third truck joined us, driven by a military driver with several soldiers in the back. We bypassed the main cities and stayed on rural roads. As we travelled across the German countryside, I could see the leaves sprouting on the trees. It was late spring and in all its clear sky and fresh splendor, it was difficult to appreciate there was a war going on - until we got to Hamburg.

The shipyards, and the oil refineries had been bombed frequently, since the beginning of the war. As our trucks rumbled through the city, a war-torn city in chaos and destruction, it was obvious that our world was changing. Buildings were caved in and destroyed from the Allied bombing and many parts of the city were closed off for repair and clean-up. We had to detour and backtrack many times with the streets cluttered in mountains of scorched building materials. Pathways were narrow as bricks had been bulldozed six feet high, up against the ghost-faced buildings, blackened by explosion and fire. Armed soldiers stood as sentries to prevent looting and dangerous trespassing. We were halted at each checkpoint and our group sat in silence as Harms was questioned as to our presence. When cleared, and with Harms and the scout car still leading, we were allowed to pass in single file as we snaked our way towards our destination. Some buildings were gutted with only the walls remaining. Windows were blackened holes in walls without doors; even the roofs were gone. I felt like an intruder in what used to be a busy city. I was intruding in space belonging to others, except the people were missing. There was no sign of life in this silent city.

Eventually, we found our way to Fürstenmoor. It was a small corner settlement, just a rural clearing, but close to the harbour district. The transport yard was already set up and functioning as a repair garage for army vehicles. It was huge, and obvious to me on arrival, our group would be added to other mechanics, welders, painters and drivers who worked there. The complex network of railway lines and the vast harbour of Hamburg made it easy for large numbers of damaged and broken-down military vehicles to be brought for repair. Jack looked at me with the same shocked face as I am sure I had. "It looks like we have lots of work waiting for us," was all he said.

As we entered the compound, I could see the huge repair shop immediately to the right. To the left was the storage area where all the vehicles were sitting awaiting repair. In the middle of the compound was an oval track. Vehicles could be test driven there without leaving the compound and using the city streets. In the middle of the oval track, laying neatly in rows like a steel cemetery, were trucks, cars, motorcycles and other vehicles, apparently damaged beyond repair, waiting to be scrapped. Further inside the main gate and to the left was our barracks. Running behind the barracks was the boundary fence bordering the local street. There were seven barrack buildings as the camp had a large workforce of army personnel, German civilian workers, and an assortment of forced labour workers. Jack, Arie and I, and our three Belgian friends Lowie, Rik and Frans were assigned to Barracks #4.

"Stow your gear in your barracks," said Harms. "Report in front of your barracks in 30 minutes. I will have your duties and priorities worked out by then."

As ordered, we were standing outside in front of the barracks within 30 minutes and as he said he would, Harms delivered a run-down of our jobs and responsibilities. We helped a few of the labourers with whatever they were doing and slowly got a feel for our new surroundings. There were more forced labourer groups here, but we only took orders from, and answered to, Harms. He was the boss of our group. All our duties and jobs had to go through him. But for that day, we were just getting familiarized before being sent to our barracks for the night. Dinner was the same as always. It was on the table in our barracks along with the next day's breakfast. We all were tired after our day's journey and skipping our usual evening discussions, we were all in bed early. Tomorrow, the work would begin.

Our new home was one of the busiest locations in Fürstenmoor. There was a manufacturing plant down the street that built small three-wheeled cars called DKW's (Dampf Kraft Wagen). Between our yard and the car plant was a pub. There was also a dentist's office and a small grocery store down the street. Other than that, Fürstenmoor just seemed to be a collection of charming German homes grouped together as a neighbourhood. The compound was on a street corner, enclosed by a three-metre-high meshed steel fence, and topped with a double strand of barbed wire. The main gate was off a side street and guarded by armed German soldiers who checked every vehicle and person that entered or left the area. Similar to what we experienced in Braunschweig and Hannover, the compound at Fürstenmoor was a restricted area. Unless they cleaned or worked in the kitchen, the locals were not allowed to enter.

In the camp, were French, Belgian, and Dutch men. Two Frenchmen had been assigned to Barracks #4 with us. There were also women in forced labour, but they were in their own barracks. The buildings were very basic clapboard shacks, but the barracks were clean and well maintained, much the same as before. Inside each barracks were four beds on each side wall, a wooden table and chairs, a set of lockers for our clothes and a wood burning stove in the middle of the room. And, as usual, hanging on the back wall so we would not forget, was a large framed photograph of Hitler.

A large drainage ditch ran through the back of the compound. It carried the rainwater away from the camp and the surrounding neighbourhood but was dry most of the time. A large kitchen was on one side of the ditch alongside the storage area and, directly in front of the kitchen was a large bridge, strong enough to carry any vehicle crossing between the storage area and the repair shops. In the months that followed, we walked over the bridge daily to get from our barracks to the kitchen for lunch. The compound yard and repair shops were big, but so was the kitchen and the aroma of food was always present. It was an unwelcome distraction when we were constantly hungry.

At Fürstenmoor, our jobs were the same as they were before in Braunschweig and Hannover. Being in forced labour meant exactly that. We were part of a labour force intended to be used however required. We were not there by free will. We had to fix what we were told to fix and do our best to do so. Arie and I remained the main drivers.

The German soldiers in the unit were still not aware that Rik could drive and he preferred it that way.

~

We all slept well our first night in Fürstenmoor. The move had been tiring. First thing the next morning, and once again, we were assembled together as a group in orderly military fashion in the middle of the compound. A sharply uniformed commander, stood ramrod straight before us and sternly read the delivery to remind us (as if I needed to be reminded).

> *You are now employed by the greatest nation in the world and great things are awaiting you. You must do as you are told. If you disobey, you will be punished. If you escape, because you think Germany can do without you, you will be found and you will not live to talk about it.*

After hearing that, and before we began working in the garage, we were told to dig ourselves a foxhole. There had been a lot of Allied bombings in Hamburg earlier that spring and being new in the compound, we each had to have someplace to go if we got caught in the open yard. The Germans had always issued us with our coveralls and work boots, but that morning for the first time, we received a personal steel helmet and a gas mask. We were given orders to always have the gas mask with us, and the helmet had to be worn at all times. It was heavy and felt awkward on my head. The Germans needed our skills and wanted to keep us alive, but I always hated wearing even a cap, so my new helmet was going to be difficult. Jack and I picked an area where we were told to. The area was open ground near the fence at the edge of the compound. We decided that in an emergency that would be our spot. We stood looking at our shovels waiting for the others to start digging.

"I'm not a soldier," said Jack, "how the hell do I know what a foxhole is supposed to look like."

"Just start digging," I said. "I'm sure somebody will be around to tell us." We each started digging and in time a soldier came by to check the progress of our work. He told us the basics of the length, width and depth for a proper slit trench. Our holes lacked military shape and form but we were close to the required standard and we had holes that we were proud of.

"The main function of your foxhole is to reduce the likelihood of you being killed during a bombing," he said. "And, there is a reason why you were issued with a steel helmet this morning," he reminded us as he walked away. "So, wear it."

With such a dismissive attitude, it seemed that he really didn't care. We were just forced labourers to him. Before that day, especially in Braunschweig, I had been made to feel like a foreigner, but for the first time I now felt that I was expendable. We dug deeper so we could get our heads below ground level, and before that very day was over, the bombs did come. The ground shook in anger as explosions rocked our compound. I don't think our compound was specifically the intended target, but from thousands of feet above the city, Hamburg was Hamburg, and the bombs rained down mercilessly. The detonations were deafening and the ground trembled around me as all hell broke loose.

"Sonsofbitches," I thought as I cringed in my foxhole, grasping my wrists around my legs and pulling my knees up to protect my head. I was not just scared – I was totally terrified. I had always measured life in terms of months and years. But I knew by then, that in war, life was uncertain, and so was death. Both were only seconds apart, and people died in the bombings. It couldn't always be the other guy. Would I live through this day? Would I live through tomorrow? Each bomb was terrifying as the raid went on for a long time, and all I could do was hunker down in my hole and wait. It's funny how your mind works when you are terrified. It is a strange question you find yourself asking: *Am I waiting to see if I live, or am I waiting to die?*

That day, and frequently in the days to come, we experienced or at least heard some form of bombing in and around Hamburg. Sometimes only a couple fell at a time and it was over; and sometimes they fell for hour after hour as hundreds of planes roared overhead. There was bombing before in Braunschweig and Hannover, and we sometimes heard the distant thunder, but never in the immediate area of our compounds. In Fürstenmoor, the bombing released its fury where I had to eat, sleep, work, and stay alive. In the days to come, I worked on my foxhole to make it deeper and deeper. It always lacked proper form, but what I needed was a hole deep enough to keep me alive. After every bombing, I vowed to make it deeper.

I believe that the saying is true: there are no atheists in foxholes. I was always a believer but not always a praying man. I just talked to Him as though He was with me, and during the bombings, I had many monologues with my maker. I wondered if He was listening.

Chapter 12
Consequences

Fürstenmoor, June 1944

We adapted to our new location and quickly adjusted to our daily working routine. Within the first couple of weeks after our arrival, a new job was assigned to us. The army wanted a bomb shelter in Fürstenmoor. It would be shared with soldiers, compound workers and local citizens. It became our job to build it. The German army provided the plans and supervised the work as the shelter required lighting and mechanical air circulation. Local construction workers provided the materials and some labour, while men from the community took turns daily helping with the work. Our skills were essential in getting it built as quickly as possible. We were eager to complete the shelter because we needed it as much as everyone else did.

There was a large hill just outside the compound. With only hand shovels and a wooden cart to move the dirt we dug three adjoining tunnels into the sides of that hill. It took several days of digging, then the walls and roof of the tunnels were supported with reinforced concrete, steel doors, lighting and ventilation. The tunnels provided three entrances or exits for the shelter so that if one exit became blocked during a bombardment, those inside would not be trapped. They would still have two exit options. The tunnels were long and wide enough to have benches along the walls.

The work was completed in a timely fashion, and there was a grand celebration put on by the community.

Soldiers and local citizens joined together to familiarize everyone with the facility. We were not invited to attend and that suited us fine. We knew how it worked: we built it. We were not eager to celebrate the accomplishments of the German army.

~

It wasn't long before we had to use the shelter and were relieved that we had it. Within the week, our late afternoon work repairing vehicles in the yard was interrupted by the loud siren warning us of incoming bombers. We ran to the shelter and I watched as many locals hurried in the same direction. As instructed, we had to anxiously wait outside for the locals to go in first. The benches along the walls were taken up quickly by the women, children and elderly. The rest of us could stand or sit on the floor. Locals were concerned for the safety of themselves and their families and did not pay much attention to others, particularly us.

With the soldiers and local civilians squeezed into the confined space, we all huddled in terror as the bombing grew closer. People talked to one another, creating a buzz of nervousness. We all tried to reassure one another that the danger would pass us by, as it had before. The pounding and noise came closer minute by minute, leading to a thunderous crash. A little girl near me screamed. Her mother panicked and started to cry as she held her daughter and tried to soothe her fears. The ground shuddered so violently that I could see my pant legs move with the shock waves. My ears hurt and though I covered them with my hands, the noise was still deafening. The bombing felt very close and it pounded the shelter for over an hour. The walls started to feel too close together. They shook as if they were going to collapse in on us. The air became stale and dusty and it was getting harder to breathe. I closed my eyes and covered my ears and tried desperately to calm myself and shut out the screams, the dust and the fear that was growing inside me. I could almost smell the terror. I wondered if I would survive.

Finally, it stopped, and it was quiet as we waited nervously for the all-clear siren. No one spoke as I'm sure they, like me, wondered what we would find when we emerged from our protective cave. What would be left of our world? At last, we were relieved to hear the all-clear siren, signaling that it was safe to leave. All three exits were open and everyone pushed their way to the doors and fresh air. I stepped outside and greedily filled my lungs. But, fresh air was not to be found. The bombings had not only caused destruction to the compound buildings and houses in the area but the heat and explosions had robbed the air of oxygen. Everyone was coughing and choking, trying to breathe in the hot pungent air as we staggered about. I wondered if my gas mask would have helped if I'd had it with me. I was stunned to see the damage in the compound and the surrounding area. Our garage had sustained only minor damage but it took days of hard work to replace the windows and clean up before we could return to vehicle repairs.

~

With first moving and then surviving the bombing, I did not have time to think about the punishment that I was yet to receive for being with Elfrieda. We saw Harms every day, as he gave orders and instructions, but yet, nothing had been said. With each passing day, I tried not to focus on my punishment, and was hoping that Harms had done the same. Unfortunately, I was wrong.

"Pete, come to my office after work today. We need to talk," said Harms one afternoon. It was unusual to be singled out and told to report to his office. It must be about my punishment, I thought. I spent the rest of the day in fear thinking about the options Harms had at his disposal. I thought about what a ruined man Alex was when he returned from Lager 21, and the punishment imposed on Frau Schmidt and her husband for joking about Hitler. They were never heard of again. In fear, I reported to Harms as requested. His demeanour had changed and he stood behind his desk in rigid military fashion. His delivery was direct and formal.

"The consequences for your lack of judgement in Hannover, and spending time with Elfrieda, have not gone away," Harms informed me. "I have received your punishment order, and it will begin tomorrow. You are to be re-assigned for a couple of days or for as long as they need you. The bombing has caused significant ruin to the city and the clean-up is hampered by the presence of trapped bodies. The bodies must be removed before the bulldozing can begin. That will be your job. You won't be alone, there are other forced labourers in that detail. Compared to the work that you do here, the job will be difficult. The soldiers in charge will not be friendly, the conditions you will work under will not be pleasant, and nobody will care. But that's what your punishment will be. You will need to be careful, the work is treacherous and your days will be long and hard."

There was nothing I could say. Harms had always been strict, after all he was a German officer - patriotic and loyal.

This would be my punishment, and it was out of his hands. His role was to ensure that the punishment happened. He was now very abrupt with me, and I saw a side of him that I had not seen for a long time.

"Tomorrow morning at 7 a.m. you will report to the Transport Section of the compound, and they will provide you with a truck and directions as to where to go. On arrival at that destination, you will be given further instructions. That's all. You are dismissed."

I left Harms' office in a state of shock, fear and in trepidation. What had I brought down on myself? Why had I not taken the signs seriously. They had been very specific.

> *Foreigners are not allowed any contact or fraternization with the local girls. Disobedience will result in severe punishment.*

As a young man, I didn't believe they were meant for me. What would I have to endure in the weeks to come?

~

The next morning, at 7 a.m. sharp, I reported to the Transport Section. On arrival, I went to the soldier at the front desk.

"Are you from Harms' unit?" he asked. When I replied, he said, "Follow me." Instead of walking me out to the yard as I anticipated, he escorted me down a hallway to a kitchen area. "Sit here," he said, "I'll be back to get you later." I was confused by what happened next. I was served a breakfast of eggs and bread, followed by strong tea. The tea had rum in it: lots of rum. I quietly enjoyed my breakfast, and by the time I was done, I was feeling lightheaded. My escort returned and took me out to a dump truck that was parked outside the door. The soldier gave me a list of instructions as to where I was to take the truck and where I should report on arrival. "Wait a minute," he said. He left me sitting in the truck and returned quickly. He handed me a small basket with four bottles of beer in it. I looked at him in disbelief.

"I was told to give these to you today. Be discreet, keep them hidden and make sure that no one is watching you," he said, "but make sure you drink them today. Now, be on your way." With that, he turned sharply and was gone. I knew better than to ask questions.

I had no idea where I was going, but my drive took me deeper into the city. I was halted frequently by soldiers at checkpoints and was surprised by how smoothly every check went. The truck was recognized as a German military vehicle and the papers given to me by the transport soldier that morning were never questioned. I drove on into the abyss of rubble and devastation, eventually coming to the final checkpoint. I was told where to park and was escorted to a soldier who appeared to be in charge.

My German had improved over the past year and I could understand most of the words in his instructions, but anything I missed seemed to be of little importance. There were other civilian workers present and I presumed I could follow their example.

"Start here," he said, "pull the bricks and debris away until you can see the bottom of the rubble, then move over to another area. We have machines to help you with the steel and heavier materials but under it all, there are bodies. Get them out."

I was standing in the middle of the ruins of a factory that had been totally destroyed by the recent bombing. What a horrific scene. I struggled forcing my mind to absorb what I saw. There, amidst the ashes and the rubble, I could distinguish human arms and legs. As I got closer I saw horribly bloated bodies covered by large swarms of hungry flies. With their features so distorted, the corpses looked ghoulish, almost not human. These charred and mangled bodies must be those of the factory workers who could not, or were not allowed to, leave their posts to run to the safety of a bomb shelter.

The area was a hub of activity. There were several pathetic and weak looking political prisoners dressed alike, hard at work cleaning up the debris. I watched as one of these men received a swift but severe thrashing from a soldier carrying a baton. There were several soldiers supervising our duties. All were carrying batons or rubber truncheons. After he had delivered the beating, the soldier saw me for the first time. He looked at me and angrily made it clear that if I did not get to work immediately I would receive the same treatment. In the midst of the machines and the commotion I didn't hear his words, but his body language was clear.

As the debris was moved aside, bodies were dragged out and laid in a flat bulldozed area. "Get your truck," I was told by one of the soldiers. I had to move my truck closer to where we were working. As the bodies were pulled out, they were dragged to the truck. It often took two workers to handle the job of lifting the heavy bloated bodies, or sometimes, it was just body parts like a shoe with a foot still in it. It was all just thrown into the box of the truck like discarded trash.

When my truck was full, I was directed to a large, freshly dug pit some distance away. That was to be the final resting place of those we had gathered up so far. As I went to my truck, I could see blood and other dark coloured liquids dripping out of the tailgate.

At the pit, I was guided backwards towards the edge by a soldier in charge. I backed up until my rear wheels touched a wooden block. I jumped out and raised the box using a hand crank, then dumped my load. As if in a trance, I watched as pieces of humanity fell into a pathetic grave. I was sick to my stomach, retched beside the truck and after cranking down the box, I climbed back into the driver's seat. Cautiously, I quickly drank one of the beers that I had hidden under the seat. I hoped it would give me the false courage I needed, knowing I would have to do it all again.

Returning to the rubble pile, I parked the truck and was immediately struck by the sickening smell of the rotting flesh. It was almost overpowering. The weather was warm and the bloated bodies were getting soft in the sun. I tried not to breathe through my nose in order to deal with the stench, but then I was afraid something would land in my mouth. I felt dizzy and wished I could rest, but the sight of soldiers armed with rifles and bayonets, some accompanied by dogs, convinced me that I should get back to work. I resigned myself to the gruesome task. At the edge of the rubble pile, I tried to pick up the body of a man and put him in the truck. As I lifted his legs they became detached from the rest of his body and then his torso hit the ground with a squishing sound. It was a gruesome mess and I struggled to pick up the pieces of what used to be a human being.

By late afternoon I could feel my body ache from the physically exhausting work and the emotional toll that the job was taking. I noticed one of the labourers nearby was also struggling with his task. He was obviously weak and malnourished and this demanding work was too much for him. The poor man fainted. One of the nearby soldiers ordered him to get up and return to work. He did not move. The soldier hit him with his truncheon and the man moaned quietly, but could not get up.

The soldier, stepped back, and to the dog that stood obediently by his side, he gave a quick verbal command.

The well-trained animal jumped onto the prisoner and without hesitation sunk his teeth into the man's throat and shook him violently, tearing his throat out. Having accomplished the task, the dutiful beast licked his lips and shook his head as he looked up at his master. Work stopped as we all were stunned by what happened next. The soldier calmly patted his dog and looked up to make sure he had our full attention. With a sick malicious grin for his captive audience, he slowly unbuttoned his pants and pissed on what was left of the face of the dead man. I felt light-headed and nauseous with shock. Never had I witnessed such grotesque lack of respect and compassion for another human being. I forced myself to move and I bit my lips to rid my body of the urge to faint. My punishment had become a nightmare.

It couldn't come soon enough, but after another couple of loads, and another couple of beers, the day was finished. As I headed back to the compound, I went back through the checkpoints again without question. Once clear of the city, I pulled over on a side road and took a few moments to gulp my last beer. My hand shook as I drank and tried to make sense of the events of the day. As my eyes rested on the beer bottle, close to my lips, I noticed my hands. My hands were encrusted with blood reminding me of what I had handled all day. Bodies, that if I was fortunate, had stayed intact. If not, my hands had been immersed frequently in blood, entrails, body fluids or sometimes maggots. The smell was unbearable at times and breathing was sickening, causing me to gag and have bouts of dry heaves. I was dreading having to return tomorrow, and I knew then why the rum had been given to me that morning. Was that usual? Who, in this dreadful place, cared about me enough to give me liquor to survive such a horrific experience?

My trip home was a blur of emotion and confusion. I pulled into the compound and parked the truck. As I walked across the yard heading for Barracks #4, I was surprised to see Harms waiting for me. "Are you all right?" he asked. Although he did not want any details he seemed to be genuinely concerned for me. All I could do was nod as words to describe my day were lost.

My friends were surprised to see me. "We thought that you had been sent away to a prison camp, or even Lager 21," said Jack with concern. I gave them a general description of my job for the day and, even though sensing that I had left out many of the gory details, they did not ask any questions. The more I talked, the more solemn they became, and the less they asked. Even Lowie listened quietly without comment.

"Well, we are sure glad that you made it back Pete," said Jack. "Harms didn't tell us where you went, but he mentioned your name several times today, as if he understood why we might be concerned about you."

It was a comfort that I had friends who were glad I was home. But the best comfort I found that day was the shower. Hot water wasn't abundant but I stood in the shower scouring myself with gritty pumice soap, long after the warm water was gone.

I felt that my body was covered in death and the gruesome images haunted me. Even if I was able to rinse the experience from my body, it was impossible to rinse it from my mind.

As I lay on my bunk that night, I relived my day bombarded by the sights, the smells and the horror. Eventually, sleep took me, but it was short lived. I woke up screaming. I was unaware that my bunkmates were awake and watching me. I sat upright in a cold sweat and panting. The room was dark and I was still in a sleepy state of semi-consciousness. But, I was there on the rubble. The soldier was there. The dog was there. I was biting my lip and praying loudly, "Oh God, don't let me faint… please God, don't let me faint."

That was the first time that I had ever been awakened by such a nightmare but, it would not be the last time. Everyone has their demons, and I was meeting my own.

Chapter 13
Survival Skills

Fürstenmoor, June 1944

In the days following that horrendous clean-up detail, I was glad to be back at work in the scrap yard with Arie. He had a way of finding the humour in almost any situation and the days passed quickly in his company. We had to scrap a small amphibious military vehicle that was beyond repair. The Schwimmwagen's floor pan had been torn open and the vehicle was no longer functional. Lowie did the cutting and Arie and I spent the day hauling the pieces of steel to a truck. Together, we dismantled several destroyed vehicles and soon we had a full truckload that had to be taken to the smelter to be melted down. The smelters were in Denmark and as one of the few drivers in the compound, I was to make the delivery. I had never been there and was looking forward to the trip, even if I would not be alone. As usual, I would be travelling with a soldier.

I eventually made several trips to the smelters and, each time, I became more aware that the German presence in Denmark was less noticeable. The people there did not seem to be suffering as much, as I had seen in Holland and Germany. They didn't appear to be experiencing the shortages that had become a part of everyday life for us. People seemed to be more relaxed, carefree, almost normal, as though this dreadful war had not yet affected them. In my two years in Germany, I met many young people in forced labour from many different countries, but I never met, or ever heard of anyone from Denmark. I didn't know why, but Denmark seemed to be experiencing a soft occupation. As ever, I never asked any questions, I just did my job.

When delivering a load of scrap metals and vehicle hulls to Denmark to be melted down, I was accompanied by an officious armed soldier. But I was always left to travel home alone. I soon learned that I could use my return trips from the smelters to my advantage.

Though I was directed exactly where to go, on my return trip through Hamburg, I was always on the lookout for areas that had been recently bombed. After my delivery I would drive through those areas and search for anything that I could use. Sometimes I could find panes of glass that survived an attack. I would carefully cut as large a piece as possible and hide it in my truck to be traded later. If I could salvage drapes, dishes or anything else out of the rubble, it could be valuable to someone in Fürstenmoor in exchange for food. I was always hungry, and they were always in need of materials, due to the bombing damage. I could not collect these materials in broad daylight of course, but I could sometimes use the excuse that I had trouble with the truck. To make a delivery and come back after dark did not arouse suspicion.

~

Seizing an opportunity and using it to my advantage was not a new behaviour for me. The Germans had occupied Holland in 1940. Goods became increasingly scarce where I lived, testing the character and the resiliency of the Dutch citizens. Desperate times bring out the best and the worst in people, and during these impossible years, two very powerful and clandestine operations took root:

the resistance and the black market. As supplies became scarce, there was a huge market waiting for a provider. At the time, I was a truck driver for my uncle, and I knew I had the skills to survive, but what I needed was a network of supply and demand. Then I met Rene de Groot. Rene was a farmer, and often had milk and garden vegetables that he sold locally. He was a very likeable man, with a lot of connections in Amsterdam.

"I've got the supplies," he said to me when I met him, "but what I need is a partner with a delivery truck." Rene hated the Germans and thoroughly enjoyed defying them.

At 18, and partnered with Rene, I had my network.

I continued to make my regular trips to Amsterdam by truck, delivering coal, grain, or milk for my uncle. My trips were quite routine, but as the war continued and the rationing became more strict, people became more desperate for supplies. Some were willing to pay or barter for the goods they needed, and before long, we realized that we could make more money bartering the extra goods. Though we could not do it often, it was always a bonus when I could make an extra evening delivery to Amsterdam for my uncle. Then, Rene could pack extra vegetables between the milk cans or grain. The trips to his contacts were profitable for Rene and I learned to be resourceful earning an extra wage.

As supply dwindled and the demand increased, the soldiers and the inspectors became more diligent, checking every truckload. Weights and quantities were checked more carefully and permits were required. The soldiers sensed that we were up to something and suspiciously asked questions. They didn't trust us, but they couldn't catch us doing anything wrong. When the Germans imposed a 10 p.m. curfew, only those with special permits could travel at night. The inspectors got lazy working the night shifts and were more concerned about proper night permits than load contents. I had such a permit because I was in the trucking business and the restriction opened up new opportunities for Rene and me. The German inspectors knew me, knew I had a permit, and didn't bother checking. They just accepted the weight and content of my load. Rene and I took advantage of their complacency. I worked all day legally trucking for my uncle, but, in the evenings, I made occasional black-market trips back to Amsterdam with Rene. The days and nights were long but profitable. On occasion, I bartered for other groceries and my mother often found meat, soap or flour on the kitchen table in the morning. She did not ask me where it came from but with seven children at home, she was always grateful.

~

I relied on the same skills to survive in Germany. The small pub in our neighbourhood at Fürstenmoor was allowed to sell us beer. As foreigners, we were hesitant to go in there at first, but in time, the locals got more receptive to our presence in their lives. We had worked with them to build the bomb shelter, and when we were all huddled together in a near-death experience, we were all just people trying to stay alive.

In the pub one evening while I waited to be served, I overheard the locals sharing their day-to-day struggles, and of course how the war was affecting their lives. They all were suffering with the rationing and were frustrated with having to do without. One older woman complained that the soldiers repeatedly came to her door and disciplined her (and others) for light-infractions. Households were not allowed to show any lights after dark. She was annoyed by their frequent aggression. She needed blackout curtains. Hers were damaged by bombing and it was impossible to replace them. I was glad to hear her story and the trade value of functioning blackout curtains gave me an idea.

It was usually dark by the time our workday was over and I paid particular attention for a few days to our surroundings. "What is that building?" I asked as Jack, Lowie and I walked across the compound to our barracks one evening. I had previously noticed a small building near the back fence.

"I don't know, nobody ever uses it that I have seen," Jack replied to answer my apparently simple curiosity. "Maybe they plan to use it for more workers, or something... I have never seen anyone go in or come out of there."

"You never see a light on inside the building either," I said, "and the building is never locked. I have checked it several times. It has blackout curtains. Why would an empty building need to have blackout curtains? Who would miss them if they were gone?"

"Oh no you don't," said Jack, "I am not getting involved with one of your schemes. It'll get you into trouble. Haven't you learned anything from Elfrieda? You are still being punished for that adventure."

"But that was different," I said. "According to them, that was fraternizing."

"And this is theft," said Jack. "Damn you Pete, you'll be in shit again."

"C'mon, help me," I said. "All I need is a look-out."

"You can get somebody else to help you. You're crazy." By now, it was getting to be a laughable discussion. "I'm not doing it. I am outa' here."

"I'll do it," said Lowie, "only because it will inconvenience the bastards."

Under the cover of darkness and with Lowie standing out front to keep observation, I relieved the German army of their blackout curtains. Knowing the frustrated lady who complained in the pub lived nearby, Lowie and I secretly offered her the curtains and later received a fine meal for our efforts. We knew we would have been in trouble for taking them and she would have been in trouble for feeding us. Survival involved risk for all of us.

~

The situation of the war in Germany was getting worse. Allied bombing seemed to be more frequent, and often came closer to Fürstenmoor. We were now required to wear the cumbersome gas masks all the time at work. They were uncomfortable so we tried to avoid using them, but Harms insisted that we obey the rules. The soldiers would grab our masks and pull, testing for tightness. We were of no value to Harms if we were dead.

One evening as I was finishing up my work, the siren sounded to signal the approach of bombers. The shelter was too far away and I only had time to run to my foxhole. With my helmet and gas mask on, I jumped into my hole with my head down. While impossibly trying to get comfortable, I observed a sheep grazing peacefully on the other side of the compound fence. The sheep was on a long chain just a few yards away from me and was totally unaware of the danger as the bombers approached. There were so many planes the sound was deafening and all I could do was keep my head down and wait for the bombs as they fell to earth. With the ground shaking incessantly, bombs fell around me with ear-piercing explosions. Battered by flying dirt and debris, I was glad that I had worked hard to make my foxhole deeper. I vowed that before the next time, I would find something to make a roof-like covering to protect my head.

Finally, the earth stopped shaking, the dirt stopped falling and the all-clear signal sounded. At first, I was afraid to move. I felt no pain so I carefully wiggled my arms and legs and tried to free myself from the dirt that pinned me down. Slowly I worked my way out of the rubble. As I surveyed the damage in and around my foxhole, I approached the area where the sheep had been grazing. All I found was a smoking crater. I stood there in disbelief and wide-eyed amazement. I was almost giddy. It was as if God was reminding me that I could live to be another day older.

I am alive, I thought.

The fence that had separated me from the sheep … was gone.

The chain that held the sheep … was gone, and the sheep … was gone.

Chapter 14
No Overtime Allowed

Fürstenmoor, June 1944

We were all hungry for news. Mail had been banned and we had no idea what impact the war was having on our families and friends in Holland. Most of the locals in Fürstenmoor were cautious about discussing German political issues, or the war across Europe. You never knew who was listening. The few that did talk to us usually spouted some Nazi propaganda about the triumphant campaigns of Hitler.

Occasionally following our workday, we were told to report for a mandatory assembly. There, we would have the "privilege" of listening to the Führer speak on the radio. I was fairly fluent in German by then and I could understand the basics of his speech. Hitler was a compelling orator. Although his message about the "Master Race" was disturbing, the conviction in his voice was, nonetheless, fascinating to listen to.

Because we were paid a wage, we were expected to fill out and submit a weekly time sheet to account for our hours of work. The submissions were routine and Harms seldom questioned the accuracy of them. After listening to one of Hitler's lengthy speeches one such evening, we sat together as a group and filled out our worksheets. Jack was usually respectful with orders, but that night he was in a defiant mood. Jack hated Hitler.

"I resent being forced to listen to those long speeches," he said. "If it wasn't for him, I wouldn't be here, and I begrudge having to give up my time," and with that he added an extra two hours to his work sheet.

"Be careful, my friend. You won't win that argument. You could be punished for that," I warned him jokingly, as he had often warned me. Everybody at the table was tired and we understood. Everyone else agreed with me.

"Yes," said Lowie, "and then they'll start watching all our time sheets more closely."

Disregarding our warning, Jack added the notation: *"Forced to listen to the Fuhrer."*

We tried to discourage him but he was determined.

~

The next morning, as we expected, Jack was called into the office.

Harms was livid. According to Jack, Harms "wasted no words" reminding him that, he was expected to be respectful, and he should keep his thoughts to himself.

"Remember Frau Schmidt and her husband in Braunschweig? Remember what happened to them? You WILL change your worksheet," demanded Harms.

It cost Jack a week's pay, and whether Jack appreciated it or not, Harms was looking out for him. He was a German soldier, but he wasn't SS and he wasn't cruel. He was the boss and in his own way did the best he could for us.

~

When we were transferred to Fürstenmoor in May, I had been in Germany for 14 months. Braunschweig and Hannover had been busy. While there, we were introduced to the routines of our jobs and to the German people. People in Braunschweig and in Hannover were cruel and resented us being there. We were foreigners in forced labour and they took pride in reminding us of it. But, the people in Fürstenmoor were different. We realized that we were treated differently. Bert, the bartender at the pub down the street from the compound, told us, "not all people here are Nazi sympathizers and they don't care much about all the rules. People here are more relaxed. Many are just tired of the war, the bombing and the suffering, and they just want it to be over. If you can help them, they are ok with you," he said. "But, don't forget, there are Nazis here as well, and they are not kind. Just be cautious. Be mindful as to who you are talking to, and what you are talking about."

Fürstenmoor was also different because it was a bigger compound and the work was more expansive. Our unit had more vehicles to repair than in Braunschweig and Hannover, but as a driver, I was away a lot. Between my trips to Denmark, I was also assigned to drive a truck to deliver food and other supplies to local work camps. However, I was still on my punishment detail. I was still made to go back into the ruins of the city at times, to pull away the rubble and haul out the poor wretches who had been caught in the bombing. Frans also was taken away from us when an electrician was required elsewhere, and Arie was sometimes away driving as well. We were lucky when we all were in the compound at the same time. When we were all there, we took turns going down to the local pub at night with our empty pail and Bert would fill it with enough beer for all of us. One evening, it was Frans' turn to go, and we all sat around waiting for the beer. When we finally heard footsteps on the porch, Lowie opened the door for Frans, to help him to come in carrying a full pail.

"It's about time," said Arie with a laugh. "I'm thirsty."

"Sorry," said Frans as he put the pail in the middle of

the table and took a seat. "I was talking to Bert. But more than our conversation, I was interested in listening to the discussion the locals were having at a close table. They said something about an armed invasion. Apparently, troops have landed in France, and they are moving inland. The Allies are coming." Our conversation took off with rapid enthusiasm.

"When did they land?"

"Where are they now?"

"What countries are involved, who are they?"

"How big of a force is it?"

"What are the locals saying, how do they feel about it?"

"I don't know," said Frans. "I couldn't hear all that well but I heard enough to know that liberation is on its way."

"Damn, all we ever hear is that crap in Hitler's speeches," said Jack. "I want to know what's really happening. Why did they have to ban our radios?"

We were all so excited, the cold beer was gone in no time.

"We need more beer," said Arie, "I'll go." If it involved beer, Arie was always eager to volunteer. I liked Arie. He was a good guy, a good worker and we all liked to be around him.

While we waited for Arie to fetch us some more beer, all we could talk about was the invasion. Jack was so frustrated his voice was louder than anyone else's. "Damn," he cried, "if only we could get a radio."

Rik got up and looked over his shoulder. He walked over to the window and looked out. He then stepped outside the door and returned before speaking.

"What are you doing?" I asked

"Just checking to ensure there is nobody outside that can hear me," he whispered, "because... I have a radio."

"What?" Again, everybody was talking at once.

"Where did you get that?"

"Where is it?"

"Does it work?"

"Why didn't you tell us?"

Suddenly there were loud and hurried footsteps at the door.

"Shhh, shhh," said Rik. He looked terrified as if he had said something that he now wished he could take back. We all looked in surprise, thinking that soldiers were going to burst in the door. In a flurry of activity, the door opened, and Arie came in.

Breathless, Arie said "What, what did I miss?"

"Quiet," said Jack, "Rik has a radio."

"What?" Arie exclaimed in surprise. "Where the hell did you get that?"

Over another pail of beer, Rik told us his radio story. He was a quiet sort of man about my age, and a gentleman. His story had been a secret, but it was not a surprise. He had been visiting a local girl that he had come to know quite well. Fortunately, the girl's family was very anti-Hitler and they did not discourage the relationship.

He visited her often and sometimes had evening meals with her and her parents. He talked about the frustration of personal radios being banned and it was impossible to hear reliable news about the war. "We only hear a radio when Hitler speaks," he had told them. The girl's family was quite fond of Rik and they trusted him. They had an extra radio, but it was broken. If he could fix it, he could have it. Without us knowing about it, Rik smuggled the radio into our barracks. We were often subjected to random barrack and locker inspections so he had to find a secure hiding spot for the radio. Rik had hidden it beneath the floorboards of the barracks, under his bunk. It was wrapped in canvas and sat on a pile of stones to keep it dry. We all drank our beer and talked about how exciting it would be to know how the war was progressing. It took all evening but within a measurable time, and thanks to Frans' electrical abilities, the radio was repaired, set up and working fine.

"I dunno," said Jack with his usual caution, "if they find out, we'll be punished. They will kill us."

"I got it for all of us," said Rik. "I wouldn't have told you if I thought you wouldn't go along with it."

Despite Jack's concerns, we did go along with it, and in time, Jack was as eager to secretly hear the news as we were. In the evenings that followed, we would take turns standing guard at the window and at the door of the barracks, watching for any approaching soldiers. It was illegal to listen to any broadcasts from Britain, from the Allied forces or from the Dutch government in exile. Legal or not, we were able to listen to the news in all three languages, Dutch, German and English, and we listened to it all. We did not have a full appreciation of the geography of Germany and what was happening around us, but we learned about the earlier invasion that had taken place in Normandy. It had taken place in June and, although we had no understanding of military strategy, we understood that the operation to liberate Western Europe was well underway. We were excited, but nervous too, because in order for the Allies to rescue us, they would have to destroy the German will to fight. That fight was coming to us, and we too could be in danger. As if the Allied bombing wasn't enough for us to endure, the ground war was heading our way as well, and we could be caught in the middle.

Chapter 15
THE FLYING DUTCHMAN

Fürstenmoor, July 1944

Arie and I were standing in the yard with our suitcases early one morning, waiting for our trucks to be loaded. Harms had come to our barracks the night before with an assignment for us.

"Be ready to leave by 8 a.m. tomorrow morning," he said to both of us. "You will be making long distance deliveries, so pack a suitcase with whatever you think you'll need. You'll be gone for at least a couple days."

"Where are we going?" asked Arie.

"You are going to different camps with supplies. Your trucks will be loaded and ready to go in the morning and your escorts know the routes." His only parting words were "do not be late in leaving."

~

As we stood together in the yard the next morning, waiting for supply workers to finish loading our trucks, I noticed Arie frequently looking at his watch. It was only 7:30 and we were plenty early, but he seemed nervous.

"What's the matter, are you worried about leaving late," I asked. Arie wasn't usually a worrier, he took things in stride.

"Oh no," he responded with a smile on his face. "I'm just looking at my new watch."

"Nice watch," I don't remember you ever wearing a watch?" I asked, realizing that I had not noticed it before. It was quite a piece of jewelry for a watch.

"Thanks, and no, I've never had a watch before and usually, I don't care what time it is. If I need to know, I ask somebody. I won this beauty in a crap game in the Reeperbahn last week," he said. "Some guy ran out of money, bet his watch, and I won. I got the loser's watch."

"The where: where did you go?" I asked. I thought he had gone to another city for some reason.

"The Reeperbahn - the entertainment district in Hamburg," he said, surprised that I knew nothing about it. "It's an amazing place. Just walking around there, you forget there's a war on. It's in Hamburg, but it seems to seldom get bombed. If it does, it gets fixed and repaired quickly. There seems to be a lot of money there. There is also lots of girls, lots of beer and lots of loud music. But, the best part is that I discovered gambling; I've never gambled in my life before - it's addictive."

"How did you find that place?" I asked naively.

"I went with the two Frenchies, have you never been there?"

"No, never heard of it," I said. He seemed surprised by my answer.

He told me that the two Frenchmen from our barracks took him there. They had the connections to get into some of the backrooms of the clubs on the Grosse Freiheit, a street off the Reeperbahn. "The guards know we are allowed out after work hours on Saturday nights, and they keep records on when we leave camp," he said. "They don't know where you go, and don't care as long as you are back by curfew. You can go for a walk; stay in Fürstenmoor and go to the local pub; or, as the Frenchmen encouraged me to, you can go to the Reeperbahn. You should come with us sometime."

"No, thanks," I said without hesitation. I was in enough trouble already for breaking the rules in Hannover.

"Everybody there just wants to escape the war," he said. "As long as you're back by curfew nobody knows." A loud command from one of the soldiers ended our conversation.

"Drivers, get to your trucks and let's go."

The soldier in charge directed me to a large three-ton transport truck that was loaded with supplies. I knew it was going to be difficult. They were big and challenging to drive at any time but fully loaded it would be even more difficult. Arie and I stayed together as we wove our way through the bombed-out streets of Hamburg. Once outside of the city, we separated and headed in different directions.

Sometimes, the soldier would have me stop and he would take a look-out position on the front fender. He watched the sky for advanced warning of planes. German military trucks and equipment on the roads had been more recently attacked by Allied planes. Arie and I had been told that if the soldier jumps off, we were to stop the truck and take cover.

My first stop was at a military post where I was happy to stay in my truck as usual, while civilian workers unloaded the supplies. On previous trips, the time spent in any camp was no more than a couple of hours, just long enough for the prisoners to unload the cargo. I was always ordered to stay inside my truck and avoid contact with them. I had never been away at a camp overnight before. It was daunting enough when I could stay in the safety of the truck, what would happen to me when I had to spend the night at a camp?

~

The whole day passed quietly as my soldier escort was constantly checking his map and was not interested in conversation with me. Lunch was a sandwich on the move. I drove slowly, followed his directions and by late afternoon we arrived at our destination. The camp was surrounded by a tall fence with a very heavy gate. The armed guards at the gate directed me in and I could feel the muscles in my shoulders tighten when I heard the dull clunk when the steel gate locked behind me. As a forced labourer, I had restrictions as to where I could go and when. I had never been locked in like a prisoner. That locked gate and the fenced enclosure told me: *You are not free. You are ours.* A soldier, standing about fifty feet away, motioned for me to bring the truck towards him. He told me to park the truck near a warehouse. I exited the truck and left it there to be unloaded. I was escorted to a large two-storey barracks, taken to the second floor and put in a small room by myself. A wooden bunk, a dirty worn-out mattress without a blanket and an old table was the only furniture in the room.

In an abrupt voice, with as few words as necessary, the soldier said, "Sleep here tonight. I will fetch you in the morning. Supper will be brought to you; stay inside and mind your own business." The guard left and I was surprised that he did not lock the door. As I waited for my food, I studied my surroundings or at least as much as I could see through my window. I was in a larger camp than what I had seen before, and I recognized the tattered blue and gray striped uniforms worn by the political prisoners. I had seen them before at other camps. There were several people outside but oddly no one was talking. The political prisoners - referred to as undesirable - were thin and filthy. They all walked as if their feet were too heavy and each step was painful.

They seemed to be in a daze as if they were shutting out the world around them because it took all their energy just to complete the task at hand. There were groups of people doing a variety of jobs, one more bizarre than the next. I watched as two people worked together very diligently trying to fill a loosely woven wicker basket with water, using a hand pump. When they stopped for a short rest they were whipped by a watchful guard. I saw another group building what looked to be a long stone fence in the middle of the yard. As they worked hard carrying the heavy stones and fitting them together, another group was just as diligently working at the other end, dismantling the fence and returning the big rocks to a large pile at the side yard. It gave me a dreadful feeling to watch those poor prisoners working so hard, under the ever-watchful eye of soldiers. The soldiers were armed with guns and some carried horse whips. It was an eerie place.

As the sun started to set, I could feel a heavy foreboding in the air. There was no lantern for light and my room was getting dark. My simple supper of dark bread, jam and tea arrived. I was starving, yet I could hardly eat. The sight of the weakened prisoners doing senseless tasks and guarded by armed soldiers bothered me. I opened the door to get some fresh air. The view from my door looked out onto a courtyard and, in the centre, I noticed a couple of tall poles that were about two feet apart.

They did not serve any purpose that I could see but, in the twilight, they cast long eerie shadows across the yard. The prisoners were heading to their barracks. It was abnormally quiet and spooky. I laid down on my bunk and tried to relax.

Startled by the sound of loud voices, I got up and looked through a window towards a group of men outside. It sounded like a friendly argument going on, but I couldn't hear exactly what was being said. I heard enough to realize that the guards were drinking, laughing and joking. I moved to the open door to see what was happening. A few of the guards were standing together near about six or seven prisoners. They were pushing these men into a straight-line formation, one behind the other. The one at the front of the line was shivering and sobbing. I watched as the guards stood back, except one who positioned himself directly facing the line of prisoners. He made a comment to the other guards, and they all laughed. He then lifted his rifle placing the muzzle within inches of the first man's chest and fired at point blank range. I stood there frozen in shock as several of the men slumped where they stood, and fell dead. To my horror the guards laughed as they took a body count of the fallen, and I watched as they exchanged money and congratulated each other. I had witnessed a game of chance measured in human lives. They had made bets as to how many men the bullet would penetrate before it stopped. It was, to them, simple entertainment without remorse and without accountability.

~

In the morning, we headed out again. I didn't know where we were, and I was relieved to be accompanied again by the soldier. He was a rigid individual who did not talk much other than to give me direction. All I wanted was to drive and take some comfort in listening to the rumble of the old truck. By noon, we arrived at another compound. It was not a prison camp, but looked like a military post in a wooded area of the countryside. It was fenced as usual, the gates were guarded, but I had never been to a place like this before. We were bringing supplies to the soldiers who were stationed there. I was given some lunch and some water and told to stay in the truck. The soldiers unloaded our cargo of supplies and within an hour, I was dismissed. I was sent back alone.

When the truck was empty, a soldier was no longer required as an empty truck wasn't worth risking the safety of a soldier. Without him, I could follow a map, take my time and just get home, home to Fürstenmoor.

~

On arrival at our compound, I stopped before entering the gate, but by now, the soldiers knew who I was. Recognizing me and the truck, they pulled up the barricade without question and allowed me to pass. I parked the truck outside the Transport Section and, taking my suitcase in hand, headed off towards the barracks. My supper and my friends were waiting, and so was my bed. I was glad to be home.

"Hi Peter," I heard someone say, in German, and I stopped to see who it was. It was Alfred. He worked with us frequently and told us stories of his previous adventures. He had an interesting history. Alfred was born in Germany but as a young man had lived for a time in the United States. He liked the States but was jobless as a young man during the depression. He spent a time hopping trains all over and riding the rails looking for work. Alfred had heard how the German economy was thriving and he decided to answer the call of the fatherland. He returned to Germany. At first, he was excited about all that Hitler promised to those who sacrificed for the cause. But, when the war broke out, he was forced to join the German army. Now he worked as a machinist in the compound. He also was a painter and re-painted the vehicles when repaired. Alfred knew us all and he knew that I was Dutch.

"You look tired Peter, where have you been?" he asked. In spite of Alfred's coveralls, covered in old paint, it occurred to me how strange it was to be having a conversation with him. He did not fit the mold of what I had seen recently of Nazi soldiers.

"I've been here and there," I said. "I've been to various camps. I've driven through various parts of Germany, and I have seen things that are hard to believe."

"Well, you do get around," said Alfred. He still had a wet paintbrush in his hand and as we talked, he reached out and painted a few words on my wooden suitcase. I stepped back and was uncomfortable. A German soldier had just painted bright red words on one of my only pieces of personal property, in a language that I didn't know or understand.

Recognizing my discomfort, Alfred laughed and quickly reassured me that I had nothing to fear. Apologetically, he explained that without thinking, he had printed in English, the words *The Flying Dutchman* on my suitcase.

"Why in English?" I asked Alfred as he stood smiling, admiring his work. "I don't know any English, and you no longer speak it?"

"I don't know," he replied as he stopped to spit between his boots, "just a dumb impulse. I guess I was thinking in English," and we both stood there laughing. Alfred was one of the few German soldiers that I would learn to like.

I continued my way across the compound, careful not to have my leg brush against my freshly painted suitcase, and I saw Frans standing on the step. He opened the door and stuck his head in. "It's just Pete," he whispered. Confused, I stepped into the building. It was in darkness, blackout curtains were drawn, and the guys were all sitting on the floor. A dim glow was apparent in their midst.

"Quiet Pete," said Rik. "The radio's on."

Everyone in the barracks was listening to a Dutch news broadcast and stood up as I entered. They seemed happy about the news, but Rik shut the radio off and quickly stowed it away under the floorboards beneath his bunk. We never kept the radio on very long because it was too dangerous. Even when turned low, the muffled sounds could be heard through the thin walls of the barracks and if a passing guard was alerted to what we were doing, it would be just one of the many things that would result in punishment.

"What did you learn? What's happening?" I asked, wanting to share their enthusiasm. My friends were excited, wildly excited, eager to share some news but yet, maintaining low voices: "The Allies are winning in France," said Lowie.

Chapter 16
Resistance

Wognum, July 1944

By the summer of 1944, the German occupation in Wognum was more oppressive. The German soldiers were becoming more aggressive. They demanded compliance and that made times hard for us. In the beginning, men aged 18 to 40 would receive letters, just like Peter did, instructing them to report as forced labour. But by now, the letters had stopped and men were simply picked up and collected by way of roundups. The *razzias* happened frequently and without warning.

I met Marta one day while I was out running errands in the neighbourhood. "Did you hear the *razzia* on the street last night?" she asked. Surprisingly, I hadn't heard the *razzia* but I knew that she and her family were afraid for her younger brother. He had just turned 18 and could now be picked up and sent to Germany. "We were so afraid for Co. His only alternative had been to run away to escape. But living in the marshes like some of the other boys, afraid of capture and punishment, was not a very appealing option," she said, as she continued her story.

Co had resigned himself to soon being taken, now that he had come of age. He had a bag already packed and was sitting at the kitchen table waiting for the soldiers. They were so close that he could hear the clatter of the heavy army truck and the pounding of their boots on the brick street. They were banging loudly on front doors and shouting demands as they moved from house to house in rapid succession. Co listened in fearful anticipation as they pounded at the door of the neighbour's house. Without waiting for the neighbour's consent, the soldiers entered the house. Co heard the commotion as they barked unrecognizably at the neighbours, and searched each room of the house. Beds were overturned and furniture was thrown around as they looked for their targets. The Manshande house would be next, and Co waited in anxiety and fear.

"Oh no, what happened to him?" I asked in eagerness.

"That's the strange part," said Marta. "For some reason, maybe because of an emergency, the soldiers jumped into their trucks and left, not just our house, but the entire neighbourhood. It took a few minutes to realize what had happened but Co had been passed over. It was such an ordeal. Our fears turned to unexpected joy so quickly all we could do was give Co a hug. We were all crying and shaking when the soldiers left." Co had been missed, and for now, he was one of the lucky ones.

~

I knew a brave man by the name of Nico Broers. He was a couple of years older than I was and when he was called to go to Germany he decided to join the resistance instead. The resistance was active in hiding people, sabotaging phone lines and generally disrupting German control. If Allied pilots parachuted from, or crash-landed their aircraft, the resistance would help to hide them from the Germans so they could safely return to England. At the beginning of the occupation, if the Germans discovered people involved in the resistance, they put them in jail. By mid-1944, the Nazis ordered the soldiers to shoot all accused resistance members. They also committed revenge attacks against innocent civilians when resistance activities occurred.

Nico took part in a raid on a distribution office where ration coupons were kept. A few days later, a man who had worked at the centre saw Nico walking down the street and reported him to a nearby German soldier. Without hesitation or question, the soldier walked over to Nico and shot him dead on the spot, in broad daylight. His body was left on the street and removal was forbidden. It was a warning to others. As if we needed reminding that we were powerless.

~

On another such occasion, a German officer was found dead on a country road just outside of Wognum. Although the matter was investigated by the German forces, the cause of death was never explained. He may have been shot by local members of the resistance or struck by a passing vehicle. It didn't matter. One of their own was dead and the locals were made to pay for the loss. At random, a local citizen was stopped while simply walking down the street, and picked up by the soldiers. His hands were forcibly tied, and he was lashed into the back of a truck. Again, as a warning to all of us, the soldiers drove about town beating and assaulting the poor man in plain view. To ensure that we all would be aware of what was happening, the soldiers used a bullhorn to let everyone know the consequences of any similar activities. After they had beaten him nearly to death and toured about town while doing so, they unceremoniously dumped his bruised and battered body into the middle of the street. They left it there as an example of what would happen if another soldier got killed. When retaliation took place for actions made against them, the Germans were arbitrary as to who suffered the penalty. Their justice was aimed randomly at anyone. Our obedience was expected, and it would be obtained through fear.

Chapter 17
No Choice

Fürstenmoor, July 1944

Once the radio was safely stored beneath the floor, under Rik's bed, our crew sat around the table in the bunkhouse talking about the exciting news we had just heard. The Allies were steadfastly moving across France, pushing the Germans back. My thought was they couldn't get here fast enough.

"How was your delivery?" asked Arie. His face looked tired and his voice was unusually meek as he leaned across the table in a whisper. "Mine was horrible. You won't believe what I saw."

"About the same as you, I think. I couldn't believe what I saw either."

I went on to tell Arie and the others about what I had witnessed on my trip; the soldiers shooting a line of prisoners as a contest. I did not leave out any details in my description of the terror that I had seen in the faces of the men used as game pieces. Everyone at the table listened intently and they were shocked at the details of my story. They were speechless and sat in quiet astonishment at the atrocity of it.

As I finished, Arie sat shaking his head from side to side as he told us the details of his trip. "I get it, Pete. I saw that too. Like you, I didn't know where I was and like you, I was told by the German soldier to leave the truck to be unloaded. I was taken to a room for the night, told not to leave it, and to mind my own business. My supper was delivered and as I sat on the bunk eating, I hoped darkness would come. All I wanted to do was escape by going to sleep. But I couldn't. The commotion outside the window drew my attention."

"Prisoners were being dragged out of their sleeping quarters by the Nazi guards, ridiculed and tortured for no apparent reason," he said, almost repeating the circumstances that I had witnessed. "The prisoners were lined up in an orderly fashion and made to watch as one of them was picked out. That person, to the horror and fear of those watching, had their fingers or toes broken, while the drunken guards just laughed. The prisoner was forced to stand on a wooden block extending toes or fingers over the edge, while a guard pounded with a heavy hammer, breaking the bones. Others were chosen and sharp pins were jammed under their fingernails and toenails. Sometimes the nails were ripped off. It was the screaming of the prisoners that was horrifying, and it was the screams that I will never forget."

"I can't believe how those prisoners suffer," I said. "The terror inflicted by the soldiers in those camps is totally unchecked. Unbelievable."

"That's because the camps are not run by German soldiers like we have in our compound. Those political prisoner camps are controlled by the SS," said Arie cupping his hands around his mouth and whispering as if it was a secret, "they are sadistic brutes."

None of us slept well that night, disturbed by the stories that Arie and I had just told. The stories left us with horrible visions on everyone's minds. I lay there reliving what I had seen in the past two days, and thanks to Arie, now I had more visions and nightmare tales. The prison camp guards were Nazi SS willing to torture for no other reason but to display their arrogant supremacy.

~

In the days that followed, I remained troubled. I was tired but could not sleep. I was hungry but could not eat. Before I had a chance to recover and get back into the routine of the compound, Harms pulled me aside while I was working in the garage. He reminded me that my punishment was not yet over. I would have to return to Hamburg the next day and help with recovering bodies. *When will this damn war be over?*

The next morning, I was provided with a hearty breakfast that I could not eat, but I sipped my mug of tea, laced with rum. I retrieved a truck from the Transport Section and, as before, the soldier provided me with a box with four bottles of beer.

"Don't ask," he reminded me. "Just make sure you drink it yourself and have it gone before you come back tonight."

I headed back to another recently bombed area of the city and my stomach churned at the thought of what I would find in the rubble. With the destruction, the fires and the explosions, the citizens of Hamburg had been trapped and died. The bombing was relentless and the devastation done to the city was more than the recovery efforts could fix. The structural timbers and steel girders were pulled aside by bulldozers and heavy equipment. But beneath tons of bricks and broken windows were the bodies. Old people, men and women; all who had died when the bombing was indiscriminate. Maybe the military had arrived quickly to take away those in uniform, I don't know, but I never found the body of a soldier. It seemed to me that the consequences of the bombing were heavily suffered by civilians.

I parked my truck and joined the other forced labourers from the factories, the political prisoners dressed in their blues and grays and the soldiers standing guard. Then I felt my whole body tense as I recognized one of the guards. He was standing nearby, his dog obediently sitting at his heels. He was the same arrogant soldier who had on an earlier day, encouraged his dog to kill one of the workers in such a brutal manner. The earlier experience with that soldier and his dog attack was distressing and I had nothing but hatred for him.

The heat of the day was already making the stench of decaying bodies unbearable. Flies and rats were everywhere. When everything around them is destroyed, rats find a way to survive. They enter a corpse through any orifice they can find and eat their way into the body. In the pile of bricks where I stood, I found a victim and I kicked at the man's body to scare away any rats. As I grabbed his legs, I caught a glimpse of a light blue material and I carefully moved the bricks aside to see what it was. It was another body. It was a young woman. She was well dressed and could have been going to work in an office, or heading out for lunch with friends when the bombing came. Her long blonde hair was caked in blood, still braided and meticulously pinned above the laced collar of her blouse. The light blue colour that I had seen was her knitted sweater. She was stunning and I moved closer so I could see her face. Her eyes were closed as though in peaceful sleep and I was momentarily struck by the tracks of her tears. They scarred her beauty as they had trickled through the dust and across the side of her face. Suddenly, my fixation was shattered as she opened her eyes and stared directly in my face.

I lost my balance and stumbled as I fell back. I was shocked and quickly restrained myself so as not to draw the attention of the guard. I was terrified and struggled to stifle a scream. To help her would be futile. She was near death for sure, and I knew from watching others, that helping any casualty would result in a beating from the guards. I took her hand and softly held it for a second, but I had no choice. We were there to recover - not to rescue. It was one of the most difficult things I had ever done, but I forced myself to stand up, step back, and turn towards the truck. Painfully, I walked away.

At the truck, as the bodies were brought out of the ruins, I busied myself in loading them. It was all I could do to maintain any sense of conscious ability as I was witnessing such brutality. The things that I had done and the things that I had witnessed were unbelievable. I kept thinking about home, family and life before the war. I wondered about the families of these victims. Would they ever know what had happened to their loved ones? In my trips for this detail, I never witnessed any attempt by those in charge to identify the dead. There seemed to be no accountability. Another worker helped, and for the next couple of hours, we stacked the dead bodies like cordwood in the back of my truck as blood drained from the tailgate. The war was over for them and I would soon take them to the open pit for mass burial. Then, I realized that this load was going to be more difficult than the others, because in the pile of corpses, I saw the blue sweater.

The young woman reminded me of Elfrieda. I wondered if Elfrieda ever thought about the punishment that I was forced to endure because of her? It was unjust that the wholesome experience with Elfrieda would lead to such a painful experience for me, including finding this young woman. I had to detach myself from any compassion for her to get the job done. I had to deliver her and that load of bodies to their graves in an unmarked pit. I hated that job. But I was luckier than she was because I was still alive.

Unfortunately, the price of survival in this war was to be left with memories.

Sometimes, when the bombing was severe and the trapped casualties were too difficult to reach, the bodies would be disposed of differently. It was more efficient for the soldiers to just use flame throwers to ensure death, dump lime into the aftermath to quicken the decomposition of the bodies and bulldoze the entire mess. The victims were just part of the debris that had to be cleaned up.

When I returned home to the compound that day, Harms was waiting for me when I pulled into the yard. His concern for me was comforting, after all the death and misery I saw that day, and each day, at that job. The basket of beer that I took with me in my trips helped to divorce my feelings from the work, but I never knew where the beer came from. I suspected that it was ordered by Harms. I was learning that he was a good man who genuinely seemed to care about us as a team. Harms was not like the soldiers that I had seen in the prisoner camps. He was not a fanatical Nazi: he was a disciplined German soldier… and soldiers go to war.

Chapter 18
Hände Hoch

Fürstenmoor, July 1944

I was learning that you sometimes have to experience the bad to appreciate the good. Next morning, I awoke to a cloudy day with fog and drizzling rain. Despite the weather, we all had a positive outlook for the day. The body recovery details were usually put on hold in miserable weather and I was glad to stay at the compound. Any day that I was not sent on body recovery was a good day. Cloudy days were also safe days: safe from Allied bombings. The bombers normally flew high to avoid being shot at and they needed a cloudless sky to accurately identify targets. On cloudy days with reduced visibility, the bomb runs were scrubbed. They were good days as we could look forward to a routine day with simple tasks of repairing vehicles.

The jobs required us to go to the centre of the test track where the parked vehicles were sitting, waiting to be scrapped. We would take our time removing the needed part and carry it back to the shop. Then, we needed to test drive the repaired vehicle around the track or out of the compound and around the streets of Fürstenmoor. Despite the rain and clouds, vehicle repair was a safe and easy job when not interrupted by bombings. The job gave us the chance to work as a team. Arie always lightened the mood, Lowie liked help so he didn't have to work as hard as when he was alone, and of course, there was Jack. Jack was a solid friend, supportive and wise. We all spent our smoke breaks together as comrades, discussing the war, our lives in Fürstenmoor and what we had left behind us at home.

"How about the Reeperbahn tonight?" asked Arie, as he inhaled broodingly on a freshly rolled cigarette. "It's Saturday and we need a break from here," he said.

I really wanted to go but I had to work that night. We were expected to take turns doing yard duty. This involved carefully searching the yard for fires or any unexploded bombs. It was time consuming and dangerous, not a job that anyone enjoyed. Our compound had a very large yard, which meant a check took a long time. An unexploded bomb made a ticking sound and had to be reported right away so that it could be defused and removed.

"I can't leave," I said, "I'm on the list for night duty."

"Sneak out," suggested Arie, coaxingly. "Just use the hole in the fence: I have done it before." Jack just shook his head. "Are you guys nuts? You'll get caught and we'll all be in shit." He got up and walked away.

~

There was a hole in the fence at the back of the compound. It was not visible to the guards at the front gate but almost everyone except the guards knew it was there. No one ever talked about it but everyone had used it at one time or another. I had not used it and I didn't even know it was there. I was a little apprehensive about going. Yard duty was important and I knew I would be in trouble if they found out I wasn't there.

But, after what I had seen at the ruins, and with the relentless bombing, I was now afraid every day that I would end up in one of those piles. So, I went. I went through the hole. Arie and Lowie knew how to get to the Reeperbahn and I did not. As agreed, they were waiting for me at the corner beyond the compound. We walked to the streetcar line, caught the next car passing and rode it to the suburb of Harburg. From there, we took the train to a small station in Hamburg. The Reeperbahn was pretty much a seedy place, but it was also a fun place. Everyone was there for the same reason: forget the war, forget the problems with the uncertainty of life, and enjoy the moment, because you never knew what was coming tomorrow. You never knew what was coming for you.

The weather was warm, the evening crowd was pleasant and soon we were getting comfortable walking about. I found the streets to be alive with a culture which I had never before experienced. The bars were vibrant and lively. The music was loud and could be heard everywhere – the beer and schnapps were flowing.

Walking through the Reeperbahn for the first time was startling. It was worth the trip just to see the working girls on the Grosse Freiheit. As we picked our way along the crowded street, two girls walked out of the crowd immediately in front of us. Their tops were transparent, openly revealing their breasts, and their unabashed behavior was very exciting as they met us with a warm and friendly smile. Their skirts were seductively short. As they approached, they pulled a cord, opening the front of their skirts revealing everything. As they passed us walking away, another cord opened the back. The girls of the Reeperbahn were certainly not shy.

"Wow, nice tits. Did you see that, Pete?" said Arie. "Maybe we should catch up to those girls and talk with them. They smiled like they wanted us to."

"Don't be stupid, man. They'll show us a good time for sure, but all they really want is our money," I said, "and if you are anything like me Arie, you don't have much money."

"Maybe it's worth it though," suggested Lowie, with a full-faced grin.

"No way," I said. Getting caught once was punishment enough. As much as I would have liked to, there was no way I wanted to get mixed up with German girls again. They were young and beautiful. Like anyone else, they were willing to do what they had to do in order to survive the war. But it wasn't going to be with me. I just wanted some beer.

We found a promising bar. There were several tables with chairs for two or four patrons at each, and we waited in line for a vacant one. Each table was identified by a large number card on a pole extending above it. We were seated at table eleven. Also, on each table was a telephone. The people at one table; guys, girls or mixed company, were welcome to phone over to another table and offer to share their beer, a dance or their company. It was always in fun and always a friendly choice to accept or refuse any offer. Couples were dancing to the music of a live band. It was hard to believe we were still in the middle of a war. Like us, they wanted to escape the bombing, the destruction, the death and the horror. Like us, they wanted the comfort of being social. We took turns buying rounds of beer for our table, as vendors walked about selling cigarettes, taking group photos and offering schnapps for additional prices. We were paid a minimal wage for our labour and I kept train fare aside. Other than that, I spent all I had before the night was over.

At one point in the evening, our drinking was suddenly interrupted by a commotion at the door. There were several German soldiers doing a random ID-check on the patrons and anyone outside. This was not a regular occurrence but we had been warned to carry proper identification papers at all times. Any civilian who was non-German was forcibly escorted out into the street. We were lined up and herded into an alley. Then were told to face the wall, raise our arms and be prepared to present our identity papers. "Hände hoch," they yelled. *Hands up*, "Hände hoch."

My hands must not have been high enough and a soldier struck me on the back of the head. I was knocked off balance and I dropped my papers. This obviously annoyed the soldier and he kicked me just as I bent over to retrieve my papers. His heavy army boot hit me hard, right in the middle of my chest. The pain immediately took my breath away and again the soldier screamed at me to raise my arms. The pain was unbearable as I tried to catch my breath. I fell to my knees, holding my chest, and the soldier walked away, satisfied that with or without papers, he had made his point. Finally, after the whole group had been checked, we were released. We returned to the bar to find our table was occupied and our beer was gone. It was just as well, as we needed to catch the train to Harburg and then the last streetcar back to the barracks. If we missed the last streetcar, we would have a long walk back to the compound. That could take hours, when every step I took caused me pain and left me breathless. It was to our good fortune that we did catch the train but as we left the entertainment district and disappeared into the night, the gentle rocking of the train caused a piercing pain deep in my chest. The comfort of my bed couldn't come fast enough.

~

When I woke up the next morning I was hurting so badly that I couldn't get up. Work was never something that I would neglect, but that morning, I could hardly breathe or move. My chest was in such pain that all I wanted to do was lie still. Jack knew that the German soldiers in charge of our compound would have no sympathy for me. He knew what had happened to me, and also knew that if I couldn't work, I was useless to them.

"Get your ass out of bed," said Jack, and he reminded me of the story of Alex, the labourer in Hannover, who was unable to work and was sent to Lager 21. That memory was the convincing that I needed. I had difficulty breathing that day and for a few weeks after, and I was sure that a bone must have been broken in my sternum. It caused an odd lump on my chest and, thanks to that moffen, *(Dutch derogatory term for a German – like Kraut),* it remained there for the rest of my life.

Chapter 19
The Red Tie

Fürstenmoor, Summer 1944

By July 1944, work at the compound had become routine and steady. Compared to Braunschweig and Hannover, we each knew our individual jobs better and I could pace myself, allowing my chest to heal. If there was something that needed lifting, one of my friends would jump in to help. We had become a supportive team. The days were busy as we woke early and worked all-day repairing vehicles. I had to drive a few times to make camp deliveries, but I was glad not to go back to the body removal detail for several weeks. My chest pain was slowly going away and my breathing was becoming bearable, but lifting heavy bodies would not be helpful and the soldiers would not be tolerant.

I was not tempted by the Reeperbahn for quite a while. Arie and Lowie went a couple of times and always on a weekend, never during the week. On Sundays, soldiers had time off so we did as well, as they wouldn't let us work without supervision. I don't know why. We knew more about motor mechanics, welding and vehicle repair than they did, but I often wondered if they feared sabotage if we were left alone and unsupervised. Not that the thought didn't enter our minds, as it would be satisfying to know that a vehicle broke down during a critical moment in battle. And battle was coming, we knew it. We cautiously listened to our radio in the barracks at night and learned of the Allies' advance. They had captured the harbour at Cherbourg and were continuing their march eastward across France.

The bombing of Hamburg continued and I adjusted my foxhole whenever I could to make it safer. I dug the hole deeper and, having scrounged steel rods and wooden timbers from around the compound, I laid them across one end to provide roofing and cover. I took straw from a neighbouring farm, and stuffed it under the roofed end to make it more comfortable to lie in. Early one evening near the end of the workday, we were interrupted by the scream of the alarm signaling to us to take cover. Compared to the bombing of Hamburg, air raids over Fürstenmoor were less frequent, but it only takes one bomb to kill you. I was closer to the bomb shelter than my foxhole and quickly followed the line of locals into safety. As we shuffled through the door, I was immediately tense. Breathing was already difficult; the air inside was stuffy. People were pushing and shoving to find shelter from the imminent danger. Soldiers, local citizens and foreigners on forced labour from several countries were all squeezing through the door to find safety. People were shouting in several different languages, children were crying, mothers were frantic and the raging alarm was ear-piercingly loud. Despite the soldiers shouting and trying to keep order everything led to chaos. I pushed my way to a bench in a corner and took a seat. I hoped it would not take long as I hated being in there. Arie and Jack were close by and in the darkened abyss, I could see Rik and the two Frenchmen. Lowie was not in sight.

Sitting next to me on the bench was an old man. He was dressed in a well pressed white shirt and a black suit jacket. Unlike the rest of us wearing work boots, he wore dress shoes, and at his throat I could see a perfectly knotted crimson red tie. He smiled at me, as any gentleman would smile at a stranger. Who knows why in all the madness of war, a gentleman would be well dressed for a bomb shelter. War is crazy.

We didn't speak as we huddled together in the noise and chaos. He sat with a woman close to his age, presumably his wife because she sat protectively close to him.

She, too, was well dressed. She had on a black dress and she had a single strand of pearls at her neck. Her fashion sense was as impressive as his. Together, they seemed different to the other locals that were there.

The sounds of the bombing became louder and the shelter shook as the bombs impacted closer. The air got thinner as the oxygen was sucked out of it. The dust hung in the air beneath quivering ceiling lights. I could still see the old man and his wife close to me.

She was watching fearfully as the old man struggled to breathe. He leaned over straining to get air. His eyes were filled with fear and panic as he tried to take short breaths. I watched helplessly as he slumped over, clutching his chest and gasping in pain. His wife screamed and looked around frantically for help. In the hazy chaos and confusion no one saw her, and it was so noisy with so many screaming, no one heard her. We were cramped in such a small space there was little I could do.

To assist her, I held the old man under his armpits, loosened his tie and tried to keep him upright. On the floor he could be trampled. She shook him and tried to revive him. In the tension and fear, it appeared that he had suffered a heart attack, as he now sat limp and motionless in my arms. She pulled him away from me and I let him go. She held him close and rocked him gently back and forth, as she wept. When he did not respond, she calmed herself as if accepting what had happened. It was over as quickly as it started. Now oblivious to the noise and chaos around us, his wife held the old man tenderly as I watched his red tie sway back and forth in the flickering darkness. I forced myself to look away; I was an intruder in this intimate moment. As I turned away, I took a breath and thought about how much death I had seen in just the last few months. When the all-clear siren sounded, we filed out of the shelter and I left the old man in the care of his wife, his friends and a few soldiers. There was nothing I could do to help him. The old man's war was over.

~

Arie, Jack and I walked together back to the compound. As expected, Harms was waiting for us. He had not been in the shelter we had built; he and the other senior rank soldiers had another concrete bunker for safety.

"Everybody make it out ok?" he asked. Again, I appreciated his question.

"We didn't see Lowie," replied Jack.

"He's ok, he's over by the bridge. Find him and get back to your barracks. I'll see you in the morning," he said curtly as he walked away towards his office.

We found Lowie standing at the bridge, leaning against one of the rails; smoking a cigarette. Jack and Arie walked on to wash up and I asked,"where were you Lowie, I didn't see you at the bomb shelter? I was worried. I thought you didn't make it."

"Yeah, I was there," he said. "I saw Ella from the kitchen. She was alone and scared so I sat with her."

With the whole camp being fed at the same kitchen, it took a lot of help to make it run. Some of the cooks were trained soldiers, but a lot of kitchen jobs were handled by locals and Ella was a young woman whom we all knew.

"Oh, I should have figured that," I said teasingly, "you sit with Ella whenever you get the chance."

With a smile of embarrassment, Lowie went on to tell me his story. Before the bombing started and things got noisy in the shelter, Ella asked a favour of him. She wanted some dishes. Not for herself, but for her aunt. From the bombing, her aunt's dishes had all been broken and with the strict rationing, she couldn't buy any new ones. Ella knew the army kitchen was well stocked and a few plates would not likely be missed, but working with others, she couldn't secretly take any.

"I want to help Ella," said Lowie "but, I can't do it alone, I was hoping you would help me."

"Are you crazy," I responded. "I know why you want to help Ella, but what's in it for me?"

"Her aunt says she has a ration card and living alone, she has enough food to share. She can get us a ham."

Food was always on our minds. The army fed us but it was barely sufficient to keep us alive. Living on black bread, mouldy tasting cabbage soup and some kind of brown water they called coffee forced all of us to constantly be on the lookout for more.

Lowie told me his plan. Each day after our warm meal at lunchtime, we would each steal a dish or a plate, and we could hide it in our coveralls. He would arrange it with Ella so that she would be standing by at the wash rack so other kitchen staff wouldn't interfere. Then, instead of handing in our dishes, we would walk past Ella as if we did.

"Then what?" I asked, "We can't keep dishes in our barracks." Because random checks of our personal lockers were always a threat, Lowie would have to find a secure hiding place for them away from our barracks.

"Already found a spot," said Lowie. It was apparent that he had put some planning into this already. "There is tall grass to hide them in growing around the fence at the back of the compound. It is close enough to the kitchen that we could walk over without attracting attention. Ella can get them from the fence after dark."

Stealing from the German army would be considered a serious offence for an *Ausländer.* But I never thought of it as theft. With the things that I had seen and experienced, every day was a struggle to stay alive. It was that way for everyone. Tomorrow you could be dead. All my time in Germany so far had been driven by two powerful feelings: fear and hunger. I did what had to be done for survival. My bartering opportunity with the blackout curtains to a local resident had paid off with extra bread and cheese. The thought of sharing a real ham with Lowie was a strong motivation. So, what the hell, I agreed to help him.

~

The next day as we walked to the kitchen for lunch, I was nervous. *What did you get me into, Lowie?* I thought. We ate with the soldiers and other camp labourers, and as I ate, my full attention was on the soldiers. *Did they know our intentions? Were they watching and waiting for us to slide a plate into our coveralls?* Suddenly, I was wishing that I had not volunteered to help Lowie with his deception. With the meal finished, I saw, and was sure that every soldier in the room saw Lowie smile and nod at Ella. As we got up to leave, Ella moved to the stacking table by the wash bins to receive our plates. With my back to the soldiers, and inching towards Ella in the lineup of workers, I slid my plate into the front of my work clothes. Each worker put his plate on the pile and, his knife, fork and spoon in a large metal bowl of water and his cup beside the plates. Lowie did the same and as I approached her, I saw Ella watching my hands. I followed the normal routine with the exception of the plate. Ella smiled at both of us.

As we walked away, I thought my shoulders must have been touching my ears, I was so taut with nervous tension. *What if it was a trap? What if Ella was intentionally trying to have us punished for some reason, and the soldiers would have been only too happy to investigate if she reported an infraction.* Lowie was still ahead of me as we approached the door. I was starting to relax and just as I reached the door a soldier quickly walked up behind us.

"Warte," he said, *wait*, and I froze.

I had forgotten my hat and gloves at the table, and he reminded me that they had been issued, and that I should take better care of them and not leave them lying about. I thanked him as he cut in front of me and walked out. If he was looking for signs of misconduct, I felt sure I was exposed. I was sweating, my legs felt like rubber and I was unable to speak except for a feeble "Danke."

Like the others, we walked about the compound for a couple of minutes after lunch for exercise and to breathe the clean air. Lowie and I walked towards the fence and, once behind the building, I gave Lowie the plate. *You hide it,* I thought, helping me feel less of an accomplice and reducing my responsibility for our deception. He quickly buried the plate in the long grass and we walked on, undetected. I breathed a sigh of relief and was glad that was over. We were careful. We didn't steal plates every meal but enough to provide Ella's aunt with several plates. Every time we delivered the plate or dish to the fence; the earlier cache was gone, as planned.

Chapter 20
MIDNIGHT RUN

Fürstenmoor, August 1944

In August, I had to return to the bombing detail. My punishment remained in effect for much longer than I wished, and certainly longer than I thought was deserved. At least I had a few weeks throughout July for my chest injury to heal so the pain had become minimal. The work intensified in the compound as well. Vehicles of all types and descriptions came to us for repair. The days were hot, long and busy as we repaired engines, wheels and twisted fenders, with the pressure to get them returned to service as soon as possible. Our radio provided us with welcome news. We knew that the Allies were moving inland on one front, and the Russians were pushing westward on another. Germany was being squeezed.

Work in the compound was frequently interrupted by bombing. It challenged us to stay focused on our work, when it came without warning. Gas masks and helmets became a regular part of our work gear. We were not soldiers and wearing special equipment, especially a hot and uncomfortable mask, was not something that we were used to. Our safety was less important to them than the need to keep us efficiently working.

~

We were awakened early one morning by the sound of a siren signaling us to take cover immediately. Everyone in our barracks jumped up to seek shelter. Everyone except Jack.

"Get up, before you get killed," I yelled as I struggled to get my boots on. But he didn't move. "Leave me alone," he complained, "I'm tired, I need sleep." I tried to get him up but he wouldn't budge. In frustration, I watched him pull the covers over his head, as I reluctantly ran out of the barracks, to the safety of my foxhole. The siren only sounded when there was danger, but we all had been through so much, I understood. There were frustrating days when every one of us had taken chances. That day was Jack's day.

The recent improvements I'd made to my foxhole were helpful but not comfortable. I was afraid and I got in as low as I could get. The bombs were getting closer and heading towards our compound. I hoped that our hidden radio would not be exposed or damaged by the bombing. But more, I worried that Jack would not be safe. The bombing stopped as quickly as it had started and I could tell by a blast of hot air that one bomb had hit somewhere in the compound. I was afraid of what I would see from the safety of my foxhole. The raid was unusually quick and more of a nuisance and I waited for the all-clear signal to be sounded. My view was lost in the smoky dust and my heart sank as I ran for the barracks. I could not believe it. Barracks #4 had been hit. The wall opposite the bunks behind the lockers had been demolished. There was debris everywhere, and in the middle of the rubble, I could see Jack's bed. I could see his blanket and under the blanket, I could see Jack. I ran in screaming towards my friend. "Jack, Jack," I repeated; then, I saw the blanket move. I was stunned and relieved as Jack rolled over and lifted his head. He was pale and he was shaken, but he was not hurt.

Our lockers and bunks were still intact; our precious radio was still out of sight. The only damage seemed to be the one wall that had collapsed and fallen outward. It was, of course, the wall where Hitler's portrait had hung.

Jack stirred to get up and stumbled towards me. "That's the best thing that could have happened," said Jack secretly to me, almost with delight. "I hate that son of a bitch. If it wasn't for him, I wouldn't even be here." The humour of it all, was, when the soldiers came to repair the damage, the first thing they did when the new wall went up, even before they installed the windows, was to hang up a new picture of the Führer.

"Shit," said Jack. "Same bunk, same blanket and the same locker. But I have to look at a new picture of that asshole!" Despite Jack's dangerous breach of protocol, we had a chuckle at his reaction. We were all safe and that became a day to remember.

~

Working in the compound, we kept ourselves busy enough to avoid complaints or punishment, so it came as a surprise when Harms himself came walking about one afternoon as if inspecting our work. He pulled Jack and me aside. That was unusual and I had no idea what was coming. "My family is here in Hamburg and with the constant bombing and destruction, I want to go home to check on them. I need you to drive."

He continued, "the gas supply is diminished here right now, so we'll take one of the trucks that runs on wood. After work, clean yourselves up and come to my office with one of the trucks." Jack and I both knew how the trucks ran on alternate fuel like wood or coal, but the conversion generator was tricky. We knew that Harms wanted to go home and get back again without fail. Having two of us who understood the mechanics of the truck increased the likelihood of that happening. When our workday was over, we quickly washed up and changed into our cleanest dirty clothes for the trip into Hamburg. We got the truck from the compound as Harms had authorized and picked him up at his office. "You drive, Pete," said Harms, as he and Jack squeezed in as passengers. Harms sat silently on the far seat and except to give me directions or show his identity, he did not interact as we passed through the roadblocks making our way to his family home.

"Stay in the truck," Harms told us, upon arrival. "My wife has made a meal for us and I will bring it out to you in a little while." Jack and I sat in the truck taking advantage of the situation. The opportunity for friendly conversation was an unusual benefit for us and we made the most of it. We talked about home, family and how much we missed Holland. We wondered what was happening there. We appreciated having the radio at the barracks, so that in the evenings we could hear the news of the Allied forces moving inland.

As he promised, Harms and his wife eventually came out and approached the truck carrying a couple of plates of food. "This is Hilda," Harms said, as his wife passed our food through the passenger side window. "It is not much," she said, "but Herm wanted me to make his favourite dinner for tonight." It looked delicious I thought as we thanked her.

The meal was a full plate of sausage, mashed potatoes and green beans with some apple sauce and a slice of homemade bread on the side. It was the finest meal I had eaten in months and I was eager to enjoy it. While we ate, they talked to us until Harms stepped away from the passenger window. "I'll bring you some coffee and apple tart," he said with a smile, and he walked away towards the side door of the house. The trip home had obviously made him happy. While he was gone, Hilda engaged us about the war and its foolishness. She spoke openly about what she thought about Hitler and his antics. I got the impression that she hoped it would be over soon.

Harms was always very cautious about discussing the war, and as he returned, he overheard Hilda speaking openly with us. He handed us the coffee and tart. It was the first time in a long time that I had tasted a dessert. I relished it without paying further attention to Hilda's conversation. But Harms was listening carefully. He cautioned his wife about what she was saying, wrapped up our conversation and hustled his wife back towards the house. He spoke in general terms, not committing himself to any expression that would be disloyal. Harms was a good man, but he was also a good soldier and I thought it wise to remember that. It was great to have had a nourishing meal and, afterwards, it was wonderful to experience a leisurely sleep in the truck, rather than on a bare floor or a straw cot.

~

Sometime after midnight, Harms returned and in silence again, we headed back to the compound before we would be missed. In the early hours, there wasn't much traffic in the city. Having the most driving experience, I stayed at the wheel. Harms was concerned about getting back to the compound. "I stayed too long," he said, "but I wanted to know that my family is safe." With that, he encouraged me to speed up.

The narrow streets were dark with blackout restrictions, no streetlights were on and lights were not visible within the building interiors. The truck too was equipped with blackout lights. The normal headlights had a shroud over the top of the lamp like the peak of a hat. The lens was covered allowing only a narrow horizontal strip of light: just enough to see, but not to be seen. It also meant that I couldn't see too far ahead. We bumped along silently, passing deserted and bombed out buildings along the sidewalks.

Suddenly a motorcycle appeared from the right and darted out in front of us. I didn't hear the motorcycle over the noisy engine of the truck and the bike had only blackout lights as well. I didn't see it coming. A German soldier travelling quite fast down the side street had obviously not expected us, or any other traffic to be around and had passed the small intersection without stopping. I was driving faster than I should have and had no more warning of his approach, than he did of ours. It was all over in seconds as I hit him broadside. The noise of the crash echoed off the buildings sounding like a catastrophic alarm. I stopped the truck and all three of us bailed out quickly to check the damage. The truck had a big front end covered with a heavy bumper and a couple of push bars. The damage to the truck was minimal, a couple of small dents and visible scars, but the bike had not fared as well.

The motorcycle and its sidecar were entangled under the truck's front bumper and grill. Jack and I worked feverishly to pull it away as Harms stood back in the darkness, with a worrisome look on his face. The bike was twisted and heavily damaged. We disengaged the sidecar and backed the truck away from the motorcycle so we could get to the rider.

"Is he dead?" asked Harms.

"I think so," I said. All I could see was his face covered in blood but when I removed his helmet, his head fell backwards out of control. His body was limp. In the dim light of our shrouded headlight I recognized the distinctive metal plate carried on his chest by a heavy neck chain. The scroll on the plate said *Feldgendarmerie*. The soldier was a German MP – *Military Police*.

"I think he might still be breathing," said Jack.

"No," said Harms noticeably shaken and becoming officious. "He is dead."

"We should help him," insisted Jack, pulling open the soldier's field coat. "I think he is still breathing."

"I said, he's dead. Leave him," barked Harms, obviously in command. "Get in the truck and let's get out of here."

Jack and I reluctantly pulled the rider's limp body off the roadway. We pushed his crippled motorcycle and sidecar beyond the curb, leaving everything to be found in the coming daylight. Climbing into the truck as ordered, we were given strict instructions to drive on. Harms had insisted that we leave the man. He knew that he was badly injured and that, if not already dead, he soon would be. The collision and our presence in the city at that time of night would have required some explanation.

"If we stay," explained Harms, "we will all be in shit. I am not supposed to be here, and neither are you. Drive on."

As we distanced ourselves from the scene, Harms explained that he was supposed to be on-call at the compound. The fatal collision with the soldier would lead to questioning and hardship for him as well. All three of us were outside our designated area, in the wrong time of day and in a vehicle that he would have been responsible for.

Harms issued a severe caution to us. We, all three of us, should never discuss the incident again. No argument. No negotiations. He told us to make it a priority to repair the truck quickly in the days to come. "If anybody asks, all we have to do is tell the story right. A few dented scratches are just routine damage," he said. "As to the accident, if we don't say anything, we might just get away with it."

Once again, in order to survive, I was pulled into a world of secrecy. The rest of the trip home was made in silence as we slowly found our way back to the compound in the pre-dawn darkness of Hamburg.

Chapter 21
Too Much Death

Fürstenmoor, September 1944

For days, I waited fearfully for any repercussions from the motorcycle accident. Every time an unknown soldier entered the compound, I wanted to run, hide or disappear, especially if the soldier was an officer or was escorted. The reality was that Harms was often visited by his superiors to check on the progress of our work, or the bombing damages, but until then, I had never paid attention to their comings and goings. Now, it was different. Now, in my guilty mind, every senior officer I saw in Harms' office was there as part of an investigation. But, somehow, Harms must have successfully deflected any concerns as I never heard about it again and I never talked about it with anyone.

Thankfully, my assignments to the body details in Hamburg became minimal and I was hoping that (for me) the job was over. I could never erase the sights from my mind - the bodies collected and disposed of like trash. What I saw in the piles were faces of mothers, fathers, sisters, and brothers. But more, what I saw were lost souls. Civilian casualties not mourned and lost without any identification or records as to where they might have gone. It was punishment that I would re-live over and over again for the remainder of my life.

I was always content when I was given a map and told to head out on my own and make a delivery. I could relax and just drive. But after my days of body removal details, I was often too upset to eat the meals provided at the compound. Sometimes I was famished. If I didn't pass any orchards, in desperation I stopped to ask for food at any clean-looking house in the country. The first time I tried that approach, I was hesitant and afraid. I wasn't sure what my reception would be but I was starving hungry and decided to take a chance. I knocked sheepishly on the front door, unsure who would answer.

A pleasant looking older woman cautiously opened the door. When she looked out and saw the army truck she seemed confused, but not afraid. After all, I was not in uniform. I explained that I had been working in the area and was on my way back to Fürstenmoor; but it was a long drive and I really needed something to eat. Did she have anything to spare? She hesitated for a moment and then she smiled, and without any more questions she made me a couple of cheese sandwiches and a jar of hot tea. That was the first time that I had begged a stranger for food, but it was not the only time. Other times, I had the door slammed in my face. More than once, I was chased back to my truck by an angry housewife armed with a frying pan or a broom. They were neither impressed, nor intimidated by my army truck, but I continued trying. Hunger can be a powerful influence on behavior.

In making the deliveries, I never knew what my cargo was. It had been made clear to me at the outset that my business was to drive. What was in the back was loaded and unloaded by other people. In the driver's seat, I had no business or concern. It may have been food or supplies for the soldiers and civilian workers at one of the outreach camps, or it could have been arms and ammunition. I didn't know. If the load was of high value, I always had a soldier with me as an escort. On occasion, I travelled again with the same old soldier. I never knew his name but because he was older, he was more passive, and like me, he wished the war would soon be over. He slept a lot and again like me, he just wanted to go home. He understood when I had talked about the meagre rations and how hungry I was. The soldiers' rations at the compound were getting smaller as well, and they were not fed much better than we were. I told him about my efforts to ask local farm wives for food, and that I was not always successful in getting anything.

"Let me try," he said. "I know it is difficult to beg, but if we stop together, a German soldier, in a German army truck might have better luck. Some farmers might feel obligated to help out and might be pleased to be helping the war effort."

With him along, we tried our luck together and, more often than not, we were successful. It was rare but for once, I was glad to be accompanied by someone wearing a German uniform. He was calmer and less authoritarian than others I had encountered. He remained unknown to me by name, but he was friendly. He became a friend at a time when I needed one.

~

In the fall of 1944, as the war raged on, my delivery trips to the camps, or the outposts became more and more dangerous. The loads delivered from Fürstenmoor became bigger as the camps where we took supplies were getting larger. More soldiers had to be fed and supplied. I was warned to be cautious and always on the lookout as a moving army truck would be a likely target for Allied fighter planes.

The standard accompaniment of a soldier grew to become two soldiers. At times, they would order me to stop the truck so they could leave the cab. They could see better and avoid danger if they were sitting outside the truck. With one on each front fender, facing in opposite directions, they were to protect the truck and its load from attack. I was never sure who their enemy was or from where the attack would come, but I had to remain alert as the soldiers watched from their fenders for any indication of attacking planes. If planes were observed by the guards, they bailed from the fenders, and took refuge in the ditches. If that happened, I had to bring my truck to an immediate halt and take cover as well. I could only go back to the truck when they did and continue to our destination, once they had determined it was safe to do so.

Some trips were routine supply deliveries to military camps and were usually uneventful. But I hated going to the civilian prisoner camps. They were usually some distance from Fürstenmoor and always involved an overnight stay. It was heartbreaking to see these prisoners. The camps were for "undesirables." Anyone who, because of race, religion, political affiliation or behaviour contrary to Nazi ideology, ended up there. They were kept in overcrowded conditions, poorly clothed, poorly fed, and they were poorly treated. Not by German army soldiers, but by SS soldiers, who were young and fanatical. The prisoners were neglected and barely kept alive. At one of the hundreds of such subcamps - those smaller camps which surrounded larger camps - I again witnessed Nazi atrocity.

As usual, I was shut away in my own room where I was to sleep and be ready to move on in the morning. I was always warned before being left for the night to mind my own business and not interfere with the goings on in camp. But curiosity again took control of me as I heard soldiers shouting outside my room. Carefully peeking from the window, I could see the soldiers controlling a group of ragtag civilian prisoners behind an adjacent building, a short distance away.

Prisoners were made to line up and stand at one end of a pond, filled with raw sewage from the latrines. Under control of the guards, and upon a start command, two prisoners were made to jump in and paddle, wade or swim through the raw sewage to the other end. Already weakened by the long days of work and poor diet, they had to somehow make it across the pond to save their lives. The winner was challenged to do it again, against a new competitor. The loser was shot, killed, then hauled out by the winner.

I had watched a race involving human beings in an open latrine and what I saw made me so angry that I was sick to my stomach. I immediately lost the food that was in my body and I was shaking in fear. Soldiers fought wars and soldiers died fighting wars. I understood that. But I could not understand why civilians should die just because of who they were. These people were not combatants, they were civilian prisoners and were killed with malice and without accountability. Why?

I spent the remainder of that night near to tears in my desolate room with only a blanket and a straw-filled mattress. I was left shivering in the cold as I mourned the deaths of those innocent prisoners. Who were they? All I had heard was that people from all over Europe were being held there. I too was a civilian in a camp of soldiers and every noise outside awakened me from any sleep. In my mind, every sound I heard was the soldiers coming for me. The next morning, I was fed some bread and coffee, then set out alone with an empty truck to go home. I lost track of time as I drove mindlessly on, across the German countryside, and away from that camp. I only hoped that every turn and every signpost was getting me closer to safety and I was glad when I saw the familiar landscape around Fürstenmoor. Upon arrival I parked the truck and immediately went to the barracks. My team was still working but my workday was over. I was hungry and glad to see my supper on the table. I ate quickly and I fell into my bunk, thankful to be home.

~

Maybe it was the way the barracks faced the sunrise or maybe it was the lack of trees about the compound, but mornings often dawned brightly in Fürstenmoor. Every day was a new day and I tried to start every new day with a positive attitude: an outlook for a positive adventure. But it didn't always go that way.

"You and Arie are driving together to make deliveries this morning," a soldier from Harms' office explained. It was going to be another day on the roads of northern Germany but at least it was just a day trip. We would not be staying anywhere overnight.

Arie and I reported to the Transport Section and were told to wait beside the trucks until the four soldiers who were accompanying us were ready to go. They were standing close by and making plans. All seemed to be friends, enjoying a pause and a little planning discussion over a cigarette and a few laughs. When ready, they told us that we were travelling separately in two enclosed Opel Blitz cargo trucks. We were to set off in the same direction and I was to drive the lead truck with a few civilian workers in the back. Arie was to follow in the second truck, loaded with supplies. A soldier opened the tarp and half a dozen civilians climbed into the back of my truck. They took their seats on wooden benches along each side. With their plans completed, the soldiers climbed up into the cabs and we were set to go.

"Stop - wait," shouted a soldier, coming across the yard from Harms' office.

"The commander wants to see you, Peter." With that announcement, plans were changed. Arie was told to drive the lead truck with the civilians and I was to follow with the supply truck after talking to Harms.

"What did you do now, Pete, you in shit again?" asked Arie teasingly, as he climbed into the lead truck. "I get to lead the parade today, so try to catch up," he added with a laugh.

"I have no idea, but I won't be long. Wait for me when you get there, and we can come back together, it's safer," I replied. Arie waved goodbye. And then he was gone.

The soldiers jumped down from the cargo truck and were happy to hang around and have another smoke as I walked away towards Harms' office. It was unusual that he called us to his office and I was curious as to why. Why could he not have waited until I got back that afternoon?

On arrival, I was told to have a seat and wait outside his door until Harms called for me. The headquarters office was busy with important looking soldiers walking about quickly and administrative staff typing in a whirl of activity. I hoped not to draw attention to myself and was content to just stay out of the way. I waited for what seemed to be a long time for Harms to finish his business, and after what seemed to be an hour, he called me in. Over the office clatter, I heard Harms' distinct voice. "Enter," he said, in more of a command than an invitation. Harms was seated behind his desk and I noted it was clean of any papers or business. His posture was stern and his voice reflected the same demeanor. "When were you at the Reeperbahn?" he asked and without waiting for my response, he lifted his left hand. In his hand was a picture, a picture with me in it. "And, don't tell me you have not been there," he said. I was speechless. Where did he get that photograph, I thought, as my mind raced for an answer? I didn't want to tell him that I had been there, but he had the evidence in his hand.

"This photograph has been presented to me, and I am told that the photo was taken at the Reeperbahn. More so, it has been alleged that it was taken several weeks ago, on a Saturday." I started to speak although I had no idea what I was about to say.

"Be quiet," stormed Harms. "It is also alleged, that on that date, you were supposed to be on yard duty … here," he said. "There are no gate records of you leaving the camp."

I had no defence. I had no explanation. It was me in the photo, sitting at a table, in a bar on the Reeperbahn, drinking beer with a friend of Lowie's.

"You went through the hole in the fence, didn't you?"

I didn't know that Harms even knew about the hole and if he knew, it instantly became useless for us all. Again, I stood there without comment and tried to hide the guilty look that I am sure was on my face.

"Damn you, Peter," said Harms. "I should be disciplining you for this offence. It was your turn to be on yard duty and your neglect must be punished. What if something had happened? What if there was a bombing or a fire? Leaving the compound with disregard for your responsibilities could have had significant consequences for all of us. When are you going to learn that rules are made to be followed? Did you not learn that from your behaviours in Hannover? Has your punishment removing the bodies from the bombing sites not taught you anything? You are a good worker, and a skilled mechanic. You and Jack are alike. You mind your own business and you do your work. I don't want to lose you or see you punished. But somehow, I need to handle the matter of this picture."

I felt disappointed in myself for getting caught. *Who took that picture?* I thought. My mind was racing as I tried to imagine what punishment was to follow. I was not prepared for what he said next.

"Fortunately for you, this photo has no date on it. It shows that you were there, but it does not show when. It does not conclusively prove that you were there while you were supposed to be on duty here. Consider this discussion to be a warning; and consider this discussion to be your discipline. But remember this and realize that somebody is watching you," he said. "Clean up your behaviour, and be smart about it. I cannot always cover for you and if I have to haul you back in here again, you might be facing a harsh punishment."

Sternly and without a doubt that the matter was over, he said in a demanding voice: "Now, get out of my office, get to your work, and tell no one about this conversation."

The Evidence Photo at the Reeperbahn (Pete on right)

I left Harms' office in shame, being called out for shirking my job. He was a fair man, but if necessary, he would do what had to be done. I thought Harms was setting an example of the relationship we were now in. My behavior would be shrouded in silence, just as the motorcycle accident was. A secret only remains a secret if no one knows there is one. We both had secrets to keep.

Returning to the Transport Section, I was unable to leave until the soldiers were ready. They had been given another job in my absence. I stood by the truck, revisiting in my mind Harms' caution to me, and once again, I realized, fortunately, another predicament had worked out in my favour.

~

By the time the soldiers returned to the truck it was approaching mid-day and they were anxious to leave. They gave a nod of approval, climbed into the cab, and I drove off. The German countryside was quiet and the trees were starting to show early fall colours. The yellow leaves stood out against the green fields bordering the roadway. I drove along in silence for a couple of hours, my mind wandering back to Harms' office repeatedly, as if his message was slowly sinking in. It would have been a beautiful drive, if the soldiers had not moved out to sit on the fenders. They were watching the skies and reminding me that there was a war on. As we came through an area of heavy bush on both sides of the road, we rounded a curve and I pulled over. I was shocked at what I saw on the side of the road ahead.

A German army truck lay awkwardly in the ditch, a burned-out wreck. I recognized it immediately. It was my truck: the one I was supposed to have driven. The one that

I would have driven if Harms had not called me off to talk to me. The one that Arie took for me. My soldiers jumped off their fenders and took cover in defence. I stopped the truck and quickly joined them in the ditch. All I could do was lay low while determining what had happened there. The vehicle had been strafed by a low flying Allied fighter, and the truck had crashed and burst into flames. Although the fire had burned itself out, I could feel the heat. The truck lay motionless with flickering flames still licking the tires. When the soldiers determined that the danger had passed, they cautiously began to move forward. I followed them as they approached the truck. Carefully pulling the shreds of burned and melted tarps aside, the soldiers checked the back of the truck while I fearfully crept forward alongside towards the driver's door. The door was too hot to touch but the window was shattered and glass lay about where I stood. Through the open window, I could see the driver. He had died in a fiery crash and his face and clothing were badly burned. I wasn't sure if it was my friend or not. His upper body was hunched forward over the steering wheel. His hands lay motionless on his lap. On his wrist, I recognized the watch. It was Arie. My friend was dead.

We could see that the occupants were all dead. Escape had been impossible and I felt queasy with the heavy smoke and the smell of the burned flesh. The soldiers were horrified and struggled with their emotions as they grasped the reality of how the other soldiers, their friends, were dead, lying face down in the ditch near the truck. In that moment they became ordinary men, like me, caught in a hellish war. There was nothing we could do for any of them.

Fighting back our feelings, we returned to the truck and each soldier took up his position on the fender as I climbed back into the cab. My hands were trembling and I was struggling to deal with the realization that my friend Arie was dead. Had it not been for Harms wanting a meeting with me, it would have been me driving that truck. It was hard to leave but harder to stay. I took a deep breath, started the truck and I turned to return to Fürstenmoor. The tools in my truck were of no value today. As I drove along, I felt lonely, lost and far from home. I thought to myself, why must every day be filled with some experience of cruelty, distress and death?

Everything I did, and everywhere I went, I was surrounded by death. At 20, I had seen too much suffering; fear and distrust; more tragedy and despair than I would see for the rest of my life. It was all around me and I couldn't control it - I couldn't run away from it. I couldn't even talk about it. I was so tired of war and needless misery I wanted so much to get back to Holland - back to Wognum.

Chapter 22
The Retaliation

Wognum, September 1944

In Wognum, the harshness of the German occupation was increasing. Everyone had suffered in some way at the hands of the military, and we had each in our own way been transformed by the experiences of war. Many young men had joined the resistance in defiance of the German regime and their efforts continued to interfere and disrupt German authority. Everyone remained fearful as to how it would ever end.

Peter's parents and his family continued to welcome me and I had clearly become an accepted member of their family. Their support gave me hope and it was always a pleasure when I visited them in the evening, before curfew, and had tea with his mother. I was so appreciative, and with Elisabeth's love, I never felt alone. I had always known Peter's dad to be a warm and friendly man. Jan spoke with his eyes and could inspire me with a look. His face always had a sparkle that invited conversation. But lately, his usual jovial demeanor had become just dim resignation. Elisabeth, too, seemed to just resolutely carry on. She was in her late forties and was blessed with a quiet strength and stoic perseverance, as she fed, clothed, and kept her family together during such unpredictable times. Peter's brothers had grown from boys to young men, still too young for the *razzias* and so continued to work at local jobs, helping to feed a family of seven children. It was difficult, at the best of times, and the family all spoke with such pride about their mother. But even Elisabeth was becoming worn down. I noticed that her steps were slower and she was tiring. The joys and the fun family times that I had shared with them just two years ago seemed so far away.

The rationing system made it challenging to provide enough nourishment for any family. We could only use ration cards to obtain food, clothing, or supplies and the daily adult food allotment was down to 1600 calories. Jan's family were fishermen in Medemblik, a fishing village to the north. As a young man, Jan had learned how to weave fishing nets by hand and he could repair them if they became worn or torn. Luckily, he could still sell his nets, or barter for fish with some of the Medemblik fishermen. If there was plenty, Jan could use some of the fish to trade for vegetables or meat with local farmers. Meat rations were particularly scarce. Whether rich or poor, people could not ordinarily buy more than their ration coupons would allow.

When a farmer was able to secretly butcher a pig, or a cow, meat became available to buy without using coupons. The news of extra meat quickly spread about the neighbourhood. By communicating with each other and sharing what little they had, the people of Wognum were surviving.

~

In September, another German soldier was found dead in a ditch outside of town and the soldiers angrily carried out an even more terrible revenge than usual. On a chilly, cloudless evening an army truck stopped in front of the Roemer family home. Tinus and his wife were downstairs, while I was upstairs with the children. My attention was drawn to the sounds of soldiers yelling, and the familiar thumping of their boots, as they ran about on the street out front. I looked out to see several soldiers lined up and standing guard by a truck as their leader, stomped across the front yard towards the house. He pounded fiercely on the front door with angry determination,

"Raus, jeder raus," he said. *Out, everyone out.*

Tinus rushed to the door and tried to make sense of what the soldier was saying. He was pulled outside and brutally thrown to the ground. The commander looked at Tinus, pointed to his watch and then held up seven fingers. After more yelling and arm waving sign language, the officer's intentions became obvious. Tinus understood. He would be allowed seven minutes.

"To do what?" he asked in Dutch, raising his hands in confusion. "What do you want?"

Again, the soldier pointed to his watch and held up seven fingers. He pointed to a line of a dozen soldiers standing back in the evening shadows. Each soldier stood at attention, with a gas can at his feet, awaiting further instructions. The horrific reality was shocking. Tinus realized that they were going to set fire to his house. He had seven minutes to remove his family and anything they wanted from the house. He ran back to the door and entered the house screaming loudly. "Trina, Trina," he yelled. "Grab your stuff we have to leave. We have to get out of the house."

"What's happening?" his wife called. "Why?"

"Just grab some clothes and any valuables and get out quickly, they are going to burn down our house."

"Corrie! Get everything you can carry," he yelled, "get the kids out, get your clothes, and their clothes and do the same – get out. Everyone get out."

We all were in a state of panic as we rushed back and

forth from room to room, trying to collect what treasures we could accumulate in just minutes. I ran to the kids' room and started emptying their closets. I just desperately threw their clothes and shoes out of their bedroom window. I then quickly grabbed what I could of my own belongings. I wanted to save as much as I could. I stuffed things in my apron and as I grabbed a blanket off the bed for more, I heard the soldiers' thundering footsteps coming up the stairs. Seven minutes were up, and I had to get out with what little I could carry.

"Raus, Raus," they yelled loudly, pushing the children and me downstairs and outside.

With tears of fear and confusion we all made our way out of our home. All we could do was stand on the road, crying, as the soldiers moved quickly, emptying their gas cans throughout the house. The soldiers then threw flares into the house and stood back as it immediately erupted in a firestorm. Whoomph! They waited to ensure the job was done and the house was fully ablaze. With nothing more than a few treasures that were precious to me, I stood on the roadway with the Roemers and their children. I had my favourite coat from Peter, a few clothes, pictures of my mother and father, some keepsake jewellery and a pair of mismatched shoes, The Roemer home had been in the family for three generations, and due to their compassion and generosity, it had become my home. Now, in front of our eyes, our home and everything we owned, except what we could carry, was being reduced to ashes. It wasn't until then that I realized I had forgotten to bring my Braunschweig letter from Peter. I was heartbroken to realize it may have been my last personal contact from him and now it was gone. As the heat and smoke grew, we had to move further back and down the road. We all were coughing and struggling to breathe as the flames consumed the oxygen. Mrs. Roemer fell to her knees screaming in terror as Mr. Roemer fought back his own tears, trying to calm his wife with his hand on her shoulder. The children were in an anxious state and fought to understand why this was happening. Tina was hysterical. In the terror and anxiety, she had forgotten Dolly. Despondent with the loss of her best friend, she was determined to rush back into the house to find her. "Dolly! Dolly's on fire," she screamed, a pitiful four-year-old distraught and confused, standing on the road in darkness.

My heart was broken for the entire family. They were a strength to the community: well established for generations with a successful trucking business. Not only did I enjoy working for them, but I enjoyed living with them, as part of their family. They were a faithful Catholic family and I was always comfortable with them because their faith in God mirrored my own. Standing there in tears with a loving family, I questioned my faith and challenged what the nuns had taught me in Zoeterwoude. I had been taught to put my faith in an all-loving, all-powerful God. But I doubted. *Why would an all-loving God want this to happen? Why would an all-powerful God allow this to happen?* That night, my faith was crushed.

With the fire raging and lighting up the sky, the soldiers callously looked at us as they climbed aboard the truck in strict orderly fashion. They drove off without a single soldier looking back, as their retaliation had been achieved. Local fire fighters came to protect other homes on the street but were unable to save the Roemer house. Another family across town in Wognum suffered the same fate that night. The soldiers had chosen the two largest houses in Wognum and burned them both to the ground sending a clear message that crimes against them would be strictly and quickly dealt with. This time, for someone killing a soldier, two families who didn't even know one another, were forced to pay the penalty. The Roemers had no choice but to walk away from their blazing home. We all took refuge with the generosity of the neighbours and were able to stay there overnight. The following day, Mr. Roemer found temporary housing for his family with relatives across town. I was welcome to stay as well, but I felt awkward there. The house was smaller and there was not much need for a maid and so it was a difficult time for a while; not only had I lost my home but I had also lost my job.

~

In time, and with the Roemers looking out for me, I was able to find a temporary job close by, at Café Stam. The café was owned by some relatives and was always a popular spot, even still during wartime. I worked as a waitress and helped with the general cleaning and all the other duties required in running a restaurant. I was a friendly person, and I was used to hard work, but I was uncomfortable being so close to German soldiers. It was common for them to come into the café for a drink. I had never been a waitress. I did not drink, and never had. My teenage years had been spent growing up in a convent in Zoeterwoude, where my development had been monitored by nuns. I had not known men, and certainly never experienced their, sometimes rowdy, behaviour when drinking. But I was resilient and adapted quickly. The café served two kinds of beer. The better brew was held back to serve to the locals and the inferior brand was reserved for strangers. Generally, the soldiers knew the policy and accepted it as a matter of how the business was run. Sometimes the younger soldiers would angrily try to convince me to pour the better beer for them. I innocently pretended that I was confused and would apologetically pour another beer from another tap. They thought that I was giving them the *goed spul* - good stuff, but I never did. After all they had taken from me, it was just a simple retaliation to deny them, no matter how trivial the denial.

Chapter 23
Letters

Fürstenmoor, September 1944

By the time I left the crash site and got my truck back to Fürstenmoor, it was dark and well after the workday was over. The barrack lights were on but nobody was around and it seemed strange to me that the world around the compound was empty. I dropped the soldiers off at Harms' office, drove the truck into the Transport Section and backed it up against the fence in one of the two vacant spaces. The Transport Feldwebel – *Staff-Sergeant* – was very particular as to how the vehicles were to be parked in his compound. He often said, "Just because there is a war on, that's no reason to be sloppy." I jumped down from the cab, slowly made my way over to the office and dropped my papers through the after-hours slot in the clerk's door. Standing at the door, I yelled, "I'm back," into the empty office, more to amuse myself than anything else. That's what Arie would have done and I missed him already.

From there, I walked straight away across the compound to the barracks. My supper was still on the table, but again despite my hunger, I was too emotional and could not eat. All the guys were getting ready to go to bed, a couple were already in their bunks. They were not surprised that I was alone.

"We heard about Arie," said Jack, "what happened?"

The soldiers had reported the entire incident to Harms. The commander had broken the news to Jack and the rest of the team, but of course, they wanted details as to how our friend had died. I related the story of the truck, the apparent strafing, finding Arie, the soldiers and the dead civilian workers. The details left everyone sad and speechless. It was Lowie's suggestion that we all go to the Reeperbahn soon to have a beer as a tribute to Arie. "He liked it there," said Lowie, trying to give us a positive thought. Some Saturday nights were clear for all of us and everyone agreed that we would go soon.

~

Following Arie's death, the routine around the compound quietened down for a few days, and we were thankful for that. We continued with our jobs on vehicle repairs and regained our emotional strength within the unit. Damaged vehicle bodies were welded and straightened by Lowie. Rik and I replaced parts and carried out repairs by replacing brakes, axles, and other parts while Jack worked on motorcycles. Jack knew everything about motorcycles. As an electrician, Frans was usually away in other parts of the shop, but in the evenings we all had a chance to sit together, talk and tell stories about Arie and how much we missed him. We waited to learn more details as to where he was taken or if his family had been told, but we were never apprised. All we knew was that he was gone and without any follow-up, it was a cold reality. It made it clear that as foreign workers, we were expendable.

Lowie and I followed up on our barter of kitchen plates for Ella's aunt. True to her word, she did what she said she would. At the fence, as we delivered the last plate, Lowie found a package wrapped in cloth. We were pleased with the deal we had made and were anxious to share our prize. I stood guard alongside the back wall of the kitchen as Lowie opened the wrapping expecting to find the glorious ham. I could hear his voice erupt in a series of unfamiliar Flemish swear words. "We have been duped," he said. In the package was a very large ham bone that had been cooked and picked clean. There was more bone than ham. There wasn't enough ham to feed one person, let alone everyone. But, what could we do, complain to the soldiers that a local woman had tricked us? Our reward for theft had been a fraud and all we could do was laugh about it. We never spoke of it again.

Some days, not often, but occasionally, we were given other jobs to do around the community. When our absence from the shop would not affect the work schedule, we were loaned out on local projects. The soldiers would help local farmers and contractors to rebuild what had been destroyed by bombing. Quickly rebuilding essential structures and providing food for the kitchen provided a boost to morale and were some small steps in rebuilding the Third Reich. To the benefit of Germany, we were forced labour intended for their use, however it was required. Jack and I were taken to a construction site on one occasion and, for a while, our job was to help dig and pour a concrete foundation. On another occasion, we were sent to a farm to dig potatoes for a few days. It was hard, manual labour and we returned to our barracks every night exhausted and tired. There were forced workers there from many countries: Poles, Belgians, Russians, French, Dutch and others. Everyone it seemed, spoke a different language, and for them, this work was their role.

We always remained under the strict monitoring and control of the soldiers. Some had dogs and they would never let us forget who was in charge. But, for Jack and me, it was different work. The change of scenery was a temporary relief and we could relax from the daily stress of the compound. In the evenings, I often took a walk around the familiar surroundings of Fürstenmoor. We had to sign out at the front gate of the compound, and we had a curfew, but being away from the confinement was good for my soul. I wasn't a free man, but out there, my mind was free. I had a chance to think about Wognum, my family and Corrie. Would I ever see them again?

~

Rik accompanied me one evening. We walked, and we talked about my home: his home, and how weird it was to be here now. The war had changed the world. Rik was Belgian and like me, just wanted to be back home. We cursed the Germans, the whole idea of forced labour, and how so many of us were here from all the occupied countries of Europe. We were all doing the best we could to survive German oppression. Rik knew I had been to a few camps making deliveries, and again wanted to know what I saw, what they were like and how they were set up. As we walked, I told him all that I had seen and heard. Rik was quiet and listened to my every word without interruption. I think he was shocked at what I had seen and experienced.

All he could say was, "damn: that's horrible: and horrible for you as well to have seen it." He injected such responses frequently. We agreed that we had it better than the political prisoners that were held in those camps.

"There are many forced workers in our compound," said Rik, "from several European countries. I think we are all treated better than the prisoners of the camps. I think we have skills that they need."

I agreed. "There are a lot of men here, but you really only get to know the ones in your own work unit."

"Not so," Rik injected. "I know many of the men in the other jobs. How about the Russian women, do you know any of them?" he asked.

"The Russian women?" I asked in surprise, "I know they are here in the compound but I don't know any of them. I don't speak Russian; how would I even talk to them?"

"Many speak German. But unless they speak to you, or you hear their language, how would you know?" asked Rik reassuringly. "You may not know them, but they know you," he said, and I tried not to look flattered. Rik obviously saw more of the compound than I did.

Rik told me that the Russian women were aware that I was one of the Fürstenmoor drivers, and that I was sometimes tasked with making deliveries to the various prisoner camps. One of these women knew that her husband was being held as a political prisoner in a camp that I made frequent deliveries to. She was desperate to get in touch with her husband and had written him a letter. She gave it to Rik in the hope that if he gave it to me, I would deliver it to the camp. I was skeptical and refused. There were too many unanswered questions. Rik was a friend, but could I trust him? Why did Rik know the Russian women so well? The rest of us knew they were in the camp, but otherwise, we knew very little about them. What was Rik's interest in this plan: what did he gain by it? I needed to be careful; maybe Rik was a Gestapo informant. The woman I didn't know at all. I had no idea what the letter contained and I didn't know the person that I would be giving it to. I wanted to believe in the woman's position and I understood her desire to learn of her husband's situation. But, what if she, and Rik both, were working for the Gestapo, or even maybe the underground. Maybe she was part of an escape plot for the prisoners. Regardless, I knew that if I got caught, I would be punished for my part in the plan. Trust is not easily given in war and my mind raced with the negative possibilities of the scheme. The more we walked; the more Rik tried to convince me. "All you have to do," he said, "is get the letter into the camp. Don't worry about who you have to find to give it to. He will find you." I felt sorry for the woman. What if Corrie knew where I was and wanted to get a letter to me? It could be dangerous, but every day here was dangerous. We were caught in a war. I agreed to deliver the letter.

~

The next morning, I headed to the Transport Section, with my Flying Dutchman suitcase in hand and the letter tucked away safely inside. My guards this time were young soldiers who were very passionate and started the day with an enthusiastic "Heil Hitler," before climbing into the cab. I nodded without emotion, put the truck in gear and we started off.

The guards by now had learned of Arie's misfortune and were vigilant in their look out for threats. Keeping an eye out for enemy planes depended a lot on the terrain. They moved back and forth between the cab and the fenders. They did not pay much attention to me and that suited me fine. We made stops at a few camps to deliver what looked like large bags of potatoes, and as usual, I stayed in my truck as ailing, gaunt, and haggard prisoners were forced to unload the vegetables. The soldiers visited with other soldiers at the camps, and stood around, smoking, talking and laughing. We travelled further and stopped for the night at another camp that looked familiar to me, and I knew that I had been there before. I believed that this could be the camp where some Russian political prisoners were being held.

I was now regretting my promise to deliver the letter and, because the camp was comprised of several barracks, I had no idea where to go to deliver the letter. A soldier interrupted my thoughts and startled me. I thought I had been found out. "Park the truck, grab your case and follow me," he said with authority and without emotion.

I tried not to look guilty as he showed me where to park the truck and took me to my sleeping quarters. It was a single storey isolated shed nearby the parked truck and I had no bed or blanket. On the floor was a stained and spotted canvas mattress bag filled with straw that other drivers must have used. The mattress smelled chokingly mouldy, and I opened the small window to allow fresh air into the room. The guard left and I waited for the supper he said would be coming to me soon. I noticed that, once again, I was not locked in. I was free to move about which was a welcome break after being in the truck most of the day. My supper arrived and I ate it quickly. It was the usual hardened dark bread with cheese, something considered to be meat and a cup of hot tea.

As it was turning to dusk, I peeked through my window and could see countless prisoners moving freely, almost aimlessly, having finished an evening meal served in the fenced yard. They were wandering about slowly as they moved towards their barracks and I thought it would be a good time to make my delivery. Hopefully, I would not be noticed. I slowly opened the door at the side of the shed and carefully stepped outside. I stopped and methodically removed my cigarette package from the front pocket of my coveralls. I took my time to obviously remove a cigarette. Cupping my hands against the evening breeze, I lit the cigarette and took a deep breath as

I dropped and stomped out the match. I stood there for a minute studying the camp construction. The camp was very large in size with many barrack buildings and surrounded by barbed wire fencing. The fences were at least 3 metres high with an additional metre of barbed wire stretched inwardly from the poles intended to discourage any prisoners from climbing with ambitions to escape. A single wire, about half a metre off the ground, was strung around the camp, parallel to the fence and about 3 metres inside the fence. The area in between was defined as prohibited and watched closely by the armed guards high in their towers. As I stood there, I noticed a disheveled prisoner across the yard. As he slowly shuffled towards the area of the barracks, he seemed to be watching me. When our eyes met, he continued to stare momentarily, then curiously and cautiously, turned and approached me in the deepening evening darkness. I greeted him in German, but he did not respond. For a few awkward seconds, he looked at me, as I looked at him, for a sign of trust of some description. Discreetly, I pulled the letter from within my coveralls, clearly showing him the Russian man's name on the front of it.

Without any surprise or emotion, he nodded, took the letter and turned away. With the exception of my greeting, neither one of us said a word. I was relieved, quickly butted my cigarette and stepped back inside before anyone else had the opportunity to see me.

Over the next few weeks, when I knew that I was going on the same overnight supply delivery, I told Rik and within a couple of hours he had a new letter for me. I delivered three letters and they always had the same man's name printed neatly on the envelope. I was never comfortable about it, but it got easier each time. After I ate, I slipped outside my door for a smoke and was met by the same prisoner. We never spoke. He never showed any emotion. I never met the woman who wrote the letters, and the delivery of them was a mindless process that hopefully meant more to her than it did to me.

~

At one of my other stops, I had a brief conversation at the gate with a soldier, with whom I had become familiar. He told me that he knew about a driver, also on forced labour, and he had been caught a few months ago delivering letters to camps. The driver was picked up by the Gestapo and was sent to Lager 21. Nobody ever heard from him again. That reminded me of Alex, the Polish labourer in Hannover. We all had seen him after the horrible treatment and suffering that he had endured there. I wanted to help the woman, but the story of the other driver terrified me, and I never delivered another letter.

It made me wonder – Rik was right. I did not have to look for the prisoner to deliver the letters. He found me. How did Rik know that would happen? Was there ever a Russian wife? I wasn't sure of the timing and was not about to ask any questions, but was it after the other driver was picked up, that Rik approached me? I had no proof that he had any underground connections, but, for some reason, somebody had been watching the other driver and could now be watching me. Following the letter experience, I tried to stay away from the affairs of others. But, that was not the problem. The problem was, the affairs of others did not stay away from me.. After that experience, I always remained cautious around Rik.

~

One week folded into another and soon our Saturday night out was approaching. Every four weeks we were all off without any yard duties. That would be the night we would go to the Reeperbahn in tribute to Arie and we all were looking forward to it. We finished work, washed, and cleaned up for our night out. We logged out from the main gate and headed for the streetcar. Jack never went to the Reeperbahn but out of respect for Arie, he was with us that night. Rik and Frans were frequent visitors and enjoyed their schnapps. Lowie was there of course. Lowie was older but a party hound. He liked beer and he liked girls. I often felt that I needed to be cautious about his mentoring. That night we even had the two Frenchmen with us. I never worked with them much and I don't think I ever knew their names. When I was with them, I just called them *Frenchie…* both of them.

We toasted Arie, drank to his memory and each time we had a drink, somebody told an Arie story. Nobody liked to laugh as much as Arie and we all missed him. I sat with Jack to keep him company but he did not enjoy drinking as much as Lowie and the rest of us. Eventually, Jack left with Frans to go back to Fürstenmoor. Both were tired and done in, having had their fill of beer. That left me sitting with Lowie, Rik and the two Frenchies. A few more drinks arrived and one of the Frenchmen invited me to join him in a different adventure. *What now,* I thought, but I was intrigued and agreed to go with him. Before we left the table, he leaned into me and with a serious voice he told me, "But you have to be discreet, my friend, or they will kick you out, and never let you return."

I followed him through the bar, down the hall, and past the washrooms to a back room. The door was locked. Frenchie knocked, and the door was opened. The door keeper, as you would expect, was a large hulk of a man who eyed us both with suspicion. Frenchie stepped forward and spoke a few words to him. The party noise coming from within was so loud that I was unable to hear what Frenchie said, but it must have been meaningful because the doorkeeper stepped aside, let us pass, and quickly closed and locked the door behind us.

Once my eyes adjusted to the dimmed lights and smoke, I could see that the room was full of local men and women, some were uniformed soldiers, and some civilians. It was a party atmosphere with lots of music, lots of liquor, men dancing with seductive women, and plenty of singing and laughter. Some looked up as we entered the room, but after a nod of approval from the door keeper, the key holder, they all returned to the business at hand. Men were playing cards and others were shooting craps. There was a lot of money on the tables. This was a private gambling club and there seemed to be no hierarchy here. As long as you were approved by the key holder and you brought your wallet with you, you were welcome. I was never much of a card player but I soon learned to shoot craps. It was addictive, exciting and for me, it turned out to be a great stress relief. Everyone involved turned a blind eye to the rules; cigars, cigarettes and all kinds of liquor were readily available. A bottle of wine was 25 Marks, schnapps was 50 Marks, cigarettes were 3 Marks each or 72 Marks for a pack of 24. The black market was in full swing here.

Some things have always remained a mystery to me and that room is one of them. It was, as I understood, open to some and closed to many. I suspected that some very high officials had their fingers in that pie because everything that happened there was illegal elsewhere and not supposed to be happening. I never asked questions because I didn't want to know the answers. I never lost the feeling that people who knew too much suddenly disappeared. That seemed to be the Nazi way.

I spent a couple of hours there with Frenchie. He knew the place and most of the people in there and did well at the tables. It was fun and for a couple of hours I forgot all about the war, and the things that I had seen. But, unlike Frenchie, I lost a lot of my money to the men behind that locked door.

By the time Frenchie and I left the gaming room, it was getting late and we had to hurry to catch the last train to Harburg. On the way home, my French companion again reminded me that we had visited a gaming room run by powerful officials and it was important that I keep quiet about the activities. I needed no reminder. I knew what I saw, I knew what I had experienced.

Chapter 24
WORSE THAN HELL

Fürstenmoor, October 1944

By the fall of 1944, Hamburg was in ruins. I continued to make deliveries to the outlying prisoner camps on occasion, travelling through a city gutted by Allied bombing. The repair jobs in the compound were frequently put on hold while we were sent into the city to help clean up the debris and open the roads. We had to work for the Germans or be punished and we had to hide from the bombing or be killed. Living in Germany was intimidating but as a unit, we grew stronger. We lived together, worked together and relaxed together sharing our individual experiences when we could. We became good friends. We lived in fear of what might happen to any one of us in the next twenty-four hours, and in sharing that fate, we became the closest friends we would ever have in our lives. For the days to pass safely, we followed the routines that we could control. We woke early, worked hard together, ate the same unappetizing meals and went to bed tired when it was lights out. Before curfew, we would retrieve our radio from beneath the floorboards and listen to a broadcast. Keeping the sound to a whisper, we huddled around the radio to hear the latest news of the war. Allied forces were slowly moving across France, Belgium and up into Holland. It was exciting news for all of us.

~

Earlier in the summer, I had met another Adolf. He hated his name and the obvious association, and so did I, but his friendship had a positive impact on my life. Like me, Adolf was a trucker. He lived in the neighbourhood, and had had a trucking business before the war. He had been forced to contribute most of his trucks to help the war effort, and was now employed as a contract driver for the army. As a truck driver with a background in mechanics, and with Arie gone, Adolf was assigned to us to make deliveries or work in the compound. We sometimes worked together and I got to know him quite well. We had a lot in common and we talked often, comparing trucking in Holland to trucking in Germany before the war. If we had to deliver a repaired vehicle back to a local army unit, I drove it and Adolf followed in a compound truck to bring me back. Then, driving together without soldiers, and coming back to Fürstenmoor, he and I had time for many conversations about trucks and trucking. Sometimes, the discussions were more personal. He was a balding plump little man in his fifties, and told me about his wife, his adult children, and how much he enjoyed his business before the war. He complained about Hitler and the whole mess that had been created across Europe. I told him about my parents in Wognum and how much I enjoyed my uncle's trucking business. If it had not been for my trucking, I would not have met Corrie. I told him about her, and how much I missed her for all this time. Our friendship grew and eventually, Adolf invited me to his home, to meet his wife and have dinner. I valued my friendships at the barracks, but overall, I was lonely and homesick in Fürstenmoor. I accepted Adolf's invitation without hesitation.

Adolf and his wife Elsa had two daughters and a son. The son was called to serve at the start of the war and was away with the army. I met his eldest daughter only once.

She worked in the city and didn't often make it home to Fürstenmoor. The youngest daughter, however, lived at home and her name was Olga. She was about my age, kind, and extremely pretty, and while I enjoyed meeting her, experience had taught me to be cautious. I was always a little nervous around her.

"I am very appreciative of your invitation," I told Adolf after dinner, "but I was punished for fraternizing in Hannover, several months ago." I told Adolf and Elsa a little bit about my experience in Hannover, visiting with Elfrieda and working for her mother. I told him of my punishment in Hamburg and about the terrible jobs that I had been given. They both cringed at my stories. I reminded them that being with them socially could get me in trouble, especially having Olga present during my visits. Adolf assured me not to worry.

"Fürstenmoor is a much more rural and relaxed place than Hannover," he said "people here don't think that way. We don't do things the way they do in Hannover."

Elsa was a good cook and I enjoyed the meals at their home. I also enjoyed the family atmosphere there, and Adolf urged me to come whenever I could. He made me feel like part of the family and I did visit their home on several occasions. Frequently over dinner, Adolf talked about plans that he had for his trucking business after the war. He slowly, almost strategically, talked as if I should be included in those plans. His daughters had their own future ambitions in the bigger city of Hamburg. Their son had never shown any interest in trucking and was unlikely to continue the family business. Sadly, Adolf and Elsa spoke of how they had not heard from their son in several months. I thought that Adolf was setting the stage towards a future partnership for us. He talked to me about his trucks and the business many times as we worked together. As a mechanic and a truck driver, I understood how trucks were used to make a living. The idea was promising and I liked it. But he understood when I talked about going home to my family and to Corrie. Hopefully, they would still be there. I had no word from them, and he and I both agreed that planning the future was a fragile effort. I was a little nervous visiting when Olga was home, but I enjoyed the company and the meals were always a special treat. My visits to Adolf and Elsa's home were positive experiences that restored my strength, but I was cautious discussing business partnerships. I thought it wise to remember that he was German. It had been a slow learning process, but my experiences had taught me to question the motives behind other people's plans.

~

I found that our work atmosphere was changing. Harms' instructions to us had become more direct; delivered with more discipline. Each day seemed to be frustrating for him and as he passed the challenge on to us, we had no choice but to accept what was.

"Today Peter, you will go to a supply depot in Hamburg, then deliver rations and uniform supplies to a local unit," said Harms. "That's all you need to know. You are the only driver we have, but it's only a day trip, and a soldier will go with you to give you directions. You'll be back by tonight. Supplies are in demand, so be careful."

I dreaded hearing the instructions to go into Hamburg. I feared that place. It was there, in the ruins, that I had to serve my punishment and dig out the bodies. I understood the need for Harms' caution. The bombing was still sporadic by the fall of 1944 and the raids could be a nuisance to us elsewhere in the surrounding areas.

I knew what I had to do so I quickly walked across the compound to the Transport Section. Gasoline had become scarce, and I returned with a large truck that ran on a wood-gasifier. Harms was waiting for me, standing rigid in uniform as if on parade outside his office as I pulled up. We were approached by a soldier, a very young soldier, just a boy actually. He looked like one of my younger brothers would have looked. His uniform fit loosely as if it was designed to be worn by someone else, someone larger. His face revealed a clear Aryan complexion and was so young and clean, I doubted if he shaved yet. He carried himself with a straight back, shoulders squared and was respectful of Harms as he approached. He proudly extended his right arm with a ringing "Sieg Heil!" - *Hail Victory* - and waited for his instructions from Harms. He then climbed into the truck and we took off. As we twisted our way through the city streets, the soldier sat quietly to my right, staring through the windshield, not speaking except to give me precise directions. I was relieved really, as I wasn't interested in conversation. I had been to these areas before and the memories tightened a knot in my stomach. I was glad to feel the healing warmth of the early October sun shining on my face through the windshield as I drove on. We arrived at the supply depot and cleared the security gate. After a brief conversation between the soldiers, my escort directed me to a loading ramp. As I backed onto the ramp, I was relieved to see that a crew of workers were coming to load the truck. These civilians were forced labourers from other countries, and I did not recognize their languages as they worked to fill the truck. They were poorly dressed. Some had overalls while others wore tattered civilian clothes. They looked as poorly kept as those I had seen at the potato farm where Jack and I had been sent earlier. Dirty, pale, and feeble, many were losing their teeth and most had thin, gray faces and huge sunken eyes. It was very unnerving to watch them, tired and hopelessly shuffling about like walking corpses. I was so thankful to not be one of them.

~

When I was 15, my father insisted that I go to trade school. I wanted to become a veterinarian, but he wanted me to be a part of his trucking business. "You will do better with a trade," he said, and I reluctantly studied auto mechanics. I did not enjoy my time there but I did learn how to repair and maintain trucks. To graduate, one had to pass a driving test and I will never forget mine. "You must maintain control of your vehicle at all times," warned the driving examiner and he had me drive a truck to an incline outside of Hoorn. Halfway up the sloped roadway, he directed me to stop and shut off the engine. He got out and put a box of wooden matches behind the rear wheel.

"Start the truck," he said, "and pull it ahead a few feet. If the matches get crushed, you fail the test." Nervously I slowly let out the clutch until I could feel the truck pulling ahead. Then before it stalled, I released the clutch and climbed the incline. I passed. In 1940, there were few people who owned or could drive a car or truck. It was a proud accomplishment for me to become a licenced driver. After trade school, I worked for my dad, and I enjoyed driving his trucks. Now, as part of the Vehicle Repair Unit, I was thankful that he insisted on me getting a trade. Our Unit rations were small and our workday was long. But compared to these forced labourers, we were given work clothes, reasonable shelter, and days off to rest. They were given nothing.

Once loaded at the supply depot, I pulled away from

the ramp, cleared the security gates and headed out again. I welcomed the screech of the heavy steel gate behind me. I was free to leave but I pitied the poor workers whom we left behind at the dock. We unloaded at a couple of locations in the city and around mid-day, the soldier ordered me to pull over and stop the truck on a side street.

"It's time for lunch," he said. We did not always stop for lunch when on the road and I said, "this is unusual, I was not given a lunch."

With a youthful smile, the soldier handed me a cheese sandwich wrapped in paper. He was prepared for this stop and had enough for both of us. The cheese was thinly sliced and the dark bread had little spots of mold on it, but once that was peeled off, it was edible. He took a metal canteen of water out of his pack for us, and still without conversation, offered me a tin cup full of water. His generous kindness surprised me. It was hardly satisfying, but it was more lunch than I would have had, if I had been on my own or with someone other than that boy.

~

Late in the afternoon, we stopped at a fenced-in area. I didn't know where we were, only that we had to bring supplies to the soldiers who worked there. I knew that the truck was almost empty and I was directed to back it into an old garage that had once been a repair shop. Soldiers stood by guiding me as I reversed into the building and parked the truck straddling a concrete pit and against a concrete dock. As I did so, fear rose within me. In the distance I could hear the approach of aircraft and the repeated thumping of bombs being dropped. I could feel the effects of the bombings as the ground itself began to vibrate. I barely had the truck stopped when a siren went off with a scream. The soldiers in the area scattered quickly, as they knew where they could find shelter. Not knowing my way around, I jumped out looking for cover and slid into the pit under the parked truck.

I didn't realize it then, but looking back, it was the worst bombardment that I experienced in the entire war. It felt like it would never end as bomb after bomb exploded so close that the shock waves shook me and everything around me. When the garage roof collapsed, I was thankful that the truck was above me and centered over the pit. That pit saved me as I was lower than ground level. As I peeked out the whole world around me seemed to be on fire, not just the buildings, but the streets themselves. The asphalt road surfaces were belching red and orange flames and I watched as locals and soldiers alike scurried for cover. Many died on the spot. Overcome by the heat, the smoke, and the lack of oxygen, they fell into the fiery streets, with their clothes, even their shoes on fire. It was a terrible sight. Some ran to the river close by, and jumped in hoping to save their lives, only to be consumed in the boiling water. There was glass and debris flying everywhere, and I crouched lower in fear. I was petrified. I heard once that there are layers of terror, each one colder and more paralyzing than the one before it. How true. With the overwhelming noise, flying glass raining down around me like hail, fire and smoke choking my every breath, I huddled in the corner, over and over again, praying to survive.

The bombing went on and on. As all hell broke loose around me, I remember thinking, *this is not hell – no, this is worse than hell. In hell you are already dead.* Amidst this calamity of panic and ruin, I had to slowly wait in terror for something to kill me.

Finally, the bombing stopped, all was quiet and my soul was awakened. I was alive and I knew that I had survived, physically at least. I was shaking, my heart was racing, and I was sick to my stomach. I vomited. For what was seemingly a long time, yet likely only several minutes, I lay terrified and paralysed in that pit like an injured fawn. The bombing had scared me so much that it was nearly impossible for me to calm down and stop shaking. I had experienced that type of shivering physical response to cold, but never such an emotional shaking because of fear. I struggled to compose myself and crawl out of the pit. The truck above me had held back the roof sufficiently that I could move about. The garage was demolished and I had to crawl on my hands and knees under roof joists and over crumpled block walls to escape. But, escape to what? Around me there was destruction everywhere. Fires were burning, people were screaming, emergency responders were hustling about trying to help those who needed help. The air was so thin, so deprived of oxygen by the fires, that I could hardly breathe. I filled my lungs with acrid air and fell over without oxygen. A soldier found me and half-carried me to a temporary aid station set up nearby. Following a hasty examination, it was determined that I was not injured, and I was offered some sweetened tea and given time to rest. My tea gone, I was still shaking but was directed to leave the area and get back to my home location, back to Fürstenmoor. In the twilight, before darkness shrouded the area, workers were brought in to clear the debris from what used to be the garage, unload the final supplies, and help me to start the truck. I was thankful that the truck had a strong steel box on it, strong enough to have held up the fallen garage roof. With the exception of broken glass and some dents to the body, the truck was drivable, and alone I headed out for Fürstenmoor.

I was relieved to pull away from the gates and was glad to be on my way. I wondered what ever happened to my youthful escort, and despite the sorrows that I felt for others, today I was lucky and I knew it. The drive was long and in the dark with shrouded headlights, it was a difficult task to return home. I was still shaken by my earlier experience in the bombing and longed to see the gates of the compound. On arrival, I was met by more fire and chaos. Fürstenmoor had also been bombed. I was glad that firefighting and any immediate response to the bombing that night was somebody else's job. Mine was over and, after parking the truck at the Transport Section, I staggered my way to the barracks. Crossing the yard in the dark – as there were no lights – was dangerous. There was debris everywhere and it was obvious that there had been some significant bombing here. One of the barracks looked to be in shambles, but #4 was intact. I found the door in the darkness and checked all the bunks. Thankfully, my friends were all alive and asleep. Without conversation, I fell onto my bunk exhausted and was devoured by sleep in no time.

"Where were you last night?" asked Jack as we awoke to abnormal morning routines in the barracks. He was anxious to tell me about what had occurred in Fürstenmoor the night before and was eager to hear about my experiences.

"We spent most of last night in the bomb shelter," he said. "The bombing was relentless and went on for hours. There must have been a couple hundred planes and they came in waves over Hamburg. We were on the fringe of it, but the incidental bombing here was brutal. Just when we thought it was over, another wave of planes came in and more bombs rained down. The shelter seemed likely to crumble as the ground shook, the lights went out and we were left choking in the dark. Women and children were screaming, men were yelling for the soldiers to let us out. We wanted to take our chances outside rather than face what seemed to be the likelihood of death inside, in the dark, and terrified for such a long time. It was horrific. I was never so glad to be able to return to the barracks," he said.

I tried to explain my experience in Hamburg of the afternoon and evening before, but the vivid sights of civilians running and dying were hard to describe.

My stories were cut short by loud and assertive soldiers rushing us out of the barracks. Without the opportunity to shower or shave, we were all provided with a hasty breakfast and were hustled into the compound. Soldiers set us up in work squads to clean up from the bombing. The compound itself had suffered damages but in our unit, nobody was killed or harmed. One of the barracks had been destroyed but fortunately the workers had made it to the shelter in time. The kitchen, the offices, and the Transport Section were all shaken by the bombs. There were windows and dishes broken; furniture destroyed and some buildings damaged, but most were still intact. Some soldiers on duty had been killed and the surrounding community of Fürstenmoor had suffered death and damages as well. Our job now was to help the people of Fürstenmoor clean up.

Most of the locals had safely made it into the bomb shelter. The shelter was intact and the surviving locals were busy cleaning up. I noticed a crowd working on a partially demolished house not far from the compound. The house had taken a direct hit. We all followed the soldiers to help.

I was surprised to see that the bombed house was that of Ella's aunt, the woman who had cheated Lowie and me out of the ham. The front of the house was damaged and the debris blocked the entrance to the basement where the woman and her daughter had sought shelter during the raid. They were trapped overnight in the cramped darkness and were screaming in fear. We all worked together in haste to remove the dirt and the wreckage to free them. When the two women emerged from the ruins unharmed, we joined all the neighbours and cheered as both women cried joyous tears at being rescued. Anxiously, the concerned mother asked about her son but no one had seen him. She and her daughter had been enjoying a visit with her son when the bombing started the night before. He was a German soldier, home on leave from the front. Apparently, several neighbours had attended to talk to the celebrity.

Our neighbour and her daughter chose to go to the safety of their basement, and the woman encouraged the son to join them there. He had refused, arguing that he was a soldier who had survived on the front line. He did not need to hide in a shelter with the women and children. He decided to sit on the front porch to watch the bombing.

The porch where he had been sitting was gone and all that remained was a pile of rubble. The crowd turned somber as the shocked woman fell to the ground and again burst into tears. We were moved on by the soldiers as her friends and neighbours began a frantic search for their local hero. Sadly, very little could be found. I was told that only seven pounds of his remains were ever recovered. The woman had cheated us with the ham, but she didn't deserve this. I felt sympathy for her and believed that she, like the rest of us, had just done things she needed to do to survive. Everybody did things that they wouldn't do in ordinary times, and these were far from ordinary times.

Chapter 25
DEMONS AT PLAY

Fürstenmoor, October 1944

I had been taken to Germany and into forced labour in April of 1943. My 21st birthday was in October of 1944. Nobody knew about it; I did not receive any acknowledgement and the day passed like any other. But I knew that the man I was now, was not the boy that left Holland 16 months ago. I had experienced hard days, been abused by German soldiers and had begged for food like a pauper. I had survived bomb attacks, removed the bodies of those who did not survive, and I observed torture beyond comprehension in the prisoner camps. I had seen more death as a young man than many would see in an entire lifetime. But nothing that I had experienced thus far could have prepared me mentally or physically, for what I witnessed one evening on a routine supply delivery. It was not the first time that I had seen SS soldiers act without human compassion, but it was the worst. War is grotesque.

Harms approached me one morning in the compound as I was working with the rest of the unit. In the beginning, I had grown accustomed to his style. He was always distinct and clear about what needed to be done, but his demeanour was usually approachable. But, by the fall of 1944, he had become stern. He was very brusque in his speech and his style was that he just wanted us to follow his instructions. I think he was just getting tired of it all and if his radio told him, what our radio told us, the Allied advancement was putting them on edge. The Nazi dominance of Europe was being challenged.

"This morning, there is a truck being loaded with supplies at the Transport Section. Pack your stuff for an overnight stay at a camp, pick up your truck and some lunch within the hour, and report to my office. There will be two soldiers waiting for you there. They will escort you and provide you with directions to the camps," he said abruptly as he walked away.

Rik overheard Harms' instructions to me and looked over. "I'm glad they've forgotten that I can drive, Pete. I have no interest in driving anymore. So, you go ahead, but do not tell them that I can drive. I hate that shit."

Now being one of only a few drivers left in the entire compound, I was being sent out routinely to make deliveries and often went back to the same camp. By now, I realized that in addition to military sites, there were hundreds of camps holding civilian prisoners from Germany and other countries across Europe. I knew the way but security around bomb sites changed frequently and the soldiers were briefed on alternate directions. I threw a jacket, my coveralls and some cigarettes in my suitcase and walked across the familiar compound to pick up the truck. It was a big Opel Blitz, a general delivery style truck with wooden side racks and a tarp covering. I had driven this type of truck before. I arrived at Harms' office mid-morning, the two soldiers jumped in, one up front and the other in the back where the load was stored and off we went.

As we crossed the German countryside shrouded in the morning fog, the soldiers took turns sitting on the fender looking forward, or sitting in the back looking to the rear. We did not converse but I was thankful for the safety of their presence. Around noon the soldiers had me stop the truck. They dismounted and had their lunch together in the ditch, removing much of their uniform equipment for comfort. They kept their rifles close by, just in case. I was told to stay in the truck and I had my lunch there. It was unusual but, that morning, the kitchen had provided me with some hard, dark bread with cheese. The bread was fresh, and although it smelled better than it tasted at least it did not have any mold on it this time. It was in the truck when I picked it up. Ella must have packed it knowing it was for me because I also had some cookies.

~

After a restful and enjoyable lunch, I started up the truck and we headed out again. We made some uneventful stops at a couple of military sites, but other than that, the afternoon passed without incident. I drove while the soldiers kept watch and I enjoyed the peaceful tranquility of the German countryside. The trees were turning colour, the morning fog had lifted with a cool breeze and I was actually enjoying the drive.

We arrived at a prisoner camp late afternoon. This one I had never been to before. The guards talked to the gate keepers. They were soldiers as well. We were allowed entry without any delay and I was directed to park the truck near a storage building behind the centre courtyard. It would be unloaded later by prisoners.

"Follow me," said one of the soldiers with a very curt German voice, as he walked ahead of me to another building. I was led to a back room on the upper floor. "This is where you sleep tonight," he said. "Stay here, supper will be sent to you and do not wander around. We will be back for you in the morning." Then he left. I understood German fairly well by now after hearing it for eighteen months, so his instructions would be easy to follow. I had to stay in my room until they came for me.

The room was stark as usual but at least had a bunk. The bunk had the usual straw filled canvas sack on it for a mattress and a woollen blanket. I was glad to see the blanket as the fall weather was bringing cooler nights recently. There was a small table in the room and a wooden chair. I had the luxury of an oil lamp. Supper came shortly and as I sat at my little table, I enjoyed a hot meal of cabbage soup, dark bread, and some sweet tea. It was good and more than I was used to.

With my supper over, I had a cigarette by the open window and lit the lamp with my match. I felt quite comfortable realizing that other places to which I had been sent presented more hardship. In the yard below, I could see civilian prisoners lining up for their supper. Soldiers were ladling soup from pails into each prisoner's cup and pushing them away as others tried to push their way back into line to receive another ration. The soldiers pushed the prisoners back and herded them towards the barrack buildings, their simple meal over with. They looked tired, haggard, and worn as they were beaten and shoved along. I was nervous that I was alone and yet glad that I was not part of the mob. I checked my door and it swung free. I was not locked in, but I had no desire to go anywhere. I was just wishing that I could lock it from the inside to give me some sense of safety from the aggressive soldiers. Determined to stay out of sight, I cautiously peeked out to stare at the scene below. I wanted to move away from the window to hide from view but once again my attempts to do so were interrupted by the shouts and commotion of the soldiers in the courtyard. I heard a loud scream that I was sure came from a woman. I didn't want to look, I didn't want to know, but I couldn't help myself. I wavered between being afraid and being captivated by what was happening.

In plain view, I could see a young woman being pulled to the edge of the yard by the guards. She was alone with them; the other prisoners hustled inside seeking whatever safety could be found. The woman was kicking and screaming as they dragged her towards two vertical posts at the edge of the now-vacant yard. Her screams were disturbing and my shoulder muscles tightened with fear for what was happening to her, although I felt helpless to do anything. I couldn't look away. I thought my imagination would be worse than the reality of what the soldiers were doing. I was wrong.

As the young woman struggled defiantly, a guard violently beat her with a rod until she stopped fighting. Others held her and one of them stood inches away from her and screamed commands in her face. Too far away, I didn't hear the commands but soon appreciated what he must have said. He must have told her to strip, and when she hesitated, the soldier grabbed at her clothing. Her striped uniform was so worn and dirty that it easily fell away when he pulled at her. He tore her smock off her shoulders and she fell to the ground on her knees. The other soldiers pulled her up and he impatiently tore at her dress, until it fell away and she was naked. The other soldiers were cheering him on and I heard them laughing maliciously. The lead soldier knocked her to the ground, and the others that were watching, continued to laugh again. Then, it got worse. They swarmed her as she lay there kicking and screaming. When they backed away, I could see that they had tied ropes to her ankles and wrists. Pulling on the ropes, the guards dragged her closer to the posts as she screamed and convulsed like a fish on a line. She was positioned between the posts and then pulled upright but inverted, as each leg was securely tied to hooks on each separate post. In such a position, her head was barely touching the ground as her legs were forced apart. Her arms were then stretched between the posts and then tied tightly despite her struggles of resistance. Once positioned, she seemed to quiet herself, as if resigned to her position of indignity. As if dissatisfied with her lack of reaction to their plans, one of the guards pulled her hair. Another picked up a bucket that had been intentionally positioned close by. He poured the full bucket of cold water on her head to revive her, apparently trying to make her more responsive to their sport. The poor woman shivered, cried, and struggled but to no avail. She had been so securely bound that she could barely move. She screamed louder than ever, in fear, frustration and despair. Nothing in my life could have prepared me for what happened next. One of the guards waved to another nearby, inviting his participation in their game. He was prepared. He walked feverishly up to her, carrying a long-nosed funnel and a kettle of boiling water. In the chill of the evening air, I could clearly see the steam rising from the kettle. I froze in disbelief as I watched the mad demon insert the funnel deeply between the woman's thighs, and push slowly, while methodically pouring the steaming liquid into the funnel. There are no words to describe what I heard. The agonizing, inhuman scream that came from deep within her was beyond what I had ever heard in my life. The second scream was just as eerie and horrifying. Then, as if a switch had been turned off, her screams stopped, and her body went limp. Her tormenters seemed disappointed that she had succumbed so quickly. They once again tried to bring her around by slapping her and splashing more cold water in her face. Her poor tortured body showed no response at all. Sadly, yet mercifully, the young woman was dead.

I dropped back onto my bunk. Their game was over and I could not watch any longer. What happened to her next, or what they did with her body, I did not see. It was too much for me to watch. Sleep did not provide the escape that I longed for as I woke several times in a cold sweat of fear and panic throughout the night. I left the lamp burning in my room overnight and the flickering flame was my only comfort in the darkness. Eventually the wick burned off and I was left in darkness with my thoughts. I actually felt sorry for Germany as a nation. It had surely come to the lowest point in history. For all of its demonstrated military discipline and rallies of political strength, German leaders allowed and approved such disgusting behaviours without accountability. What I had witnessed earlier was terrifying and beyond belief, but what is seen cannot be unseen.

~

As I awoke with the sun shining through my window revealing a new day, I heard someone rattle at my door. When the noise stopped, I cautiously checked outside and found my breakfast of bread and tea. I was hungry and wanted to eat, but despite my efforts, I could not. I took a sip of sugared tea and I prayed that we would soon leave this frightful place. My prayers were answered when one of my escort soldiers came to my room. "It's time to go," he said, and I was eager to comply.

Walking towards my truck, I felt a cold chill as I looked back at those posts standing at the edge of the courtyard. The posts, in the morning sun cast long shadows across the yard like dark stains of the torture that I had witnessed. It was a cruelty solely to entertain the sick minds of arrogant fanatics. After all I had seen and heard, my emotions were gutted and I walked across the yard a hollow man.

Chapter 26
Doing Without

Wognum, late Fall 1944

My work at Stam's was welcome during the hard times in the last months of 1944. The job became easier as I gained daily experience serving food; but mostly we served beer, and mostly to soldiers. The Stam family and the Roemer family were related and I continued to live with the Roemer family in a small house not far away from the café. Everyone was having difficulties, and we all were just trying to survive as our day-to-day circumstances were worsening. We hated the German oppression and the resistance was active everywhere. After four years of occupation, we were tired of living under German control.

The age for men being forced into labour in Germany seemed to have dropped. The *razzias* were frequent and unscheduled still forcing many young men to hide out in the marshes and barns. I heard of one family who cut a trap door in the living room floorboards and covered it with a rug. When soldiers were in the neighbourhood, their son would hide in a 3-foot crawlspace under the house. Despite the fact that it was often wet under there, the young man had to crawl to a corner because the soldiers would shoot their rifles into the floor if they found a trap door. Sometimes the boy had to lie there for hours until the danger had passed and the soldiers had moved on. When he was able to crawl out and be with his family again, he needed to stay out of sight until he had to crawl under the house again next time.

The first winter after I had moved to Wognum, I needed a coat but did not have any money to buy one. Peter gave me a guilder a week from his wages, and I saved enough to buy myself a new winter coat. It was a heavy coat and when I wore it, I thought of it as Peter's gift, and my thoughts brought me closer to him. But without any word from him, I wondered what would have been worse for him – going to Germany, or hiding out?

I visited his family as often as I could. Peter's family had become my family. When I visited, his mother could always find some tea and some biscuits or warm bread to share. Peter's sister Marta and I would talk about our day's events, and we mutually enjoyed the time of friendship. But to see her, I had to sneak through the backyards and side streets. I wouldn't take the chance on the main streets where the Germans might stop me and take my coat. Wognum was a small town and you could walk anywhere in town in a short time. For me, the walk took a little longer, but I was happy to keep my warm coat.

~

I remember one evening. I joined Peter's family after dinner and found several neighbours visiting at their home. Over hot tea, we all were talking about the hard times we were living in and wondered if they would ever end.

"You have to out-fox them," said Elisabeth jokingly, as she recalled the story of Jan sawing one handle-bar off his bike so the Germans wouldn't take it. We all laughed heartily and were amused to be reminded of that story.

"Show everyone your latest invention, Jan," she said moving on, and with that, he led us to the back-storage room of the house to show us his accomplishment.

Rubber was no longer available and for those who still had a bicycle, the tires were difficult to get. Some had replaced their tires with wooden wheels but Jan had taken his resourcefulness a step further. He had replaced a worn-out bicycle tire, by wiring a lengthy piece of old garden hose onto the rim. Finding a reason to laugh was difficult at times but Jan always tried to make life interesting.

"You better keep that hidden," said Betsy, the neighbour. "Although your bicycle has become so unique, not everyone would be able to ride it," she said with a laugh. "We have to hide anything we want to keep. Thanks to the national train strike, things have become hard to get," she continued, "and the Germans have confiscated blankets, coats, and even socks for winter," she said as we walked back into the sitting room. "They take anything that would be useful to them."

"Yes, but the rail strike had to happen," answered Dirk, her husband. "It was the only way to interfere with the Germans' supply lines."

"I know," said Betsy. "But now the Germans are only concerned about their own food supply. We don't get anything. I have seen children hanging around when their supply trucks come, hoping the soldiers will drop something. If they do accidently spill something, the children scoop it up off the roadway with spoons. That can't be healthy. Now the children will be sick as well as hungry."

"Yes, I feel sorry for the children," said Nora, another neighbour, and a friend of the family. "When they grow out of their shoes, parents cannot buy new ones for them. New shoes, or even leather to repair old shoes are just not available. I have seen children without toes on their shoes. When they grow out of them, parents have to cut off the end of the shoe to fit, exposing their little feet to the cold.

Children have to wrap their feet with rags to keep them warm. I heard that in the cities, children hang out around the German kitchens waiting for the cooks to throw out the garbage. They gather up discarded potato peels and take them home for a meal."

"Have you noticed strangers coming to Wognum?" I asked Elisabeth. "I've had them come to the café, asking for food."

"Yes, they leave the bigger cities," she answered. "In desperation, they come out to the farming areas and small towns on hunger expeditions. They bring watches, rings, or anything else of value hoping to trade for food. Some travel all the way from Purmerend, on foot, just to get here. That's almost 30 kilometres. I know that some come even from Amsterdam."

"That's awful," said Nora, sitting back in her chair and sipping her tea.

"And," Elisabeth went on, "if they are successful in getting food to take home, sometimes they get stopped at the checkpoints, and the German soldiers just take it from them."

I knew that Peter's mom, in spite of her own food shortages, often managed to have a warm pot of oatmeal ready on the stove in case someone came to the house needing something to eat. She told us the story of two young men, about her sons' age, who came begging at her door late one afternoon. I had heard the story before, but Elisabeth told it again for Betsy, Nora and Dirk.

The boys were poorly dressed for the weather, cold and starving. She felt sorry for them and allowed them to come in out of the weather. She gave them a warm bowl of oatmeal, offered each of them a blanket, and showed them a spot on the floor where they could spend the night in warmth and safety.

"When I woke up the next morning," she continued, "the house was cold. The fire had gone out. The boys were gone, and so were the blankets that I had given them. While we were sleeping, the boys also raided the cupboard for food to take with them and took two large bags of white beans." She felt angry and betrayed. "That was a big loss for us as a family," she said. "I've learned my lesson – I'll not put my family in such a position again."

"I know," said Betsy. "I've seen beggars on our street." She went on to tell us the experience she had, watching a young boy passing by looking for food. He was with an older man, possibly his father, walking past her house and she wondered why they didn't stop. The boy was pushing a wheelbarrow and the father seemed to be leaning heavily on his son for support. They both looked so scrawny and feeble as they moved on down the street.

"A couple of hours later, I saw them again," she said. "This time the boy was straining as he slowly pushed the wheelbarrow in the opposite direction. His burden was much greater; as now the man was awkwardly laying in the wheelbarrow, his arms dangling uselessly alongside. He appeared to be dead. It was so sad," she said tearfully struggling to finish the story. "I wish they would have just stopped," she said, "I might have been able to help them."

Jan was sitting comfortably in his chair, holding his feet near the fire. "We all want to help, Betsy," he said, as he puffed on his Meerschaum pipe. He had run out of pipe tobacco long ago and it was not available to purchase anymore. Jan grew his own in the garden and dried it out in the attic. It didn't smell as good as purchased tobacco, but for Jan, it worked. "When I was in Amsterdam last week, I saw the suffering myself. They have it worse in the big cities: worse than us. We have our vegetable gardens to give us potatoes and other vegetables. We can get fish and even some beef or pork on occasion. We can survive. But, in the big cities like Amsterdam and Rotterdam, the people are starving as they hunt for food."

"Do you mean the men are out scrounging?" I asked curiously.

"Not men. The men are in hiding," answered Jan. "They're trying to avoid the *razzia*. If they're seen on the streets and they look strong enough to work, they are picked up on the spot, and sent to Germany. It's just the women and children left now. The soldiers have taken their blankets and warm coats. Then when the little beggars get tired and stop to rest, without warm clothing they end up dying of hypothermia: poor little kids."

How much worse can it get? I thought. Since the occupation began four years ago, everything we needed became scarce. In the beginning, every family had to register to obtain a ration card. With the card, a registered household regularly received coupons to obtain food, clothing, and other supplies. But, over time, all supplies became even more scarce and even with coupons there was nothing to get. Now with the onset of winter, it was getting very cold. Some of us living in the country could cut local trees to burn for heat over the winter while others were removing doors and trim in the houses to be burned. Fuel had been cut off, to be used only by the army. It was a reality that was hard to accept, but that too, was part of our life in Holland that winter.

Chapter 27

A Stranger Waits

Fürstenmoor, October 1944

When I returned to Fürstenmoor from being away at the camp overnight, I still felt gutted. I wished that my friend Arie was still with us. He too had seen the terrible things that happened in the prisoner camps. Arie would understand and we would be able to talk about it. The experience in the last camp left me with so much hatred for the war, and for Nazi soldiers. The Nazis had caused death, destruction, hunger, and hardship for everyone. I had witnessed unspeakable and unbelievable cruelty. The world was caught in such a whirlwind. I wanted to just get away from it all. I wanted an escape.

~

We all sat together for breakfast the next morning and everyone seemed surprised that I was back.

"Did you get in late last night?" asked Jack with his usual concern. I just nodded as if to say yes.

"You are quiet. What happened?" asked Lowie

"I can't even talk about it right now. I'll tell you later, but it wasn't good," I said stirring my coffee. "I am so finished with this damn war. I thought we all had been through a lot, but what I saw on this trip makes me want to say to hell with it; I'm not working today for anybody. I just want to sit and think about why the hell we are here.

We have no control over anything, not even our own lives. I just want to get away."

"Well, you can't do that," Jack said, as if he needed to remind me that we were not there by choice. "My father used to say, if you can't fix it, you have to let it go." I knew that as a friend, Jack was trying to give me strength to carry on, but he could see that I was not listening, and his wisdom was wasted.

"I cannot believe that human beings could be so cruel," I responded.

"You have to tell us; share with us," said Jack, "Get it out… talk about what's bothering you. We're all in this together."

I told them everything. The barracks became quiet and nobody seemed to be in a hurry. I was delaying the start of our workday and nobody cared. The soldiers got on with their work, leaving us alone. Nobody interrupted me. Jack, Lowie, Rik, Frans, and the two Frenchmen all sat in horror as I relived my night of terror. I told them about the camp: about the wretched group of prisoners that were at the camp; about the woman and about the cruelty which I had witnessed; I told them about the vile acts of the SS guards and how the whole experience left me shaking in shock, anger, and helplessness. I was fed up with the world we were now living in. I was done.

War diminishes how you think as an individual. The horrifying events are too much to experience alone and you seek companionship. I was glad to be with my friends. They understood.

"You need to get drunk," said Lowie. That was often Lowie's answer to a problem and I had no other response. "I agree!" I said. "Maybe that will ease the pain."

Everyone was in. It was a Saturday and that was what we would do.

"We better get to work today," said Jack, always the leader and always the most rational of us all. "Ok," confirmed Lowie, "today we work, but tonight we go to the Reeperbahn."

The Frenchmen couldn't go as it was their turn for yard duty but Lowie and Rik insisted that it had to be that night. Even Jack agreed.

The workday was not unusual and rather routine. There were no deliveries to be made. We all stayed in camp and we all did our jobs. Jack and I worked together quietly on the motor of a light military vehicle, a Volkswagen Kubelwagen. They were quite common, so there was always one or two in the repair shop. The job was not complicated and it was just what I needed, an easy Saturday, as my mind was still swimming with the memories of what I had seen.

~

After work, we quickly cleaned up and we all signed out at the front gate, acknowledging that we would have to be back by curfew. Jack decided to stay at the compound, and switched duty with one of the Frenchmen. The Reeperbahn was not a place that Jack was comfortable with and I often felt the same way. But, tonight, I had to get my experience out of my head. I needed a distraction.

We took the streetcar to Harburg, then a train to Hamburg and another to the Reeperbahn. I was nervous as my mood was not in keeping with the fun there. The excitement was always high and as we walked the red-light district, the Grosse Freiheit, I could feel myself relaxing. The music, the women walking about, the bars and the laughter soon carried me into another world: a world of decadent fantasy. After a couple of drinks, I started to feel better and

I went with Frenchie to try my luck in a crap game in the room behind the locked door. Lowie was not interested in gambling, he enjoyed the women and the party atmosphere of the bars. We agreed to go our separate ways and meet again later. The night passed quickly as the beer and the games melted my anxieties away. I soon forgot about everything, even if it was only for a while.

"We had better go," said Frenchie at one point, "we can't miss curfew."

I was on a roll, and without looking up, I responded, "go ahead, I'll catch up with you later back at camp." In my attempt to win some extra money, I lost all track of time. It was quite a bit later before I thought to find Lowie and catch the last train back to Harburg. Almost in a fever, I reluctantly abandoned the game and ran to another bar down the street, where I had agreed to meet Lowie. True to his word he was waiting for me. Rik and the others had gone to catch an earlier train as well, leaving me alone with Lowie. He stood leaning on the bar, talking to a woman. I could tell by his awkward demeanor that he was drunk and the silly grin on his face confirmed it. She didn't seem to be too impressed and in spite of my drinking that night, I sobered quickly. I realized that it would be up to me to get us both back to Fürstenmoor safely and on time.

Thankfully, Lowie was generally a happy drunk, and with minimal difficulty I managed to get him on the train. He immediately fell asleep as I enjoyed the quiet ride while the harbour and the busy streets passed by in the darkness. I didn't look forward to waking my drunken friend but we would have to hurry if we were to catch the last streetcar back to the compound. I was right to be concerned. In spite of my prodding and desperate attempts to convince him otherwise, Lowie did not want to wake up.

"You go, I'll get home later," he slurred, curled up against the window.

"You have to come now," I insisted pulling on his lifeless arm. "There is no later. We have to catch the streetcar or we'll be walking home."

Regardless of my efforts, and just as I had feared, we approached the corner only to see the last streetcar pulling away. *Aw, crap,* I thought, *now, we'll miss curfew.* How had a simple night out for a beer become so complicated? It was true. A night of drinking might help you to escape, but beer will win any debate with your conscience.

It was a cool late October evening for the long walk home. The night air was sobering, and I felt totally revived from my evening of beer in that smoke-filled bar. As we shuffled along the asphalt roadway in the darkness, I had to steady him, as Lowie stumbled with every step. It took a concentrated focus for him to walk a straight line.

"I have to rest," said Lowie. "I have never walked this way… or this far, before."

I agreed. "We are already late, so a few more minutes won't matter," I said, as we stopped and sat down.

With our backs to a tree, we could rest and catch our breath for a while, but I kept my eye on Lowie. I tried to keep him talking, to keep him from falling asleep. After only a few minutes, I pulled on his limp body and insisted that we keep going. The rest had helped but we still had a long walk ahead of us. Several kilometres passed in relative quiet as I watched Lowie, tired and still drunk, struggle to stay awake and upright.

Finally, we were in a familiar neighbourhood and I could make out the ghostly silhouette of the compound fence in the darkness. "You are doing good," I told him patting him on the back. With that realization, Lowie seemed to perk up. His bed was within reach.

With only a few houses between us and the compound, I was surprised to find anyone on the street at such a late hour. "Help me," cried a loud voice in the quiet darkness. It was a local German, one of our neighbours actually: a man whom I didn't know by name but recognized to have worked in the scrap yard with us. He seemed to be struggling to find his way home, stumbling around in a similar drunken and confused state. He wanted us to help him get into his house.

"Be quiet," I said, not wanting his loud voice to alert the guards. "We'll help you if you just keep your voice down."

I put my arm around his waist and Lowie grabbed his other arm and now I had two drunks to keep upright and get home to safety. With a little effort, we got him up the sidewalk, up the front steps and into his house without waking anyone or alerting the guards just down the street. He was very grateful for our assistance and insisted that we have a beer with him before heading to the barracks. I just wanted to go home to bed but Lowie thought it was a polite and neighbourly gesture and for that, we would be happy to accommodate.

The man invited us into his home and as we entered, he introduced us to another man. I didn't know his name either and in fact, did not even recognize him from around the neighbourhood. *Why is a stranger here in the middle of the night?* I thought. He ushered us into a room just inside the entrance. It was a small room and there was minimal furniture. Our neighbour encouraged us to take a seat, and warmly promised that he would return with a beer for us if we would just wait a few minutes. Lowie and I both sat down at a wooden table, on a couple of wooden chairs that matched. That, and a coat rack, were the only furniture in the room. As the neighbour closed the door behind him, I heard the unmistakable rattle of the bolt sliding in the door lock. Stirred from a sleepy state, I could hear our neighbour speaking to the stranger; and although I could not hear exactly what was said, it was quite clear that our friend was not nearly as drunk as he had seemed to be. I was confused and my mind was racing for options.

"Did you hear that?" I whispered to Lowie. He was comfortably resting his head and almost asleep again. Everything was suddenly very quiet. Lowie and I were alone and in the dark. I tip-toed across the room and put my ear to the door, listening for further conversation. Quietly I slowly tried the door handle. It was locked. I felt fear well up inside me as questions flashed through my mind.

Why were we locked in? Who was the stranger that our neighbour was talking to, Gestapo maybe? Where had they gone? Would they accuse us and deliver us to the Gestapo or the SS?

The reality of our apparent situation made me panic. As foreign forced labourers, who would take our story over that of a local German citizen?

"Lowie, Lowie, wake up." I was desperate and knew we needed to get out of there fast. Without further trying to wake Lowie, I picked up my chair and smashed out the window. The loud crash of breaking glass startled Lowie and he jumped up in fear. Quickly I tried to pull out the broken and jagged pieces of glass that stubbornly remained in the window frame. I could see that Lowie was going back to sleep. Our escape was taking too long and as I struggled feverishly with the window, I sliced my hand. Blood was dripping through my fingers.

"Lowie, Lowie… damn it, Lowie," I said loudly as I pulled him by the collar and pushed him up against the wall, next to the broken window.

With blood steadily dripping from my fingers, I closed my fist to try to stop the bleeding. With the other hand, I grabbed a small floor mat at my feet and placed it carefully in the window frame. Desperately, I pleaded with Lowie. "Wake up, Lowie; pay attention," and I slapped his face. Lowie was half-awake but didn't understand that we were in danger.

I dragged him to the window, picked up his leg to push it through, and shoved his head out to follow. I heard him fall to the ground outside and I was glad the window was low. His landing was cushioned by the grass. I quickly followed him and without looking back, we ran away from the building, into the waiting darkness. I was sweating with exertion as I dragged Lowie around the corner in the direction of the compound. At the back fence, we found the hole and got into the barracks' area without dealing with the guards at the front gate. My bloody hand and our frantic state would have aroused suspicion. Tomorrow, we could say that we were back late, just before curfew and the guards were busy.

~

What had motivated the neighbour to lock us in his house? I laid awake until dawn imagining one scenario after another and I was glad when I could talk with Lowie at the breakfast table. He didn't remember much about the night before, but as we talked, the memory of the neighbour's house became clear. He, as well, had no answer as to why that would have happened. And, the question lingered, "Who was that guy?"

"Do not be asking any questions," Lowie cautiously reminded me. "Ask questions and we could be in more trouble. Just let it go. You can't go around accusing a German of anything." Once again, I was left with the questions… Who can you trust? Who will betray you?

A few days later, when we ran into our neighbour in the scrap yard, he tried to avoid us but we were determined to speak to him. When we asked a couple of friendly questions about the events of the evening, he reacted strangely.

"I have no idea what you're talking about," he said. "I was drunk. I remember talking to you on the street. I remember that it was unusual to see you when it was so late," he said almost as a threat as he walked away. "That's all I remember."

I started to follow him to ask more questions but Lowie pulled me back. "It's best to realize that we were lucky," he said. "We escaped, now leave it alone."

I was frustrated, but reluctantly I agreed with him. In Germany, secrecy seemed to be the standard, but safest option.

Chapter 28
We Go Mobile

Fürstenmoor, November 1944

Despite Lowie's advice to let it go, I could not. For days afterwards, the motive and the potential of being locked in a local's home came back to me with so many unanswered questions.

Who would want to lock us in, and why? What had I done to get locked up in someone's house?

"I'm getting scared," I said, frustratingly pulling Lowie aside in the barracks one evening. "We haven't seen any consequence of being locked in. We can't tell anybody and that guy won't even discuss it. He's acting like it never happened. If he wanted Harms to know about it, we'd have heard of it by now."

"Quiet, I told you to let it go, so forget about it. Especially in here. The walls have ears," he said walking away.

Lowie was right. We were not at war, but, we were in war, and I needed to be more careful. Maybe it was Lowie they were after. Maybe it had something to do with Ella. His comments made me think of the caution I had received from Harms when he disciplined me over the Reeperbahn picture. "Know that you are being watched," he had warned. Maybe it was Lowie they were after and I just happened to be with him? In the world I was living in, there were always more questions than answers.

~

As the days became shorter, our work routines in the compound continued and we were kept busy. We were fixing trucks as soon as they were brought in, but they seemed to be local vehicles. As soon as we had one repaired and ready to go, soldiers arrived to retrieve it and brought in another one when they came. Our rations were getting smaller. We were reduced to two meals a day. When my supply deliveries to the prisoner camps became noticeably infrequent, I wondered how the prisoners were getting their rations. Maybe they weren't.

Winter was approaching and the bombing raids on Hamburg continued. Our routines were frequently disrupted and we spent hours either in the shelter or in our foxholes. Was Fürstenmoor the target? Not likely. The intended targets may have been the harbour and the industrial areas of Hamburg, but if the bombers strayed off target, couldn't find their target or were damaged, their bombs were released anywhere before returning home. After all, Germany - was Germany. But to those of us on the ground, bombs were bombs - and terrifying, whether intended or not.

In the evenings, we huddled in secrecy around our barracks radio, anxious to know any news of the war. The German news was selected propaganda and although our listening was forbidden, we received news on English and Dutch stations as well. We were especially glad to hear the Dutch broadcasts of Radio Oranje. Earlier in July, there had been an unsuccessful assassination attempt on Hitler's life. Some of his senior officers had used a concealed bomb at a secret meeting, but it was not effective. Radio broadcasts repeatedly made it clear that despite minor injuries, the attempt had failed and the Führer was still in charge.

"Leave it to the Nazis to screw it up," said Jack. "They should have asked me to do it," he said. "I would have gladly killed the son-of-a-bitch."

We all laughed, knowing that, actually, he was not joking.

We also learned that an encouraging Allied advancement was underway and although we did not understand military plans, we could see its effects even in our compound. More soldiers were needed on the battlefront and many of the soldiers whom we started with in Fürstenmoor had been transferred out. The new soldiers assigned to work with us were very young, often much younger than us. They were disciplined to be uniformed soldiers and were respectful, but they were not fighting an enemy in Fürstenmoor. Their attitude was different. The previous group of soldiers avoided social contact with us, but the younger ones seemed to be less arrogant in their dealings with us, we frequently had conversations with them throughout the day.

~

Christmas of 1944 was one that I would never forget. As Christmas Day approached, Harms had all of us brought to his office. He was sitting behind his desk when we arrived and when we were all present with the door closed, he stubbed out his cigarette in the ashtray. Extra chairs had been set out in his office to accommodate us and he asked us to take a seat, as he stood up and rounded the desk. Standing before us, he reminded us how important it was to be careful and stay out of trouble.

"We are a unit," he said, "and we work well together. But the war is changing. I can try to save your ass," he said, "but you have to cooperate. The last thing any of us wants is to be transferred. I do not want to be in a battlefield position now at this point in the war. As for you, there are forced labour camps, and if you get sent to one, you will not survive. Ask Peter, he has seen them. Your objective, like mine, should be to stay in this unit. I am proud to be a soldier, but I have seen enough battle. Do what is required of you, and do not cause you, or me, any problems. Just do your job so that none of us is reassigned." With those words, he took his seat behind his desk, and motioned his hand towards the door. We were dismissed.

As we walked back to our job, Jack asked me, "what was that all about? Do you think they know they're losing?"

"How are they supposed to win a war with these kids?" I said pointing across the compound to a group of young soldiers. "You can see the change. We may not be out of the fray yet, but times are changing. I can feel it."

Later that day, everyone in the compound; officers, soldiers, and labourers were invited to celebrate with one another. Harms did not attend. Discipline seemed to be temporarily suspended, the atmosphere was more relaxed, and we enjoyed a magnificent meal together. There was meat, vegetables, bread and even wine. We all sat together, enjoyed each other's company and ignored the rules that normally kept us apart. After the meal we stayed at the tables, talking and drinking wine well into the evening. That Christmas appeared to be a turning point in the behaviour towards us by the soldiers in our compound. I was not swayed or convinced of their sincerity, but I thought that maybe we at least shared the sense that the war would soon be coming to an end.

~

In the new year, things did start to change for all of us. It was like turning a page in a book and suddenly realizing the plot was different. The winter weather throughout December 1944 and into January 1945 was harsh. It was one of the fiercest and coldest winters ever recorded in Western Europe and fewer vehicles were arriving at the compound for repairs. With our workload slowed down considerably, we often stayed in the barracks all day to escape the fury of the cold winds and the winter storms. Nobody cared, and it was unlikely that a senior officer would venture out in a blizzard to inspect our productivity. The conditions were hard to work in and the sub-zero temperature was relentless. Mechanical repairs were slow as parts locked up and fluids froze. Sometimes we had the availability of an indoor shop to do mechanical work on trucks and other vehicles but our job called for very few deliveries. Our Transport Section was required to give up most of our delivery trucks to be used for different purposes elsewhere.

Like that of the others, my clothing was not fit for winter. My coat was thin, I did not have any socks to wear in my cold leather boots and I was forced to wrap my feet in rags. Gloves were no longer provided to us, and only available to the soldiers. Without gloves, my hands froze quickly, making every job more difficult. To the envy of my co-workers, I wore my old cavalry pants most of the time, and I was thankful that I still had them. They were a prized piece of clothing on those cold days and it was not uncommon that I wore them even to bed, as the wind whistled through the cracks around the windows of our barracks.

Throughout the winter we had very little to keep us employed in Fürstenmoor. We did not outwardly show any change to our workload and, as Harms had requested, we busied ourselves with whatever tasks were required. We spent many hours standing in a group huddled together like chickens behind a wind break, our hands stuck in our armpits for warmth.

~

Winter finally broke and the winds of March turned winter blizzards into constant rain or drizzle. The warmer days of April followed and the buds of tree leaves were sprouting, revealing that spring was close. It was on one such morning, in early April, that Harms informed us that we were all moving soon, and we were to prepare now for a change in location. Reminding us that we were a Mobile Vehicle Repair Unit, he told us to pack anything and everything that we would need to make vehicle repairs on the go. We worked together all that day to pack our remaining trucks with our tools, along with barrels of grease and oil, any usable nuts, bolts, canvas, and wood that we would need to repair transport vehicles in the field. I was leaving with some reluctance. Leaving Fürstenmoor meant leaving without the answer to my question. Why were Lowie and I locked in that house? Now, I would never know. The next morning, our convoy left the familiarity of Hamburg and headed east towards Schwerin.

The other regret that I had in our hasty move was that I did not get the chance to say goodbye to my friend Adolf. He and his family had been a true comfort to me during my time there, and I wondered if I survived this war, would he and I have been able to build the trucking partnership that he often spoke of? But that was just an illusion. I was only 21, and my goal, if I survived this war, was to get back to Wognum, my parents, my family, and Corrie. I had been gone from them for two years and I wondered if they were still alive. I knew that the Allies were fighting their way into Holland, but we would no longer have any reliable news about the progression of the war. In our hurry to pack up and leave Fürstenmoor, we forgot to retrieve Rik's radio.

"Where is Rik?" I asked Lowie as we jounced along in the truck following Harms' Kubelwagen.

"I don't know," answered a drowsy Lowie. "I think he had to stay behind."

I took mental note that Rik did not move with us. He was in the barracks the night before we left, but now on the road Rik was not in sight. He was a nice guy, he was friendly and worked well with us. With Lowie falling asleep, I couldn't stop thinking about Rik as I quietly drove along the back roads of northern Germany.

I was driving one of the trucks and Jack was driving another. Rik could drive, but why did he not want to? How was he able to keep anyone from knowing it? Why was he not with us now? Why was our radio hidden under his bunk? Was it just because he said that he owned it? He was at the Reeperbahn the night my picture was taken. He was also there but left early the night Lowie and I were locked up. I was suspicious when Rik asked me to deliver the letters to the Russian prisoner. If Rik was part of the Belgian resistance, I would never know. If true, I felt better thinking that I may have helped the resistance somehow by delivering the letters.

~

In Schwerin, we did not have a barracks or a workshop like at our other compounds. We were totally mobile, spending a day here, another couple of days somewhere else. We slept in barns and haylofts provided by local farmers. Our workload was slowing, as the German army was not wasting any time or manpower efforts to have its equipment repaired. We had a makeshift field kitchen that we hauled behind one of the smaller trucks filled with rations and supplies. Other soldiers were in charge of the kitchen, but Harms was still in charge of our unit. The kitchen workers were female forced labourers who came with us. They were not local women from Fürstenmoor, and they spoke a different language. I spoke Dutch and after two years in Germany, I could speak and understand German fairly well. These women did not speak either and kept to themselves for the most part. I think they were Russian.

Harms gathered us together and explained that although we had less work, it was very important that we accomplish enough to keep our outfit together. He hinted at what we all suspected; the war in the west appeared to be "losing steam" in his words.

"If we appear not to be productive or you choose to sabotage any operation or job required of us, our unit could be finished," he suggested, taking a break to quickly light another cigarette. "We could all be separated and sent somewhere much worse than Schwerin. Make enough effort so we don't attract any negative attention from my superiors," he said, "and we will be left alone. Be safe and stay alive."

It was apparent that the tides of war were changing rapidly, but as Harms further reminded us, we could "not take any stability for granted." After two years of working for him we realized that he would be fair to us if we were fair to him. We respected Harms enough to do as he wished. In a humble and less authoritative manner, Harms was revealing that he just wanted to get home to his family in Hamburg. Hopefully, we all had family waiting for us.

Chapter 29
DEUTSCHLAND KAPUT

Schwerin, Germany, April 1945

We rambled around the Schwerin area for a couple of weeks. We did not stop to find a shop or a garage to set up in, but stayed mobile making equipment repairs using the tools in our trailer. The German troops were busy fighting and didn't bother us much for repairs. We established simple routines servicing our own trucks to keep us busy. The Russian women travelling with us continued to be managed by army cooks and they were able to feed us simple meals when they were able to set up their field kitchens. Harms had told us that we would be safer if we stayed on the move but we needed to be cautious. Our mobility eastward too quickly would take us away from Schwerin and closer to Berlin. Without our radio, we were not informed of any news but the few remaining soldiers in our unit talked openly about the war. They were thinking that Germany was being crushed. The Allies were coming into Germany from the west and the Russians were advancing in from the east. We did not want to be in Berlin.

We stayed on the roads in daylight, stopping roadside when required to repair any military vehicles. At night we slept in barns or sheds. Most local farmers welcomed us believing that their hospitality was rewarded by the safety of having soldiers on their properties. Others were less than cooperative, and you could tell that they were fearful and reluctant to help us.

"Why would German civilians refuse to help the German army?" I asked Harms one evening as we made ourselves comfortable in a stable, making our beds in the straw.

"They don't know who to trust anymore," he said. "Many have lost faith in what has happened and they are getting skittish. They believe their future is fragile." I remember my thoughts when he said that - *we all have those concerns,* I thought.

When the food ration got more plentiful, I realized it was because our unit was getting smaller. It wasn't a mass exodus that would draw attention, but every few days it was obvious that there were fewer soldiers. They were disappearing overnight and to my surprise, one morning the two Frenchmen in the unit were also gone. We had worked together for a long time and they escaped without a word of goodbye. They just stole away in the dark.

~

There was a young soldier named Willy who had joined us near the end of our stay in Fürstenmoor. Willy was eager to learn to drive and when the opportunity arose, I tried to teach him. My deliveries away from Fürstenmoor in the later weeks there had been minimal, but anytime that I went, Willy volunteered to be my escort. When another soldier was assigned as well, he too was usually young and eager to learn. There wasn't much opportunity for enjoyment at that point of my life but I did enjoy teaching them how to drive, as we travelled on the backroads making the deliveries.

One evening, Willy came to me as we were setting up to rest in a barn for the night. A conversation with him was not unusual as we often talked while having a break or a smoke while working. He said to me, "Peter, I'm leaving: I just wanted you to know."

"Leaving?" I whispered, so others wouldn't hear, "where are you going?"

"Anywhere," he said with a youthful smile. "Our work is slowing down to a stop. I have only been in the army for a few months and have yet to see combat. I don't want to take the chance of being deployed now to a frontline unit. Other soldiers are leaving. You must have noticed that there are fewer and fewer every day. If I am sent to a combat unit in the west, I could get killed or be taken captive. If I get sent to the east, I will be killed for sure." Emphatically, he said "Deutschland Kaput - *Germany is finished,* and I do not see any sense in dying now. I just wanted to say goodbye. You have been good to me Peter, and I wanted to thank you for teaching me how to drive."

"No," I said trying to convince the lad otherwise. "You could be shot for desertion."

"I'll take my chances," he said turning away. "By the time they notice me gone, I will be an unknown citizen, somewhere in Germany." With that, he waved goodbye. In the morning, Willy was gone, his army uniform abandoned in the hayloft.

~

Jack and I, Lowie and Frans were the only workers left. Harms and some of the German soldiers were still with us, but their ranks were dwindling, and in the days to follow, I noticed that the soldiers were getting jumpy. They knew they were losing the war and it was not unusual to see the soldiers wearing heavy backpacks, or carrying a small suitcase with them everywhere they went. By keeping a change of civilian clothes at hand, many soldiers were ready to quickly rid themselves of any identification with the German army. They hoped to escape capture by quickly becoming anonymous civilians. Everybody knew it, but nobody cared.

In the meantime, we carried on with the jobs at hand. We continued to keep our tools and equipment in the small utility trailer that we hauled behind one of the trucks. It was incredibly useful as we could unhitch it, and manhandle it into a field or other cumbersome work spot that we could not reach with a truck. To avoid thefts, Harms gave instructions to Lowie and me to build a cover for the open trailer. We located some steel rods in a local barn and acquired them in darkness one evening. Lowie heated them and we used a truck wheel to get the same arc on all four of the rods. When we were done, we lashed a tarp over them and had a covered wagon effect on the trailer.

~

With soldiers and civilians leaving the unit so frequently, Jack and I decided we had to have an escape plan if we were going to get back to Holland alive. "We need a truck, ready to go," I said, "and it will be easier if we take the one that runs on gasoline." Our other trucks were either diesel or ran on wood gasifiers. "I agree," responded Jack "and if we're going to use that truck, we better have lots of gas with us. Gasoline is rationed and won't be available once we get into the country. We'll need that trailer as well."

We worked hard to prepare for our escape. We always had an ample supply of gasoline in the unit. When we repaired a gasoline vehicle in the field we were required to fill it up before sending it back. "We don't have any work anymore and our gasoline supply has barely been touched," I said. "We could take some out of the supply and it wouldn't even be noticed."

Being careful not to draw attention to ourselves, that is exactly what we did. Throughout the day, we stole cans of gas from the supply wagon. At night, without any light, not even a lantern, we secretly dug foxhole size trenches in the adjacent fields, and buried the gas cans with a marker so we could find them again.

Just about the time that we figured we had stashed enough gasoline for our journey westward, we awoke one morning to discover the soldiers had disappeared. Jack and I, with our Belgian friends Lowie and Frans, were the only ones left. Harms and all the soldiers had left overnight, including the kitchen staff. They had taken the only truck we had that ran on gasoline and the trailer: our tools, useless to us now, were lying on the ground. Without the gas truck, we had no need for our cache of gasoline; we had done all that digging for nothing. The four of us, however, were none the less exuberant to be free. We hugged, we laughed and we danced about like children. In the absence of Harms and the soldiers, we were no longer under the control of the German army. Our forced labour was over. Our war was over.

But now we had different problems. We stayed on the move but as strangers in a foreign country, we had no idea where we were. Somewhere north of Berlin, we stopped near the town of Pritzwalk. Like any other civilians, we were caught in a war; we were without direction or purpose, without a source of food, and on our own to survive. Leaving Frans and Lowie sleeping in a barn, Jack and I walked a short distance into town. It was not unusual to find military uniforms discarded in the ditches, or left by the roadway. We checked them for money or valuables that we could use as barter for food. I thought it would add to my safety if I could find a gun, but I never found one. The soldier who removed his uniform hoping to become a civilian obviously had the same thought.

Pritzwalk was busy and I felt relaxed to be among people walking about and children riding bicycles. Stopping at a small store, it was nice to feel normal and fit in. They knew however, that we were not locals and they warned us. There was a rumour that there would be some heavy fighting near Pritzwalk in the next few days. With that news, Jack and I understood why Harms and the soldiers had left the area and were gone. We thanked everyone openly for the warning and walked towards the door to leave.

A young woman and her three children stepped out of our way and I realized all four were upset and crying.

"Are you ok?" I asked. She told me that she was terrified that she and her children would be caught in the conflict. "My husband is away in the army and I have no idea what to do," she cried.

"What is your name," I asked. She looked me in the face with tearful blue eyes. She reminded me immediately of the young woman that I was unable to save from the rubble pile in Hamburg. "Sandra," she replied. "I have to protect my children and I am afraid." Like us, she was a civilian caught in a military conflict, and helpless. I felt we had to help her. If she would make us a hot meal, Jack and I would take her home and figure out a way to get her out of danger.

Jack and I walked back to our camp. We fired up an old diesel truck, a Renault, the only one that Harms had left behind, and while Lowie and Frans chose to stay there, Jack and I prepared to head out to retrieve Sandra and her family. Once again, I threw a few items into my old suitcase, jumped into the truck with Jack, and we went back down the road into town. We picked up Sandra and took her and the kids to her little house in Pritzwalk. She made us a meal and afterwards, while the children were playing, we discussed a plan. "My uncle has a farm nearby," Sandra explained, "we could stay in a shed out in the country and avoid being anywhere near the fighting in town."

Sandra and I, along with Jack and the kids in the back, headed out into the country in the army truck. We found her uncle's farm and, after being introduced to an old couple, we settled in and spent a quiet night safely hidden in the shed. We were only a few kilometres from town but to our surprise we did not hear any fighting or gunfire during the night.

~

The next morning, we had a fine breakfast with Sandra's Uncle Friek and his wife. While Jack stayed to be company for Sandra and her children, I went back into town to see what had happened overnight. What a welcome sight greeted me. There were white flags everywhere. There were several trucks and other military vehicles about but they were not German. The soldiers that were present had just arrived early that morning. They were wearing different uniforms. Could they be the Allies? Perhaps they were Russians? I didn't know, and didn't care, but I knew that they were not German.

Suddenly, as if a light had been turned on in a darkened room, I saw now the danger I was in. I was not a soldier and I was in a German army truck. I could be picked up and arrested as a collaborator; or, with so many of them in civilian clothes by now, I could be suspected as having been a German soldier. I needed to get rid of the truck before someone saw me. I left town quickly and with a cloud of dust behind me, I sped down a graveled road into the countryside. Back at the shed, I quickly picked up Jack, Sandra and her kids. We needed the truck to get them home. Cautiously entering town from another direction, we took the side streets to Sandra's home. Once all were safely inside, I took the truck and ditched it in a field outside of town. Sandra was very thankful and fed us a welcome coffee and some cakes. We wished her well, and with her grateful hugs, we said goodbye. Jack and I felt good about helping Sandra and the children and knew that if new soldiers were now in Pritzwalk, without conflict, she and her family would be safe. Walking back to where our last camp was, we discovered that Lowie and Frans were gone. The camp was abandoned. We were alone and had nowhere to go but back into town.

It is hard to describe the mood that had taken over in Pritzwalk. I expected people to be about and busy with their lives as they were the day before. But today was an eerie quiet and there was almost nobody around. The only people moving about comfortably were the new soldiers.

The few people that we saw seemed nervous and were trying to reach the safety of their homes. There was an apparent mood of fear.

"Those people are civilians, not soldiers. Why are they afraid, why are they running to hide?"

I looked at Jack without an answer. But I was sure they had reason to be concerned. After all, no matter what Hitler had promised, and he had promised plenty, Germany was losing, or maybe by now, had even lost the war. Now who was in charge, and how would these people be treated because they were German citizens? Fear of the unknown was scary. I understood that. For the past two years, I had been under the control of German soldiers. I had survived because I understood their rules. I didn't always follow them, but I knew what was expected of me. But, overnight, everything had changed. "There aren't any rules anymore, that's why they're hiding," I said, "and who would enforce the rules if there were any?"

As we walked towards a group of unfamiliar soldiers standing close to their truck, Jack said, "we can't get out of here on our own. Do you think we should turn ourselves in to these soldiers? We're no threat to them. Do you think we should take the chance?" I was a little uncomfortable with Jack's suggestion. By now it was common knowledge that German soldiers had dropped their uniforms and were now looking like civilians - looking like us. We could be arrested as part of them. The only identification I had was my German workbook and driver's licence. But, maybe I could explain who I was and what I was doing there? We took a chance and approached cautiously. Despite the language barrier, they understood that we were civilians in a foreign land. I didn't understand *their* language and I thought, whoever they are, they might help us. We didn't know if they were Russian, Canadian, British or American and we didn't care. They gave us biscuits, chocolate, and even cigarettes. That gesture reassured us that we had nothing to fear. Without knowing who we were, they allowed us to tag along with them about town. I thought that interrogation might come later, and I would deal with that when the time came. But for now, we needed support. Later in the day, most of the new soldiers moved away from Pritzwalk, and when they moved - we moved. We kept a distance behind them so as not to be in the way, but in reality, they didn't seem to care what we did. I'm sure they had bigger problems to face than to be concerned about two wayward souls lost in a new world order.

Chapter 30
The Hunger Winter

Wognum, Winter 1944

Life in Wognum in the last few months of the war was hard. The national railway strike in September was intended to interfere with German supply lines but it forced thousands of rail workers to go into hiding to avoid the *razzias*. That left women and children to go to the countryside on hunger expeditions searching for food. German trains continued to provide supplies to the cities but food deliveries were to feed the soldiers, not the local population. People in the bigger cities were left starving. Those of us living in the country villages were not as bad off. Peter's family shared their stored garden produce with us in the Roemer household and fish was available from family in Medemblik. The stores, however, were controlled by the Germans and our ration allowance was frequently reduced. In October, we were allowed 1400 calories per person a day and, in January, it was further reduced to just 500 calories. In the large cities of Amsterdam, Rotterdam and The Hague, food supplies were almost non-existent. People were literally dying in the streets. For many, the soup kitchens were their last hope, that's how hungry they were. Thousands died.

I continued to visit frequently with Peter's family. Being alone in hardship makes every problem more difficult but sharing ersatz tea and conversation was Elisabeth's way. Jan made frequent trips into Amsterdam with his work and always had something to report on his return. Over tea one evening, with his pipe in his hand, he told us, "The daily food allowance is impossible in the cities if the bakers can't get flour," he said, "and when they don't have coal for the ovens, the flour is of little value anyway. Shoeless children crawl about on their hands and knees looking for crumbs or other morsels of food. For heat," he continued, taking a biscuit from Elisabeth, "the people burn the trim and doors off their houses. Some of the abandoned houses have collapsed in ruin because wooden structure beams have been removed. They have been taking timber from the tramlines in Amsterdam. They remove every second rail anchor for the wood."

"I think that's why the families in the cities send their children to the country. It's the only way they can help them survive," Elisabeth said, with her usual compassion. "I'm not sure what I would do if city parents came to me and asked if I would care for their children. It would be hard to refuse, they are children, but I'm not sure we have enough to be of help. Besides, the children don't know us. It would be traumatic for everyone."

"It's not just the lack of food," continued Jan. "Without coal, there is no hydro in the cities. And, without hydro, there are no pumps. The city sewage systems are plugged up and not working. The canals are filthy, the cities smell and have become unhealthy."

I understood what he was saying because we had similar problems in the country. Without indoor plumbing, many homes had outhouses. The earlier routine was for a business with tanker trucks to make a scheduled visit and empty the pots. But without fuel, the trucks stopped. In many cases, the pots were disposed of in open pits in the back of rural properties. The war was making our life primitive.

"But, there is hope," I said to encourage them. "There is a lady who lives close to Stam's where I work. She keeps a secret radio hidden in her kitchen and she comes into the café eager to share any positive news. I talked with her just yesterday, and she told me that the Allies were through France and had advanced into Belgium. She thinks that the liberation of Western Europe will come soon."

"Yes," said Jan. "I heard that in Amsterdam as well. The soldiers had quite a struggle in Belgium last fall, but the Allies are on their way."

People continued to die of starvation and cold throughout the winter. We heard that an estimated 20,000 people died of starvation across Holland that winter and in the larger cities, undertakers could not keep up with the toll. Corpses were resting in churches until coffins and body transports to the cemeteries could be found.

With food being so scarce in the big cities, many people had to survive on a meagre diet of sugar beets and tulip bulbs. I never ate them, and in the country, we were lucky. But I saw the flyers from the government officials distributing instructions to the population on how to properly wash and peel sugar beets; slice them and cook them for hours. Once softened, they could be mashed into pulp and served as pancakes or porridge. If you had any onions, that would add flavour.

For many people, sugar beets became a normal part of their daily diet as they also replaced the potatoes hoarded by the soldiers. Tulip bulbs were also prepared similarly and eaten to survive. They were generally held to be more bitter and starchy, other bulbs were officially discouraged as they could be poisonous. Sugar beets and tulip bulbs were all there was and were barely sustaining life.

~

The arrival of spring brought a renewed promise of life. The spring breeze warmed our bodies and freshened our minds with hope. Sprouting wildflowers and buds on the trees lifted our energy, and by the final weeks of April, the war was losing its momentum. The Allies were hurtling towards us and we knew that liberation was coming.

By then, the Germans knew they had lost the war and had reluctantly agreed to a plan. The Allies wanted to use bombers to drop food to the starving Dutch people, and needed a commitment that German forces would not shoot at the low flying aircraft. The German commanders of course were concerned that the planes would be armed and would target unprepared troops. As well, some Allied strategists had disagreed with the plan believing that the food drops would be recovered by German forces and used to feed their army. In the end, mutual trust prevailed.

As arranged, many of the surviving Dutch citizens of the big cities made signs and waved flags to identify drop zones. Food was dropped by aircrews for distribution. The sound of the big bombers, once terrifying, was met with joy as they flew low over the cities delivering food supplies. It was like a relief from heaven, but many of the starving couldn't wait. They broke open the cartons and cans and the gifts of food were eaten immediately. In their starved condition, their bodies were unable to process the food, making them sick. Many reacted by vomiting. Some even died.

As the food was distributed throughout the northern provinces, we all received portions of the food drop. I received a few packages of food and eagerly opened an unmarked can. I was grateful and opened it with zeal only to stare within at an unrecognizable red paste. It was the first time in my life, that I had opened a can of tomato soup. I had no idea what it was and I ate the paste right out of the can. It was delicious.

~

In early May 1945, the Allies liberated Amsterdam and the villages of North Holland. For the Dutch, there was now a lot of work to be done. Families everywhere had to be reunited and homes had to be rebuilt. The dikes needed to be repaired, the flooded polders needed to be pumped out and the welfare of the country needed to be restored. But the war was over, we had been saved and our spirits were lifted.

I wondered about Peter. Was he alive? Would he be coming home soon? I missed him so much, but would he be the same Peter who had left two years ago? Would he have changed? I was sure that I had changed - would he still recognize me? The war had surely changed us all. For those answers, I had to wait. I had to get on with rebuilding my life, while waiting for Peter's return.

Chapter 31
ON THE MOVE

Northeastern Germany, May 1945

To keep up with the new army, Jack and I needed transportation. We each had a suitcase to carry and the soldiers made no effort for us nor offered us a ride. Leaving Pritzwalk, we happened to find a small storage yard full of motorcycles. It was a sales dealership with about 30 gray motorcycles. The lot was attended by two German civilians and the presence of enemy soldiers made them nervous. They had no idea who we were and that gave me the confidence I needed. We could have been German citizens held captive by this new army.

"We need two motorcycles," I said assertively as we walked towards the men, "and we need them right now."

Jack and I were travelling home and since Hitler had taken everything from us, we figured that we were at least entitled to some mode of transportation. We made it clear that we were not leaving without the bikes. I picked an English Norton and Jack took a Puch, a German bike. The men remained quiet, watching the soldiers for a reaction. They offered no argument, standing there in dismay, as we rode off on their motorcycles.

Keeping them in sight, we followed the soldiers on our motorcycles, across the beautiful countryside of northern Germany. We had no idea where we were going, but we figured they had a destination so we would tag along with them, hopefully in safety. Besides, they had food. Though they shared it with us at times, it was hardly enough. Always looking for more, we were surprised to see how many German people left their homes unattended, hiding in fear as the army passed through their area. Jack and I gladly took advantage of their absence, and we went into their houses and helped ourselves to eggs, cheese, bread; anything edible we could carry.

~

Travelling with the army was sometimes dangerous. Occasionally they had small skirmishes with German troops who were either not ready to surrender, or not aware that the war was over. Sometimes, they took custody of German soldiers who were hiding to avoid capture. Regardless, we did not want to be anywhere near any fighting. We had just spent two years trying to avoid getting killed during bombing raids and now that the war was officially over for us, we did not want to risk getting shot on our way home. We decided to leave the soldiers and head out on our own for a while.

We stopped, late one afternoon, when we came upon a well-maintained country home. We sat at the end of the driveway and nervously discussed our intentions.

"If you're as hungry as I am," I said, leaning against the Norton, "we could ask for some food or maybe enjoy a meal with them."

"What if they have guns in the house," Jack responded being more cautious, as usual. "They could shoot us in defence, and nobody would know, or even care."

"We have been taking chances and fighting for food for two years. I'm willing to chance it," I said, mounting the bike as Jack followed. He was reluctant, but hungry as well.

The farm had a rough track leading in from the drive but our motorcycles handled the terrain perfectly. We parked the bikes side by side and timidly approached the front porch. We didn't even have time to knock when a commotion inside drew our caution.

"Get back!" screamed Jack, jumping off the porch and following the wall of the house for safety. We had nothing to fear. The noise we heard was the family running out the back door in fear of us. We watched them run across the adjacent meadow. That's how jittery the locals were. With the downfall of the regime, everyone was on their own and everyone was afraid of everyone else. We all were constantly cautious and concerned for our own safety. Feeling like conquerors, Jack and I boldly walked through the front door.

"I can smell stew," said Jack, drawn by the heavenly aroma from a pot on the stove, "and I smell homemade bread."

We had not eaten anything for over a day and we sat at the table to enjoy every mouth-watering bite. We left a kindly worded thank-you note to our absent hosts and, with our appetites satisfied, we caught up with the army once again. They provided us with gas for our motorcycles and we stayed with them for a few more days, realizing that we were not quite as capable of being on our own as we thought. It was exhilarating to be able to ride away from all the difficulties of the last two years and it gave me a newborn sense of freedom.

~

We eventually broke away from the soldiers and were on our own again, but we knew it was vital that we not become too bold or careless. We were still in Germany and were still foreigners. The local people we met did not trust us. And why would they? There was not a thread of accountability anymore. The government had collapsed and nobody was in charge. People were looting everything and anything. There wasn't anyone to complain to. The local police had gone into hiding, leaving no security. People were afraid of the conquering armies: they were afraid of Jack and me, and, they were afraid of each other. As we travelled onward, we often met small groups of displaced people walking along together. Some were homeless because of the bombings and some were just like us, trying to get back to their homes. We avoided these groups. We also did not know who to trust.

~

One of our first nights on our own, we stopped at a farm and snuck into a hayloft to sleep. We thought we were alone and would be safe there. But, sometime during the night, we were awakened by sounds and we stumbled outside in the darkness to realize we were not alone. A figure was standing beside one of our motorcycles. Loudly and in German, he commanded "Get back," as he straddled the Puch. In the dark I was unable to see if the thief had a gun but we didn't want to take any chances. The engine of the bike roared into life and we sadly watched as the rider sped off down the laneway and disappeared in the dark. We had nobody to complain to and if there was an authority what could we say? Somebody had stolen our motorcycle, the one we had stolen? Now it was going to be quite inconvenient. We were two people, with two large suitcases and only one motorcycle, the Norton.

"Now what do we do?" asked Jack with a mixed sense of despondency and frustration. Jack was easily discouraged – being more of a "the glass is half-empty" guy – "we don't have transport: we're alone in the country, in the dark, we don't know where we are, and we don't know where we're going."

We didn't wait for daylight. We just walked away from the barn and down the road together, carrying our suitcases and taking turns pushing the Norton. With the dawn of the new day, our situation brightened with the sun: as we walked past another farm, we spotted a small two-wheeled trailer full of tools in a yard. The owner yelled at us from a window of the house as we stood out front and contemplated our options. Despite his verbal opposition, we did what everyone else seemed to be doing. We needed the trailer to get home and without explanation, we took it. Two grizzly looking strangers and only one timid peasant farmer. What was he going to do? The odds were in our favour. We left his tools and other supplies on the grass but took a sturdy piece of heavy rope out of the trailer. Attaching the trailer to the Norton with the rope, we were happy with our new arrangement and we proceeded on our way; with no authority to stop us, we were free to go as we liked, as long as the gas lasted.

We travelled on country roads. We felt safer on the back roads than on the busier highways, and there were always more opportunities to find food and shelter outside of towns and cities. At times, having the freedom to go wherever we wanted was quite exciting. After two years of our lives being controlled and experiencing the horrors we had seen, those days of complete freedom were a welcome change, and an exciting adventure. We were still not sure exactly where we were; we knew we had travelled eastward with the army and were now somewhere north of Berlin.

We had been on our own for a while and had not paid much attention to road signs or the geography of the area.

It occurred to me that we had not seen many travellers in the last while and maybe it was time to start paying more attention. While we were stopped looking for clues and trying to determine where we were, we surprisingly became aware of the approach of a different group of soldiers. Instinctively, we pulled the bike off the road and hid both the bike and ourselves as we watched them move closer. Now we were uneasy. These soldiers were wearing different uniforms again from those we had been traveling with before. We realized we had travelled so far east that we were possibly quite near the Polish border. We were going in the wrong direction.

"I think they could be the Russians," said Jack. We never knew which army we were dealing with.

"I agree, and if they are Russians, we could be in danger," I said. "We don't know how they'll treat German civilians, and if they think we're soldiers, they might kill us. I don't think we should wait around to find out."

We hid until the soldiers had safely passed and we headed back from where we had come. This had been an exciting time, but it was now time to focus. We turned around, to go west to Hamburg, and then onto Holland. We both had family to get back to and it was time to concentrate on getting back home.

Chapter 32
Vengeance

Northeastern Germany, May 1945

The sight of two men on the same motorcycle, pulling a trailer with only a couple of suitcases on it and tied to the motorcycle with a piece of rope, would appear comical in any other time and in any other context. But in our world at that time, nothing was normal. On the first night of our journey westward, the sky became black and ominous as evening approached - a storm was brewing. We hoped to find shelter in a barn or an old shed, but we were just outside of a small town when the skies opened up and it started to pour. Driving in the pouring rain was uncomfortable and dangerous, so we had to adapt. Jack found a phone booth on a side street. "It's not ideal, but it's all we have," said Jack.

It was hot, humid and steamy inside the booth but it was shelter from the constant rain. If we left the door open we could get some fresh air but one of us would get wet. It was a small space for both of us. As the evening wore on and the storm raged outside, we realized we would be spending most of the night in the booth. We improvised using a small wooden crate from the trailer as a stool so one of us could sit and sleep while the other stayed awake, standing and watching over our motorcycle. It was a long uncomfortable night trying to stay dry while keeping our bike and trailer safe.

We knew that we were going in the right direction, hoping that the Allies were somewhere west of us. The freedom of a motorcycle and the wind in our faces felt wonderful as we rolled through the countryside of northern Germany. But we still faced the challenge of finding food and frequently stopped at rural homes to ask for something to eat. Sometimes the farmers were generous and other times we just helped ourselves.

~

One evening we passed a farm with cattle in the field and as we stopped to rest, the grazing animals slowly moved across the field towards us. Watching them, I had an idea. There was an old barn in the field and, taking the bike, I left Jack with the approaching herd. I searched the barn for a pail. The best I could find was a large can. I washed it out using a water pump, and returned to Jack with my prize. After grabbing handfuls of luscious grass from the ditch bank, we stood at the fence as the animals came toward us.

"They appear eager for food, Jack. Let one eat from your hands," I said.

While Jack cautiously allowed one of the animals to graze from his hands, I slipped the rope around its neck and tied it loosely to a fence post. I slowly climbed the fence and approached her, running my hand gently across her face. I touched her ears, then her neck and as she got used to my presence, I moved my hand slowly down her side and underbelly. Jack continued to feed the animal while I milked her, filling the large can. That evening, we enjoyed fresh milk with our bread. It was a rich and creamy delight.

"How did you know how to do that?" asked Jack surprised at our fortune.

"I learned as a boy," I said, and told him a story of my

childhood as we bedded down for the night in the barn. When I was a young boy growing up in Wognum, we lived near a local farmer by the name of Luuk Groenen. Old Luuk had about six cows and a horse. I always loved animals and I went to the barn every day to see them. During one of my visits, when Old Luuk was milking, the flies were especially bothersome and the cow kept swishing her tail in Luuk's face. He asked me to help by holding up the cow's tail until he finished the milking. He could tell that I enjoyed being around the animals and I was not afraid. Over time he taught me how to care for and gently approach cows for milking. By the time I was about eleven, I could milk them by myself and I often did. It was a part of my life that I had long forgotten about.

~

Somewhere west of Pritzwalk, we stopped at a farm near the edge of a town. We wanted some food but also were running low on gas. Shutting the bike off at the end of the laneway, I could see a small group of people in the yard close to the barn. Some looked to be crying and all spoke in hushed tones as we drew near. We walked up cautiously and approached the group, although at this point we no longer trusted anyone. Our intention was to see if the farmer had any food or gas to help us out, but nobody stopped or approached us. The barn door lay open and they stopped talking, watching us in silence as we entered the barn.

The barn was empty. Nobody was there. We were about to leave and go back outside to talk with those gathered there, when in the dim light of the darkened interior, I perceived the shadows of things that were out of place. There were things hanging from the rafters. I was confused and I drew closer for a better look. Figures hung from the beams and I couldn't take my eyes off them. I moved closer, my vision adjusting to the darkness. I was overcome by what I saw and reeled back in shock, stumbling into Jack as he stood behind me. He too had seen them.

At the end of a beam, close to one wall of the barn, hung the body of a young boy. The boy looked about ten. His eyes were closed and his face was looking downwards towards me. He appeared as though peacefully sleeping, but the rope around his neck tethering him to the beam told me otherwise. His tongue hung from the corner of his mouth making me want to cry in sympathy, yet scream in anger, at the sight of such youthful death. He hung there silently and around his neck hung a hand-lettered sign, strung across his chest.

On the sign was a simple inscription… # *1.*

Next to him about a meter away, hung another body. This one was a young girl, perhaps in her mid-teens. She was dressed in a nightgown as if awakened in the middle of the night. Her dark hair was neatly turned up in a bun and her face was forward and down. She too was quiet in sleep with her eyes closed.

Another makeshift sign hung from her neck and the bold letters were … # 2.

My mind raced with the terror of it all. Seeing two young children hanging from the beam by their necks was beyond comprehension, and I struggled for an answer. I could see that Jack was as horrified as I was.

"What happened here?" I asked, knowing that Jack had no answer. He did not. He and I, stood there together like statues, frozen in silent witness.

Beside the two children, again a meter away from the girl, swung the body of a woman. A mature attractive woman in her late thirties dressed in a nightgown. Her eyes were shut but her face was distorted in pain. A meter away, hung a fourth and final body. The beam creaked under the weight of a man in perhaps his mid-forties. He wore only gray serge work pants and black rubber boots. His hair was ruffled and his gray felt hat lay sideways on the floor beneath him. Unlike the peaceful look of the others, his eyes were open and the man's face expressed rage. But, like the others, the rope around his neck revealed his death. Around their necks, the woman and the man also had signs dangling loosely across their chests; the man's sign twisted and pulled sideways as though in the final minutes of life, it had been pulled at as part of an act of desperation.

The woman's sign was *# 3* and the man's was *# 4*.

Neither Jack nor I could look any longer. It appeared to have been a small family and the signage revealed a sequence in their story. We left the barn and I felt as weak as a willow. My limbs failed to respond and I was speechless. I was numb, almost hypnotized by the spectacle. Who would hang an entire family, especially children? Why? In war there are civilian casualties. I had seen them. I had removed the bodies and it was tragic. But these children were intentionally murdered, and the barbaric display reminded me that there was no morality in war.

Leaving the barn, we walked down the gravel driveway towards our motorcycle and were stopped by the small crowd of people milling about outside. Everyone was trying to tell us the tale at the same time, as if the flash flood of words in telling the story would cleanse them of what they had seen. I was capable enough with the German language, but still had to gesture for them to speak more slowly so I could understand. One person from the crowd stepped forward.

"Are you all friends and neighbours?" I asked.

"Yes, we all live close by." he replied. "We all knew this family and what has happened here is a tragedy. It is a terrifying shock for us all."

The others in the group stood by without interruption as Jack and I listened to the story. It was a difficult story to hear but more difficult to tell. The man spoke with words of fury and rage while his face revealed tears of compassion. The members of this family were his neighbours. The children of the family were friends of his children, and what had taken place here was unbelievable, even in war.

Three Polish men, in Germany as part of the Nazi forced labour program, had been sent to this German family as farm workers. The farmer and his family were well known in the area. They worked hard and were a tribute to the rural neighbourhood. According to the neighbours, the farmer and his wife were fierce supporters of the Nazi Party. They believed in the superiority of the German race, and considered Polish people to be inferior. They treated the Poles with contempt and often starved and mistreated them. We were told that the workers, upon hearing that the war was over, seized the chance to seek retribution for the suffering that they had endured from the Nazis. They broke into the house during the night and overpowered the family. The parents, bound and held, were forced to watch as their children were brutally hanged in the barn, each child, one at a time. Then, before he suffered the same fate, the husband was forced to witness the execution of his wife.

What kind of treatment did the Polish workers experience here at the hands of this family, I wondered? What hardships drove them to such an extreme act? The macabre scenario was more than an act of revenge. Revenge could be accomplished by overpowering the family and slitting their throats while they slept. This scenario was for all to see. It was a created visual expression of vengeance against the Nazis, and the German people as a whole. The Polish workers had disappeared. Four people had been murdered and there was no system yet in place to deal with crimes like these. No one would be held accountable for these actions.

War-torn and defeated Germany had become a very scary place to be. I had seen a lot of horror and death over the last two years and I believed that nothing much could shock me anymore. But I was wrong. What had taken place here was horrendous, but there was nothing that we could do. Jack and I stood speechless, then turned and just walked away. In a sea of mental despair, we were now lost, and we knew it. Confusion reigned in a world out of control.

"It is time to get back on the main roads," said Jack, "at least there, we will find safety in numbers." I agreed; I knew what he was thinking. Our only hope would be to find the conquering Allied armies. Finding our way home safely would only be through them.

~

The major roadways were jammed with hundreds of people, bodies following each other like a herd of sheep. Homeless people, displaced civilians, soldiers pretending to be civilians, and even soldiers in uniform were spread across the German countryside, all walking aimlessly, hopeless in defeat. Some had bicycles but most were walking. Many had carts, makeshift trailers, or empty baby trams. Some had a destination, while others were wanderers; many with crying children, and some left alone without their children. Highways were scattered here and there with cars, trucks, motorcycles, and anything that was available for transportation. The roads were crawling in both directions as far as you could see. Everyone was lost in that collapsed nation.

On the main highways, we began to see signs posted to help us. The signs were printed in several languages. I could not read the Russian, English, Polish, or the many other signs, but I watched for the Dutch or the German ones. Those signs I could understand. The signs told everyone, that we needed to report to one of the many transit camps. There, we would be fed. There, we would be medically checked for illness and then we would be provided transportation for our safe return to our homelands.

It took a couple of days to get back to the area just east of Hamburg and not having shaved or showered, we must have looked scruffy. People turned away in nervous apprehension as we approached. The main roads had checkpoints established to gain control over the movement of people and at one such checkpoint, the authorities made it clear that we would not be allowed to cross the Elbe River. Alone, we couldn't travel further west towards Holland. Realizing that it was time to turn ourselves in to the military and one of their transit camps, we dropped the trailer from the Norton, and left it at the edge of a sideroad. With Jack sitting behind me holding both suitcases, I operated the motorcycle and followed the signs to the next transit camp. Entering the camp, we stopped at the gate and were told that we had to surrender our motorcycle. The Norton had become a significant part of our journey to freedom and it was difficult to give it up, but it was spiritually uplifting to know that the people here were willing to help us. We set our suitcases aside and took the Norton to a compound. Reluctantly leaving it in the area set aside for incoming vehicles, we were now on foot. We were giving up our transportation such that our ability to return home, hundreds of kilometres from where we were, was now in the hands of the Allied military forces. We picked up our suitcases and followed the signs to the Verwaltungsamt – *Administration Office*.

Chapter 33
Interrogation

Northwestern Germany, late May 1945

In the camp were people from all over Europe. All had survived the war and like Jack and I were trying to get home. One goal of the authorities in the camp was to expose collaborators and deserters now dressed in civilian clothing. I had seen their uniforms tossed into ditches across the German countryside and I was sure that somewhere in the camp they were living among us, evading accountability for the role they had played over the past six years. Who would know them? How could they possibly be found out? That was the challenge of those in charge. It would be quite a feat for the conquering armies to now sort out the lives of hundreds of displaced people. We all spoke different languages, and we all had different stories.

"Well, here we go," said Jack, as we approached the main building. On a billboard at the front door, were signs in several languages, indicating the door to Registrierung – *Registration.*

"Yes," I replied, "and I'm nervous. We will have to justify why we're here."

"We worked in army compounds," said Jack suddenly fearful. "What if they think we were collaborators?"

"Don't tell them you worked for the army."

"That's a lie?" replied Jack; his voice breaking nervously.

"Everybody lies about something," I said. "You don't have to tell them all you know, just know all that you tell. Stick to your story and tell them the same story each time. We worked where we were told to work. We worked in a scrap yard, we built a bomb shelter, we helped on a farm. I'll tell them I had to recover bodies from the rubble in Hamburg. We ate and slept where the army told us to. All they need to know is that we didn't come to Germany because we wanted to. We were forced by soldiers to be here and we had to work here. We were forced labourers."

The transit camp was run by the military and staffed with civilian aid workers to help us get home. That's all we knew and while that was comforting, we were again under the control of soldiers. Most spoke a language we didn't know. They may have been Russian.

Upon entering the *Registration* office, we were shown to a larger room and motioned to join the others. The room was crowded with people of all ages and backgrounds standing in rigid lines. Several interpreters were there, provided by the military, to facilitate communication with us. It was well organized to handle the masses. As we approached the tables, large signs indicated which interpreter we should speak with. You were to select a language and then move into that line. A Dutch speaking interpreter explained to us, that upon coming here, we could not leave. Their rule was... once in - you stay in - until you are released. But first, they had to determine who we were, and why we were in Germany.

We had to answer a few basic questions about our country of origin, why we were in Germany and how long we had been there. While answering the questions, one of the workers smiled and said, "you two are so thin and dirty, you don't look any better than those from the concentration camps." His observation confirmed that we had recently been through several rough weeks in the country but had made the right choice in being there.

After the basic registration questions, it was explained to us that many displaced people, especially victims rescued from the concentration camps, were infested with lice and were suffering from various infectious diseases. A decontamination process was necessary for all newcomers entering the camp. We followed the directions of a soldier who sent women in one direction and men in another. A man and woman ahead of us in line balked at the directions and were clinging together, scared, crying and unwilling to be separated. What had they been through, I wondered. What had they survived? The aid workers knew of the horrible stories of fathers, mothers and children who had entered the showers in the concentration camps and never saw each other again. The aids were calm and guided the pair forward as Jack and I joined others who stepped back and patiently waited. Interpreters and aid workers worked to communicate and encourage the couple that it was just a shower. The husband and wife were taken to the exits to see other couples reunited following the entire process. It was painful to witness and made me thankful that the experiences of my war had not been as horrific as theirs.

Jack and I were taken into a concrete room with at least twenty showers in it. Our clothes were taken away from us and again, interpreters explained every step of the procedure. It was a slow process and many of the men cowered in fear and mistrust. Our clothes would be disinfected and returned to us afterwards. We were each given a small container of a vile smelling soap. Through our interpreter, the attendant gave us instructions. "Be thorough and cover every inch of your body," he said, as he demonstrated with his hands so we would understand. We went ahead and lathered up but the water was not turned on again, until the attendant walked about and checked each one of us to make sure we were fully soaped and scrubbed. The warmth of the water and the cleansing feeling of the soap was a luxury I had not felt in weeks. I wallowed in the feeling and took the full time allowed to enjoy it. After the shower, we were given new instructions. "Shave off all your body hair," the attendant said using a razor in his hand to demonstrate what and where he meant by *all*. As we did so, he walked about patiently to assist in the understanding and to ensure compliance. "But not from your head," he said.

Next, we were given physical examinations by a series of doctors. That was a necessary but humiliating process. We were made to stand naked in a line facing forward, as the doctors walked along in front and behind us. Each doctor had his own specialty and using instruments, they probed and examined everyone to ensure that we were sufficiently healthy to continue.

"What happened here?" asked one of the white coated doctors, as he stopped in front of me and pointed at my protruding chest bone. "A Nazi soldier kicked me," I answered.

"Does it cause you pain or breathing problems?"

"It did for a while, but not anymore." He examined me closer and listened to my breathing. "You are fine," he said, and walked on just shaking his head.

The comprehensive medical examinations took some considerable time and our clothes were not returned until all showering and medical checks were finished. The clothing had been disinfected and returned to us without confusion. Jack and I, still moving together, were sent next to the military police to be interviewed. I felt like a new man as we moved on to another building and another stage of the registration. The room was large and full of people as we sat waiting for our name to be called. Off the waiting room was a hallway leading to several smaller interview rooms. It was a one-on-one interview and a slower procedure but the room that I was sent to was relaxing. A large window allowed me to look out at the pleasant greenery of the countryside and the interviewer sat at a desk in front of the window.

"Take a seat and relax. You may smoke if you like," he said in Dutch, pointing to an empty ashtray on the corner of his desk. I took a seat in a soft chair in front of his desk, but I could not relax, remembering the warnings given to us in Braunschweig.

> *You are now employed by the greatest nation in the world and great things are awaiting you. You must do as you are told. If you disobey, you will be punished. If you escape, because you think Germany can do without you, you will be found and you will not live to talk about it.*

You are now *employed,* the warning said. That word always bothered me but what would it mean to these soldiers?

Even to a Dutch-speaking interviewer, I thought it wise not to mention my role had been working for the German army. They would be looking for collaborators and Nazi supporters. My time in Germany had not been spent under my own free will, but I was afraid that if I appeared to have helped the war effort in any way, my interview might delay my return home. Anticipation of the interview made me nervous.

Following the introductory questions of name, age and country of birth, the interviewer began to probe. "Why are you in Germany?" he asked watching me for hesitation.

"I was ordered by letter to report and I was sent here with other forced labourers from Holland," I responded in Dutch.

"To do what? What did you do?" he asked, looking me straight in the face awaiting my answer.

"I worked in a scrap yard."

"Where?"

"Fürstenmoor."

"Who owned the scrap yard?"

"I don't know."

"Is that all you did?"

"No, sometimes I was taken away to work on a farm and help with the crops."

"Where was the farm? Who owned the farm?'

"Somewhere outside of Hamburg. I don't know, I wasn't introduced. Soldiers just told us what to do."

Further questions were about my work in the scrap yard but they were easy to answer. Our scrap yard had been full of military vehicles to be either repaired or scrapped and, part of my job had been to decide which ones were salvageable. I also had knowledge of the scrap process from my travels to the smelters in Denmark. I focused on every question and responded immediately. Occasionally, the interviewer asked a question in German, as if he had slipped from Dutch by mistake. Having spoken German for two years I was fluent. I knew what he was asking, but I thought it best not to reveal that. They would also be looking for German soldiers masquerading as civilians. I tried to look confused.

The interviewer was very thorough and his questions were quite intense. Eventually, the military police officer accepted the truth of my story and thankfully, I was allowed to move on. I was exhausted. When I returned to the waiting area, Jack was waiting for me. His interview had been shorter. We were assigned to the same building and I hoped they would keep us together. We were taken to a food tent and given a bowl of broth and some delicious fresh bread.

~

Following supper, we returned our bowls and were given a blanket. An aid worker escorted us across the grassy field to a row of buildings. "This is where you will sleep tonight," said the attendant, speaking to us in Dutch and leading us into one of the tar-papered buildings. The long narrow building was similar to the barracks. Bunks were lined against the exterior walls, the space between the beds had a window and a locker. Washrooms were at each end. The building was new and still had a faint smell of lumber and paint, but overpowering that was a heavy smell of body odour. Despite the open windows, the pungent smell of perspiration from the passage of hundreds of men within the exposed walls permeated the air. "Tomorrow we will get you sorted out into a more permanent barracks for your stay," he said. "We don't know yet how long you will be here and you are free to walk about and become familiar with the grounds. But do not leave the camp."

Jack and I took a walk about the camp in the evening. The camp was quite large and held hundreds of people. It was made up of several makeshift barracks such as ours, with tents set up as well to temporarily house everyone.

"I like it here," said Jack as he re-entered the bunk building with me. "Food is provided and we don't have to look for it."

"Yes," I said, "I've almost forgotten what it feels like but, for the first time in two years, I feel safe."

Chapter 34
Fragile Trust

Northwestern Germany, June 1945

Near the military police headquarters there were some large bulletin boards that we were told to check every day. The camp organizers updated the boards daily to provide instructions about living in the camp, and to inform us of any details concerning our journey home. There were always several temporary kitchens set up and, every day at lunch time, we were given a hot meal. The rule was to eat at the kitchen closest to your barracks. The food was simple enough with everything cooked in one pot. It wasn't that tasty and there was never a lot of it but I was relieved to be eating every day, three times a day, without having to hunt for it or beg for handouts. Breakfast was usually oatmeal and fresh bread. Lunch was a stew-like hot meal, more black bread and dinner was a cold handout of bread, with some cheese or meat if it was available. Each meal always came with coffee - good strong coffee. We always had to stand in line for our meals. Sometimes the line was very long so we all just took our spot and waited for our turn to eat. The only exceptions were the survivors of the concentration camps. They were easily recognizable as many still wore their camp uniforms - the only clothes they had. It was an unspoken courtesy, which we all respected, to let those poor souls eat first. They all looked so thin and weak; they had suffered enough. Jack and I were in line for dinner one evening and I stepped back, allowing a woman to go ahead of me. She was poorly dressed in a plain faded smock, like those I had observed in the work camps. I had no idea what language she used, so I spoke softly to her in German, "Go ahead," I said, politely encouraging her to step forward. As she did so, she turned and responded in German, to say thank you.

"Danke," she replied. I responded in German again, in hopes of a conversation. "I'm Peter," I said, and I asked her where she was coming from. Everyone in the camp had a story.

"I'm Anna," she responded with a slight smile, and she went on to tell me that she had been in work camps, near Berlin, and had been left to wander when German soldiers abandoned the camp. She had travelled alone for a time, then made her way to the transit camps, with the help of the liberating soldiers along the way.

Standing in line, I introduced Anna to Jack, and as we were given our meal, I asked her to join us. Instead of taking our dinner to our barracks, the three of us sat together at one of the outdoor tables provided. Anna was quiet and hardly spoke. When she did, she spoke in German, but mostly listened as Jack and I told her of our crossing the German countryside.

"We started out with two motorcycles when we left Pritzwalk," said Jack "but we had one stolen from us."

Anna laughed when I vividly described the two of us on one motorcycle, carrying our suitcases in the little trailer, and I noticed she had a pleasant smile. She looked to be in her thirties. Her brown eyes twinkled and with unusually white teeth she had a beautiful smile. She told us that she and a friend named Greta had been transported west to this camp in army trucks. Her accent made me curious.

"You speak German very well," I said, "but there is something in your voice that sounds Flemish or Dutch."

"I hear that as well," said Jack.

"I speak German most of the time, I also speak Polish and I understand some Russian. But I have a Dutch accent, because I'm Dutch," said Anna.

"Wonderful! We're Dutch as well," said Jack, now wearing an unusually friendly smile. Immediately, her happy face blossomed and she spoke to us clearly in Dutch.

"Oh, I'm so happy to meet you," she said. "I knew there must be Dutch people here, because there are people here from all across Europe. I spoke to you in German only because everyone here seems to understand that language."

"Let's walk," I said getting up from the table. "It'll be more private."

We did. We left the kitchen area - we walked and we talked. I felt comfortable speaking in Dutch and was glad to use my first language in conversation. Speaking and hearing Dutch made me feel closer to home. As we walked, Jack and I told Anna of our work in forced labour. We stuck to our plan and only talked about our work in the scrap yard, leaving out the fact it was for the German army.

Anna was pretty, friendly and she was happy to tell us about herself. "I'm married," she said, then taking a minute to get a grip on her emotions, "my husband and my 16-year-old son were picked up in a *razzia*, less than a year ago. We lived in Maastricht, where I was a nurse. The German soldiers knew I was a nurse - they had access to all the records - and they took me with them, because I could be of some use."

"Where were you in Germany?" I asked, offering her a cigarette, which she declined.

"Many places," she replied. "They kept moving me. They called the camps *Arbeitslagers*, have you ever heard of them?" I nodded like I had heard of them. In reality, I had visited them. I had seen the work camps. But that would be for a different conversation.

Tearfully, Anna continued. "My husband and son were separated from me at the first camp. Then I moved to several camps over the past year, wherever they needed nurses. I was with nurses and other women from Poland, France, Holland and other countries. That's where I met Greta. She is Dutch too. Greta is a baker, that's why she was sent to Germany. I do not know where my husband and son have gone or if they are still alive. I have not seen them since the first camp, and I keep watching for them on my way home."

After such a sad and emotional story, Jack and I did not add anything more to our conversation. We walked Anna back to her barracks in E-Block; we were in C-Block, not too far away.

"I am sad for you and sorry to hear your story," I said stamping out a cigarette under my boot. "It must have been very difficult for you. Perhaps your husband and son will show up."

Jack and I gave her a hug and promised to watch for her in the yard tomorrow. It was a pleasant surprise to talk to another Dutch person, to use our common language and share our experiences. It felt good to give her a hug and feel that somebody cared. I felt a unique connection to a stranger entering my life, a stranger with whom I could identify.

"We didn't tell her too much, did we?" asked Jack, as we walked back towards C-Block.

"No, we stuck pretty close to our plan," I said. "But, I still think we need to be cautious."

"She told us a lot about herself, we were sharing," said Jack. "You don't trust anyone, do you? I think she is a good person."

I had listened to her tell her story, but after two years of betrayals, it was still difficult for me to trust anyone. Meeting Anna was no different. The camp was huge with hundreds of people, and everyone knew that it was a temporary lay-over. "She could be a camp spy," I said. "Her role could be to find and identify German collaborators. We want to get home and if we tell her about our time living with - working with soldiers, she might form the wrong impression of why we are here. If we say too much to the wrong person and cause confusion as to who we are, it could delay our move out of here."

"I hope you're right Jack. Anna does seem to be a nice person." I said. "But to get information, sometimes you have to give information. That could possibly have been her strategy. That's why she told us openly about herself, hoping we would do the same. We have to stay on guard."

I said that with the strangest feeling of confusion. I too had thought Anna was a nice person. She had been warm and friendly with us but the war had taught me to distrust everyone. But maybe Jack was right - maybe I was being paranoid.

Chapter 35
The BBQ

Northwestern Germany, June 1945

We spent our days resting and visiting with others but tried to share only stories about the interesting things that we had done in the last two years. Everyone had endured hardship and wanted to enjoy being free, but you never knew who you were talking to. Too much information to the wrong person could result in lengthy interrogation and delay.

Every morning in the first camp, before our breakfast, Jack and I checked the bulletin board at the barracks. We were told to watch the list for the names of people that would be moved on to the next camp. Each day we were disappointed that our names had not yet appeared, so we waited.

"Did you see?" Jack said, one morning. "Our names are on the board." I was so excited, I ran to the board and there we were. Our names appeared in alphabetical order with a few others. We had been told that when our names were posted, we had to clear our belongings from the barracks and report to the Registration building by 9:00 a.m. We each packed our suitcase with the few things we had and were at the designated spot half an hour early. I watched for Anna in the crowd as we gathered but she was not there. As planned, the trucks rolled up and, when we answered to our name, Jack and I were loaded into a cargo truck with others, and we were moved on.

~

Over the next few weeks we were efficiently moved through several camps staying a few days at each one. The construction of each camp resembled the others and the routines were also the same. At each we had to undergo the decontamination process, further medical checks and were repeatedly interviewed by the military police.

"How many times do we have to tell our story?" asked Jack as we stood in line to be interviewed.

"I don't care," I said, "as long as each interview gets us closer to home. Just stick to our story that we were forced to work in a scrap yard and we'll be fine."

Each time I was interviewed, it became more intense and it felt like less of an interview and more like an interrogation. It seemed that those responsible for finding soldiers and collaborators were looking for any discrepancies in our stories. I was very careful to tell them exactly the same story each time, nothing more: nothing less. I was glad that the soldiers were searching for those responsible for all this, but I hoped that their suspicions wouldn't delay my return to Wognum. Despite the registration process, Jack and I were able to settle in and quickly adapt to the camp routines.

~

At one of the camps we met an interesting man. He was a Dutchman who slept in D-Block, the same tar-papered barracks as we did. His name was Max. One afternoon, Jack and I joined Max and a couple of his friends for a walk around the area. We were out in the country and were now allowed to walk the country roads surrounding the camp. It was a beautiful day in late June. The sun was shining, the countryside was scenic and we were now west of the Elbe river, getting closer to Holland. Enjoying the scenery, walking, and talking was a pastime that was welcomed. We came upon a small German farm with a young pig in a pen, lazily enjoying the warm spring sun.

As we watched the pig rooting around near the fence, our new friend said, "there's a good meal on the hoof right there."

Jack and I agreed. "Yup, it's a fat little pig, just waiting for market," I said, which reminded everyone that our rations at the camps, though appreciated, were small and often left us hungry.

"We don't have to wait," said Max, and he explained that before the war he had worked as a butcher and a cook. "I have an idea," he said, and now he had our undivided attention.

I looked at Jack and recognized his sly grin. I had seen that grin so many times before and I thought, *this is going to be an interesting day.*

We spent the afternoon planning and Max told us what we would need. We all had a job to do but pillaging and scrounging was not new to any of us; being in Germany for the last two years had taught us all some new skills. Jack and I managed to acquire a large piece of canvas from one of the buildings. Max's friends secured an old mattress, which no one seemed to be using and Max himself said he would look after the bait, as he had rescued some potato peels and other vegetable refuse from the kitchen garbage. He had also borrowed a knife.

We set everything aside behind D-Block and waited to execute our plan after dark. It was midnight before we could be sure that the farmer would be asleep, and as planned, we headed out as a team. It was a quiet and very black night and we were glad that, in the darkness, we would not easily be seen. We were not locked in and all we had to do was avoid the soldiers roaming the camp on fire-picket. I still didn't know who they were. They may have been British or American, I didn't know. All I knew was that, even though they could speak German, they were not German. The MPs at the front gate were easily distracted. "What are you guys up to?" asked a sleepy Sergeant, almost startled by our presence. "Just out for a walk," said Jack. "Yeah, we can't sleep," I added, while the others skirted by in the darkness behind the guard shack. As soon as we exited the camp, we hustled down the road to the farm ahead. Cautiously we approached the pen and enticed the young pig with the vegetable peels. We needed to keep him quietly engaged so he did not squeal and alert the farmer. The pig was obviously used to people and did not seem to object to our presence, especially when he saw the food we had for him. Max assured us that if we could just open the gate he would look after the rest, and as the pig happily gorged himself, Jack and I slowly pried open the gate. The unsuspecting animal barely looked up or moved as we came near.

We all stood guard as Max cautiously approached the pig. With speed and the precision that only experience brings, the butcher quickly grabbed the pig's snout with one hand and effortlessly used the other to slit its throat with a knife. The unsuspecting animal dropped to the ground without protest, and we quickly rolled it onto the canvas sheet. Together we stumbled down the road and away from the pen with the pig in the canvas, towards the bush where we had left the mattress.

Off the roadway and out of sight beyond the camp. We struggled in the darkness, to flip the pig out of the canvas and onto the mattress. To burn the hair off the carcass, we set the mattress on fire and stood back. The fire, raging out of control, attracted the attention of soldiers from the camp and as they came running up the road, Max stepped out to assure them that everything was under control.

"Where did you get the pig?" was the only question they asked.

"We took it from a German farmer. He wasn't using it, and besides, it's the spoils of war," said Max in German, as we all struggled against the flames to pull the body from the growing inferno. To our surprise and relief, the soldiers showed no concern.

"Let us know about the barbeque," they said, "we wouldn't want to miss that."

~

In the morning Max visited the kitchen to borrow the pans and everything he needed to cook the pig and serve it up to anyone who wanted some. He cooked it over an open fire all day, and then butchered it with the skill of a professional tradesman. We invited friends, soldiers, and any onlookers who came by to join us and, afterwards, we spent time together enjoying the good company of those around us. For most, it was the first celebration in years. The freedom was wonderful, and in the atmosphere of the partying crowd, I heard a muffled but familiar voice.

"Hello Peter." It was Anna.

"What are you doing here?" I asked, jumping up from the block of wood I was using as a seat beside the fire.

"My name was posted, and here I am," she said anxiously, crowding me back towards the warmth of the lowered flames. "I watched for you at the first camp and was sad to see that you had left. Then, I was posted out but I didn't know where you went or where I was going. I wanted to see the fire and here I am. I am glad to see you again, Peter," she said with a warm and friendly smile.

Jack, Anna, and I sat by the fire for quite a while and talked. We felt comfortable with Anna as she told us about the labour camps and we shared with her our experiences at Fürstenmoor. With my distrust slipping away, I told her about Corrie, my parents in Wognum and how I had been away for over two years.

"I'm from Ursem," said Jack, "and, hopefully, my family is still there."

"We weren't able to send or receive mail since the first year, so we have no idea what's waiting for us when we get home," I added. "We heard some of the news and understand that Holland has been deprived and so many people have died of starvation and want."

"I've heard the same," said Anna. "I hope my family in Maastricht are still waiting." She talked about losing touch with her husband and son. She only hoped that they were not dead. The thought of it made her cry. "Maybe we will be able to make it home some day and again be together," was her only solace.

Jack was tired and with an apology he left us. Anna and I were alone with some soldiers and a few stragglers at the fire. We talked some more as the glow from the embers flickered off our faces. I could see that Anna looked younger than when I had seen her last. She seemed to have regained some vitality in just a few weeks. With the others leaving, I offered to walk her back to her barracks.

"This has been a wonderful surprise," I told her as we walked. "I was disappointed to have to leave you at the first camp and watched for you since. But I gave up after a couple of days. I'm happy that you are safe and here now."

As we walked slowly back to the barracks together, Anna took my hand. At that moment, I felt a warmth and a connection. In my world of distrust and expectation of betrayal, I surprised myself – I let her in. In her company,

I felt safe and secure again. I felt at home with Anna and thought Holland cannot be far away.

Too soon, we arrived at A-Block and as we stood out front, Anna turned and looked at me. "I hope Corrie will forgive me," she said, as she pulled me close and kissed me.

It was a wonderful kiss, a passionate kiss, warm and caring. It was the first time I had kissed a woman since Elfrieda in Hannover, two years ago. Anna's lips were soft and we stood embracing each other.

"It's been a dreadful time," she said. "I was alone, I was always afraid and like the other girls, I just tried to stay out of the way. We lived in constant fear of being sent to the Nazi brothels. I would have died there."

"I've seen things in the past two years that will haunt me all my life," I told her. "For now, we have each other and it feels right. Who knows what tomorrow will bring."

We embraced, kissed some more and then she left me to go inside. As she approached the door, Anna turned, smiled at me and gave me a gentle wave. Then, she was gone. As quickly as she had entered my life, Anna left it, and I never saw her again. But, she left me with a renewed spirit and a desire to move on.

~

The next morning, I was up early and after breakfast I walked to the notice board. We needed to watch for transport and daily instructions. Then, I went to the barracks. "Where have you been?" I asked Jack when I met him. "I didn't see you at breakfast."

"I wasn't hungry," he said, "I wanted to sleep instead." Lack of hunger and sufficient sleep were feelings that I had yet to experience. I knew that we could eat if we were hungry and we could sleep if we were tired. But, with my nightmares of the work camps, uninterrupted sleep was a freedom that I was yet to experience. I envied him.

"Did you hand in your money, yet?" I asked Jack. "It was on the board this morning, to turn in your German money." We both needed to cash-out as instructed, so we went together to the designated building. I don't remember how much Jack had, but I had about 1,000 German marks. In 1945, that was a lot of money for a guy like me and had it not been for my few gambling adventures, I would have had a lot more. We were not paid much but we had been paid every week for two years during our time in forced labour and with the rationing and lack of supplies, there was nothing much to buy while I was in Germany.

The military police had advised us several times, that we would be able to turn in our German money to the authorities at one of the last camps before we crossed the border. German money would be worthless to us once we were in Holland. The receipts now would be honoured later at a local bank and the Dutch equivalence would be paid to us.

"It was good to get rid of it," said Jack as we walked away from the building with our papers in hand. "Now, if we could just find somebody to take away the memories." I knew what he meant. We both had memories that would haunt us for the rest of our lives.

~

The next few days passed lazily in the welcome warmth of July of 1945. I never saw Anna again. I hoped her name was posted and she happily made her way back to Holland. Jack and I eventually saw our names posted on the board and we were moved on to another camp near Bremen. It took several weeks, staying in six different camps, as we made our way home, but we were almost there. Our final camp was in the Province of Groningen, somewhere well inside the Dutch border. At last, we were finally back in Holland.

Chapter 36
Stay in Touch

Groningen, July 1945

Just 150 kilometres away in Wognum, the Dutch were celebrating with the Canadian soldiers. My parents were rebuilding their lives and everyone was thankful the country had been liberated. I didn't know it then, but they were safe. In this, the last camp, I knew I was getting near to North Holland and I spent my days wondering if they were all okay. In Fürstenmoor, our secret radio broadcasts had kept us aware of the war and its general impact on my homeland, but I lacked personal news. I had not heard any news from Holland for two years. The war had been over for two months and still my family would not know if I was alive or dead. Being so close, I was anxious to hear about my family. There wasn't anyone there who knew them as such and could tell me anything for sure. I wanted to get home - I needed to get home.

The Dutch workers in the camp were generally busy with their duties and responsibilities but if you could find them alone at coffee, they would talk about what they had heard of the hard-fought battles and the destruction of the Dutch cities. The conversations were sometimes difficult and you could tell their stories had psychological impact as they remembered family and friends. The discussions that struck me the hardest was hearing from the soldiers how much the Dutch had suffered through starvation and how thousands had died. All that played heavily on my mind and after two years in Germany, it was frustrating to wait when I was so close.

This camp was no different than any of the others. Tar-papered buildings holding hundreds of people and with similar daily meals and routines. Camps like this were built quickly by the liberators, to handle the thousands of displaced people all across Europe. In the German camps, there had been former prisoners of war, released slave labourers like us, political prisoners, Jewish and non-Jewish concentration camp survivors, disabled people, and hundreds of Europeans categorized by the Nazis as being undesirable. But in the Groningen camp, we were all Dutch. We were all almost home. Jack and I were still together, caring for our health and checking the board every day for our final trip home.

Compared to our lives over the past few years, there was one luxury, which was beyond compare - there was plenty of hot water. Every day started with a hot shower and a shave. The feeling of personal cleanliness, together with the experience of clean clothes, was fortifying and I felt whole again.

We did not stay at the last camp for very long. We didn't have to. It seemed that the last camp was a final check on our health and of our readiness to be sent home. Most of us had come a long way by this point. Not only had we travelled a great distance but we had also become mentally and physically stronger. With three meals each day, we were regaining our lost weight. We had been scrubbed clean, medically examined, and well rested for over two months. The Allies were preparing us to return to our hometowns and former lives.

~

On the last morning before we left the camp, Jack had gone over to check the notice board to see if our names had been posted for transport. I was enjoying a walk about the fence line at the edge of the camp. It was summer - the skies were a perfect colour of blue and the sun felt warm on my skin. The fields around the camp were a brilliant green with new crops sprouting. I had not realized that I had walked away from the back fields and become closer to the front property line of a local farmer. My mind was lost in a daze of contentment when suddenly I was slammed with horror and fear. This farmer's dog, seeing me as an intruder, charged the fence and came sliding to a stop not two metres from me. The animal was crouched in a guarded stance, barking aggressively with its muscular body poised, ready to attack. Saliva dripped from its savage teeth and I was terrified - unable to move. I froze as my mind flooded back to the clean-up duties I had experienced in Hamburg. It was the same breed of dog that the German soldier had on a leash in the demolished factory. The same German Shepherd that, on command, had attacked a weak labourer and torn open the man's throat. That haunting memory was terrifying. I forced myself to move - get away and find a quiet place to sit. The fence had kept me safe from the dog but the memory caused me so much mental fear that panic rushed back hammering me like a freight train. I needed time to catch my breath and regain my composure.

To this day, that breed of dog still terrifies me. As a younger man, I wanted to be a veterinarian because I love animals, but I never owned - or wanted to be anywhere around - a German Shepherd dog. The strong memories are too real and I am afraid.

I quickly walked back to the barracks and lay down on my bunk. Shaking and upset, I needed to rest and calm myself. My rest was interrupted by Jack rushing into the barracks with news.

"We're in," he said. "We're going home today." I followed Jack as we both ran to the notice board to double check.

"Yup, we're in," I yelled aloud. "The final truck ride, I can't believe it's happening." I tried to convey that I was excited to be leaving, but my lingering fears obscured it. A part of me was still shaking from encountering the dog by the fence.

We hurried back to the barracks, and I picked up what few personal belongings I had. I threw them into the *Flying Dutchman* and left the building without looking back. The notice on the board told us to stop by the kitchen to receive a bagged lunch and then to report to the main administration building to fill out some final forms.

Throughout the morning we were assembled and re-assembled in ever-decreasing lines, as the groups were sorted by destination. The sun was slowly climbing high in the cloudless sky and the trucking area was a flat field without shade. It was hot and the people waiting were getting impatient as the soldiers called names and directed people to the proper trucks.

"I will never stand in line again," said Jack, spouting his usual frustration. "After months of food lines and now these trucking lines, I'm done," he said. "From now on, I'll sit and watch, then start my own line when it's over."

I laughed at his logic and was thankful for his friendship. He always helped me to regain my emotional strength when I needed it. I also suddenly realized then, that our companionship was in its last day. "We've been through a lot, you and me," I said. Jack turned to me and we both just looked at each other's face, as the last two years flashed by us in a few seconds. It had been a long journey we had shared and I was going to miss him. We had met very early in our war, seen a lot, done a lot, usually together and usually watching each other's back. I took my watch out of my pocket. It was all I had.

"I want you to have this," I said, "and, every time you look at it: every time you want to know what time it is, I want you to remember me, Jack."

"It's your pocket-watch: you can't go without your watch," he said.

"A watch can be replaced, a friend cannot. I'll always remember you," is all I could say.

"I don't have anything for you," he said.

I smiled. "You did give me something… you gave me memories. Good ones; I'll never forget them."

Some trucks backed up to a wooden bumper, and our line started to move. Soldiers were directing us onto the trucks according to where we were going.

"You two, over here," said a soldier as he pointed to a Dodge, idling beside the others with the driver waiting patiently in the cab. Jack and I climbed aboard and joined a half dozen others returning to North Holland. The five men and one woman with us made up our little group, some with suitcases and others with canvas bags. The rear of the truck had wooden benches and we all took our seats facing inwards. It was late July, and very hot under the canvas as we left the camp and started out across the Dutch countryside.

~

Our final journey had begun. Jack and I sat across from each other and rode along in silence looking down as if our feet provided us with some interest. The Dodge truck was loud and conversation was not easy but some of our companions were talking nervously to each other as we jostled along.

"Where are you from?" asked a young man wearing work clothes, sitting next to me. He looked younger than me, hardly old enough to be on his own.

"Wognum," I replied, not wanting a lengthy discussion. "You?"

"Medemblik," he said proudly. "Forced labour?"

"Yes."

"Me too, but I'm only sixteen so I arrived in Leipzig just as the war ended. I was never put to work. I was lucky, I guess."

Nobody was lucky, I thought, as he looked away towards the others on the truck.

As we approached the Afsluitdijk, the geography and landmarks were becoming familiar. Looking out the back of the truck I could see Friesland disappearing behind us. Entering the roadway on top of the dike and watching it run out behind us relieved my apprehensions and I knew I would soon be home. My father had worked on the dam during its construction when I was just a boy. In the early 1930s he was trucking rocks, broken concrete and earth to the site and operating machinery to put the rock base in place. I saw him come home at night after a hard day's work. His hands were cold, his work gloves caked in ice, and I saw that he was strong and dedicated to the job. He was in my thoughts as we drove across the dam and into North Holland.

The truck stopped in Medemblik to allow the boy to jump out, and I wondered if my young friend Willy had made it home safely. A couple of stops followed, leaving only Jack and me on the truck. We sat without talking – our minds in quiet reflection.

I wonder if the mass graves were ever marked, I thought. *I wonder if in time the bodies will be recorded and remembered, or will they be ploughed over and just become part of the German countryside.*

"What will you remember most?" I asked Jack.

He thought for a while and I could see the memories running through his head as he continued to stare at his feet, occasionally shaking his head.

"The motorcycle soldier, I think," was all he said, shaking his head. I knew his conscience bothered him about that night.

"Yes, that was rough," I agreed. "Do you think he was dead?"

"No doubt about it," he said as he looked directly into my eyes. "And we both know that, don't we?" It was more of a demanding statement than a question.

After a few minutes, both of us sitting quietly lost in our own thoughts, he asked without looking up, "what about you?"

I had seen so much over the past two years it was truly an effort to respond. *I've been to hell and back,* I thought. The bodies buried in the rubble, the torture of the innocents in the camps, the life-threatening bombings that we endured, and…

"The barn," I said with emotion choking my voice. "The children hanging in the barn."

Neither one of us could talk about it, we just rode along in silence for the longest time.

"What was the best time, or was there one?" I asked.

With a slight chuckle in his voice, Jack replied proudly, "my overtime sheet that cost me a fine."

I laughed and had to agree. "A day's pay, wasn't it?"

"A week's pay," he corrected me, quickly. "But it was worth it, just so I could show them how much I hated listening to that little prick, Hitler," and again we both laughed at that one.

"You?" he asked. "What was your best memory?"

"Anna," I said without hesitation. "She reminded me that I was still young and alive."

Again, we rode along in silence for a while.

"Are you going to tell your Corrie about Anna?" Jack asked, with a quirky grin.

"Yes, of course" I said, after thinking about her for a moment. "There are a lot of things that happened that I won't tell her, or anyone else, but meeting Anna was a wholesome experience. We were just two ships passing in the night, but she restored my hope for a better future." We rode along, each with our own thoughts, until we heard the driver yell back from the cab, "Wognum's coming up, be ready to jump off and be quick about it. I have to get to Ursem, and then back to my base. I don't want to be out here, lost in the dark."

~

Jack and I had been together for two years and had experienced so much together that saying goodbye was not easy. The truck pulled to a stop and as the driver got out to drop the tailgate, I shook Jack's hand. Without speaking, I climbed down and we stared at each other for the longest minute, as the driver returned to the cab. He found the gear he was grinding for and the truck jolted forward. As it pulled away, I heard Jack holler to me, "stay in touch, my friend," he said, chokingly. I felt the same inability to speak and just waved in return as I stood there watching the truck until it slowly disappeared from view. I felt bad for Jack. He must have felt lonely being the last one in the truck. But, I was glad it wasn't me.

~

I felt the rain on my face first, then, as I looked up to the sky I saw that ominous clouds had rolled in. The weather had changed since we left the camp that morning, but sitting in the back of the truck with a tarped roof over us, I hadn't noticed. The sky now was a gloomy gray and I could hear thunder rumbling in the distance.

My family home was within walking distance: roughly a kilometre from where I was dropped off. How many times had I prayed for this moment to come? And now, here it was and I was confused. I wanted to go home. I needed to go home. I knew that if I hurried, I could beat the rain but my mind was twisted with anxiety. I had been away from home for a long time, and unable to write or receive mail for over two years. I didn't know if Corrie had married, did she wait for me, or was she even alive? And, my family - what about my parents, my brothers and sisters: were they still alive? Was our house still there? I felt panic. My life was returning so quickly and my thoughts were scrambled with fear. I needed to hide, calm down and get a grip for a minute. I was so close but fear of what I might find was holding me back. As welcoming as a lighthouse beacon is to a returning sailor, a familiar sign caught my attention. It was a landmark from my past and I walked across the street towards Café Stam. It had been my favourite place, before I was taken to Germany. There were some good times for my friends and me there. With lots of music, lots of food, and lots of beer, I could always find somebody I knew at Stam's.

I cautiously stepped inside wondering what I would find now. I wondered how much it had changed. Soft music invited me in and I took a seat by the window so I could watch the weather. The rain was pelting against the glass. Curiously, I noted that something seemed different. It was the same café I had been to dozens of times but somehow today, I thought it had changed. It had the same chairs and the same tables, the same sounds and the same smells. But the café hadn't changed at all. It was me; I had been changed by my experiences in the war.

My thoughts were interrupted by the approach of a waitress. "Kan ik u helpen?" she asked. *Can I help you?*

"Een biertje alstublieft," I said, looking up. *A beer, please.* The waitress continued to watch me as she backed away slowly, and in Dutch she asked, "Peter… is that you?"

"Yes," I responded in Dutch with slight hesitation, "it's me." We recognized each other at about the same time. The waitress was my younger cousin.

"Damn, I didn't recognize you," she said. "I know you've been away. What have you been doing?"

"I have been in Germany," I said, trying to control my emotions. "I was sent to work there."

As I sat fumbling through my pockets, I realized that I didn't have any Dutch money. "I got this one," she said, as she watched me digging hopelessly. "The beer is on me. Welcome home, Peter."

I sat there alone sipping my beer, reflecting on the memories that had followed me home. I was saddened to think that the teenage innocence that I had left with was gone. I had seen more than I should have and was forced to do more than I wanted to. But that was the past and our past is what happens to us. It is not always what we plan.

Eventually, staring into my empty glass, I asked myself, *"What are you going to do now?"* The answer came quickly. *"Whatever you want,"* I told myself. *"You are home."*

I stood up from the table and picking up my suitcase I walked towards the door. I could see that the weather hadn't changed. It was the same overcast and light but annoying drizzle as the day I left for Germany.

I glanced back over my shoulder and caught a glimpse of my cousin watching me from across the bar. I gave her an appreciative nod and just as I had done over two years ago when I left, I turned up my collar to the wind, and stepped out into the rain.

EPILOGUE

I listened to my father's stories over the years and recorded them in many ways. Some were written down, others were recorded electronically and a few were locked in my memory. The easy stories came first. He was comfortable with those. Those which were traumatic, he held back. He was hesitant to revisit them and it took time for him to trust me – to trust that I would accept and believe what he had to share. The stories came randomly and were often repeated but the details never changed and so we could add the chronology later. Additionally, he was determined to recognize the others. Although he had witnessed many traumatic events and was forced to do things that haunted him with sleepless memories, he knew that many people in forced labour suffered much worse. Many were starved, abused, and beaten until they died in German factories or work camps. He knew he was fortunate to survive and return home a free man. But, Peter's story does not end there, and I asked him:

"What happened when you got home?"

He told me that by the time he walked from Café Stam to his mother's house, his whole family, a few neighbours and Corrie were waiting for him. The waitress from the café, his cousin, had borrowed a bicycle and sped home ahead of him to let the family know that he was on his way. It was no longer a surprise but it was a welcome celebration.

In the months to follow, Peter went back to trucking for his uncle. He and Corrie renewed their love for each other and made plans to get married. But the Netherlands continued to experience rationing and a lack of supplies after the war. Under those conditions, a store-bought wedding dress was out of the question. They had to be creative. A friend of Corrie's had been married right after the war and her wedding gown was made from the parachute silk of a downed Allied pilot, rescued by the local resistance. With very little alteration, it fit Corrie perfectly.

Their wedding rings were made by a local jeweler who melted the gold from a pocket watch that belonged to Corrie's father as well as a gold chain from Peter's mother. The only payment he requested was a pound of butter, which like gold, was scarce after the war.

~

With their three young children, Peter and Corrie emigrated to Canada in 1952. They raised five children, lived happily together for many years and tried to put the memories of the war behind them. He never shared his experiences with anyone, including Corrie and after almost 60 years of marriage, Corrie died. Now alone, Peter struggled to tell me his stories. As he often told me over the years, "when I allow the memories to surface, so do the nightmares. Sometimes, it doesn't feel real anymore, like I was never there, like those places didn't exist."

I assured him that those places did exist. They existed then and they exist now. I suggested that seeing Germany today with its modern, thriving cities might help to put the past behind him. In 2010, Brad and I accompanied my father in his return to Germany. We criss-crossed Germany by car, visiting the cities of Peter's war, starting in Braunschweig. He did not want to go there. "That's why you have to," I said, encouraging him to face what he described to be the scariest city in his memory.

Pete and Corrie renewed their love for each other

Braunschweig had been a staunchly Nazi city, and the German military had been everywhere. He didn't understand German then and was afraid all the time. In 1943, the locals resented the presence of forced labourers and made it clear they were not welcome. But, walking the streets and seeing the modern city without soldiers and without the swastika banners hanging from buildings calmed him and he was eager to continue. In Hannover, where he met Elfrieda, he talked about how naive he had been and how much pain and punishment came from their acquaintance.

The Hamburg area held the most vivid memories for Dad. He was eager to get to Fürstenmoor, where he had spent most of his time while in Germany. He was disappointed because Fürstenmoor was not on our map. We went to the information booth at the train station in Hamburg, and Dad stood beside me as I spoke to the attendant. "We are trying to find a small town called Fürstenmoor," I said. The attendant was a large man, balding and tall, and with an easy and confident air. At the mention of Fürstenmoor, the man looked at Dad and asked, "why do you want to go there?" Surprised, Dad reacted with a conditioned response to step back when questioned by an authoritative German, but putting his shoulders back, he responded: "I am from Holland," he said, "I was sent there about 70 years ago." Both men stared at each other for a few seconds and the attendant smiled, giving Dad a nod of acknowledgement.

"Ok, I understand," he said. "Fürstenmoor is still here but it is just a bus stop now; it's part of Harburg." He gave us directions - what bus to take and what stop to look for, as we got close.

We found it, but Dad was disappointed when we arrived - nothing looked familiar at first. We walked about the neighbourhood, now a very industrial business area, but when we found the Mercedes Benz plant, he knew it was where the DKW plant had been. From there we determined where the compound had been; now, a corner of busy office buildings. Among the buildings, we found an employee rest area and while sitting at a picnic table, he tried to get his bearings. From there, we walked a short distance and found a dry ditch - his face lit up. "This is it," he said. "This is where the compound was." The bridge was gone but he knew where it had been. He had crossed over that bridge every day to go to the kitchen and suddenly he was back in 1944. He showed me where his barracks had stood and he could guess where the pub and the store had been. The large fence that had surrounded the compound was gone, but he joked about the hole in the fence as he tried to figure out where it had been.

"This is about where Jack and I dug our foxholes," he said at one point.

"I wish I had met Jack."

"You did, he and his wife came to visit us when you were just a teenager."

"That was Jack?" I remembered the day that Dad and his friend stood up at the picnic table and walked away at the loud sound of an airplane.

"Of course, that was Jack, he visited us at home. When the war was over, we stayed in touch just like we said we would."

If only I had known then, what I know now, I thought.

"I'm glad you and Jack stayed friends. Did you stay in touch with any of the others?"

"No, I never saw any of them again. When Jack and I were near Hamburg in 1945, before we found the transit camp, we went to Harms' house. We had been there before so we knew where he lived and we were hoping to see him. His wife Hilda came to the door and told us that

Harms was not home so we left. I had a feeling that he was there, but the war was over and I don't think he wanted to see us."

"What about your friend, Lowie?"

"In 1953, Lowie went to our house in Wognum looking for me. My mother told me in a letter that he was disappointed to learn that we had moved to Canada. I'm sorry I missed him. That would have been a fun reunion."

From Fürstenmoor, we went to Schwerin and Pritzwalk, just as he had done decades earlier. I took his picture

If only I had known then, what I know now

in front of the sign for Schwerin with his hands raised in a cheer. That is where the war ended for him.

For many years after the war, the treatment of Dutch forced labourers was not acknowledged by the Dutch government or the public in general. Dad felt dismissed and, like many, he stopped talking about it. But a final, rewarding part of the trip was our visit to the Overloon War Museum, in the Netherlands. We visited the "Forced Laborers Monument", officially unveiled at the museum in 1996. He solemnly stood amongst the monument's armless and bound human figures. It was overwhelming for him to read that 500,000 Dutch labourers had been sent to Germany and 30,000 had perished. It provided some closure for Dad that the sacrifices of forced labourers were acknowledged and exhibited at the museum. As he walked through the forced labour display, he recognized many documents that he was eager to show me. There was a call-

The Forced Laborers Monument - Overloon War Museum

up letter, a German employment ID card and even a book of timesheets - all of them so familiar to him from long ago. He laughed at the memory of Jack submitting extra hours to his timesheet book for having been made to listen to Hitler's broadcast. There were Nazi propaganda posters and pictures of *razzias* herding men for work in Germany. It was all there; it was all real. I was thankful that he really was able to come to terms with his past - and be free.

"That's why I kept the suitcase," he said. "I knew I had experiences and the suitcase reminded me. You should keep it," he said. "It's empty now. I won't need it anymore."

~

My father died in 2015. The funeral had its tearful moments but there was an overriding feeling of contentment in having known a very humble man - an intriguing man with an amazing life story. He spent over two and a half years struggling to survive in war-torn Germany. And, after witnessing horrors alien to a civilized world, he returned to a life to be remembered and a life to be proud of. At the foot of his coffin, among the flowers and the photos, was his wooden suitcase, *The Flying Dutchman* still faintly visible on the side. Peter's final journey would not be complete without it.

Peter's suitcase

ACKNOWLEDGEMENTS

This book grew from a gradual beginning, following the picnic table visit in 1965. It was several years later before Peter revealed his wartime stories.

There was an earlier edition to Peter's story encompassing his life experiences leading up to the war - his childhood, family adventures and his trucking years. Our thanks to our brother-in-law Jim Cole, who suggested to us to decide on what we want. Is the book intended as a biography, a coming of age story or a wartime experience? Jim's suggestion set us on a defined path.

We are grateful to Theresa O'Donovan and Sheila Kappler, Associate Professors at Brescia University College, London Ontario, for their proofreading of the early draft of this book. Their feedback encouraged us.

We also thank our friends Marianne Brandis and Dean Robinson - authors themselves. They explained to us the strict options of the publishing process: a world of its own.

Chandra Wohleber was introduced to us by Marianne. Chandra and Martin Llewellyn, were our first copy editors.

In 2013, accompanied by Peter, we travelled to the De Goede Herder Church in Zoeterwoude, South Holland.

Mr. Hans Boers, a parishioner, escorted us through the church, the old brick gateway, and the former grounds of the Girls' Home. We viewed a photograph exhibition of the work activities and lifestyle that Corrie, as a young girl, would have experienced while being forced to live there. We express our thanks to Mr. Boers for arranging our early entry to the exhibit, as it was not yet open for public viewing. We also acknowledge the President of Stichting Oud Zoeterwoude (Old Zoeterwoude Foundation), Mr. Jos van der Poel, for allowing us to use their photograph of the old residence and Klooster building.

We are grateful for the partnership we found with our publisher, Tom Bijvoet. Tom is an author, the publisher and the managing editor of De Krant newspaper and Dutch, the magazine. He is the owner of Mokeham Publishing Inc. creating periodicals and books relating to the Netherlands and the Dutch in North America. As a publisher, Tom was eager to produce our book and provided guidance, and friendship.

Special thanks to our son Adam, for his feedback and encouragement. Further, we thank our friends and family members who supported us in the writing of the book. A seemingly minor comment of anticipation was often sufficient to motivate us to move forward.

We are thankful to Peter's sister, Nelle. When she learned of this project during our visit to the Netherlands Nelle told us stories of the many tragic hardships and the sometimes-humorous adventures that she, Marta, Corrie, Peter's brothers, and his parents endured during the time Peter was away. Each alone and as a family together, they weathered the sufferings of living under Nazi occupation.

For her frequent support from the beginning of the first draft to the manuscript becoming a book, we thank our friend Kris Middleton. When in her company, Kris would always ask for a status check. Her eagerness to see the book completed was contagious.

And finally, to our children, and to our grandchildren: our hope is for you to know about the struggles of the forced labourers, the strength of your Dutch family in wartime, and the perseverance it took for your Oma and Opa to survive.

ABOUT THE AUTHORS

Elisabeth Seltzer's story begins in Wognum, North Holland in 1950, five years after the war. In 1952, her family immigrated to Canada, leaving the aftermath of World War II behind them and embracing a new beginning. Growing up, Elisabeth was fascinated by her parents' unique background, sparking a lifelong curiosity about their untold story.

Brad Seltzer's journey led him to a career in law enforcement with the Ontario Provincial Police. Balancing his police work with part-time studies, Brad pursued a Bachelor of Arts degree, later transitioning to a role as a faculty member at Conestoga College. Married to Elisabeth, he was intrigued to share her personal quest to uncover her family's past.

For more than five decades, Brad and Elisabeth have shared their life together. They now live in Stratford, Ontario, finding joy in their family of three adult children and five grandchildren.

Appendices

APPENDIX I

MAP OF THE NETHERLANDS
with places mentioned in the book

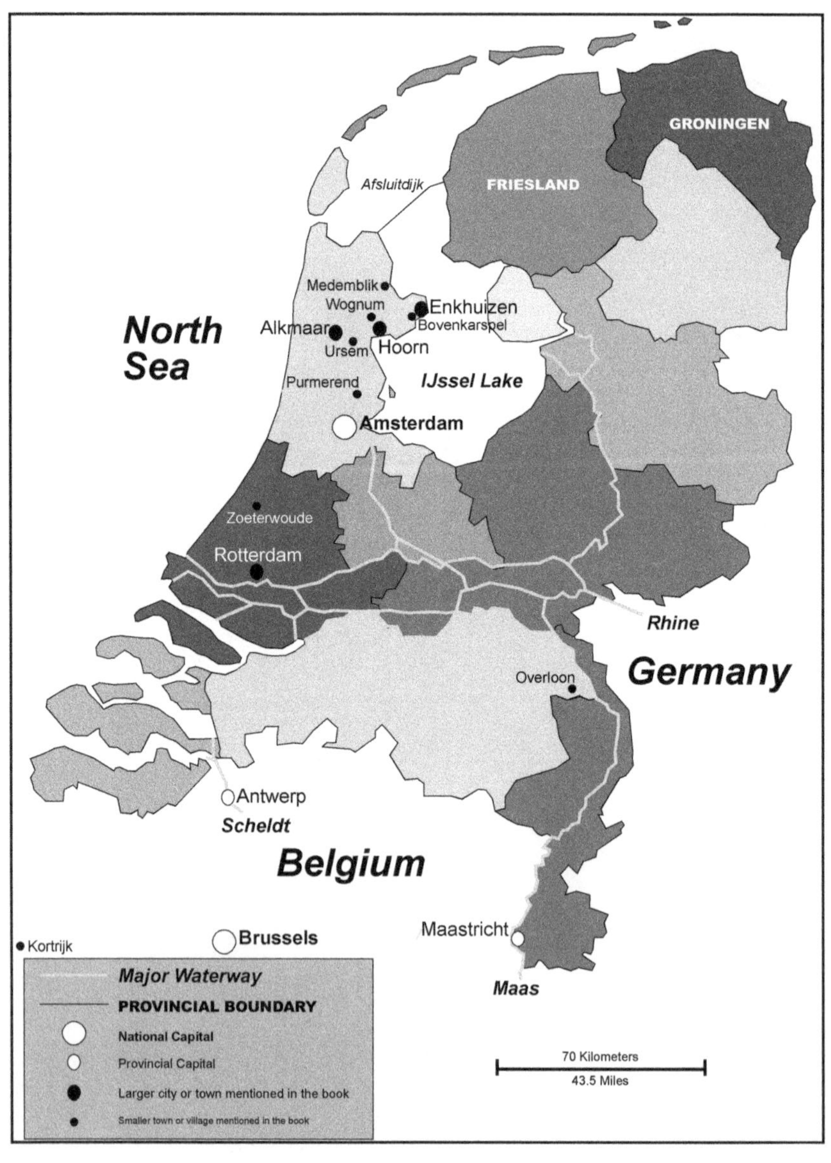

APPENDIX II

MAP OF GERMANY
with places mentioned in the book

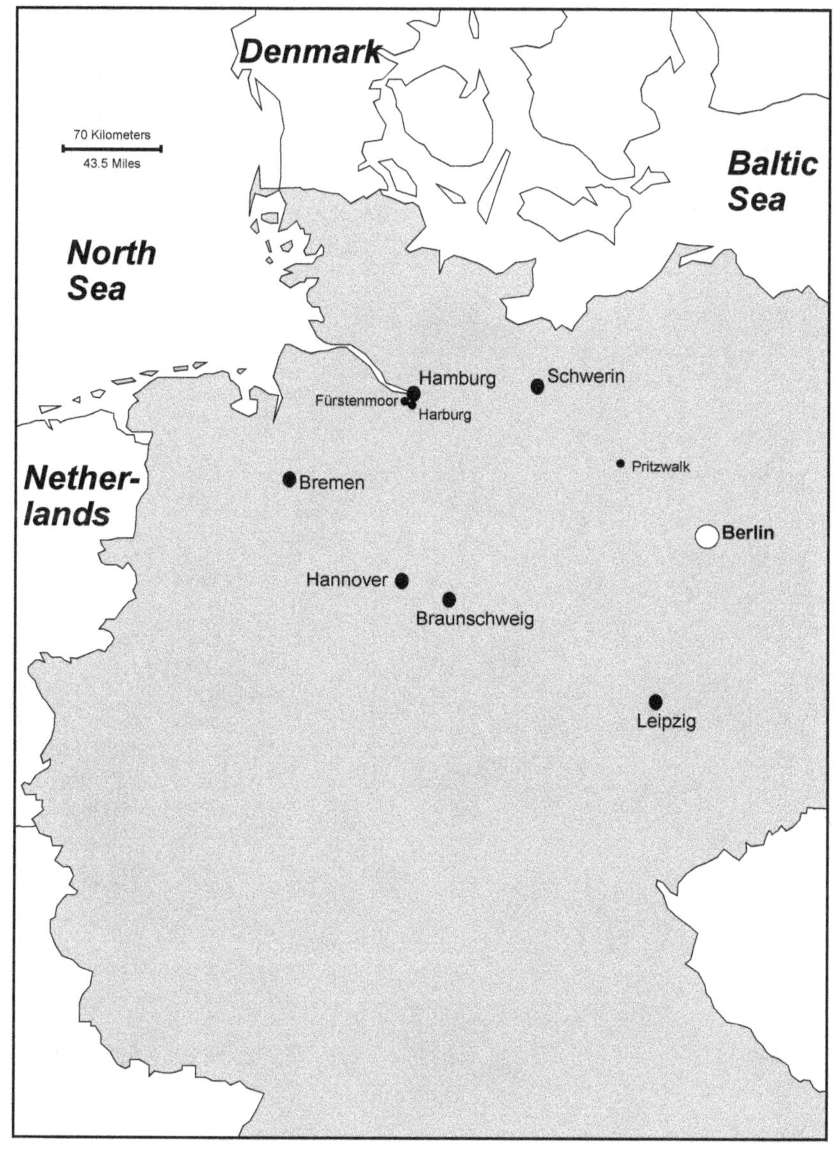

APPENDIX III
The Fürstenmoor Compound

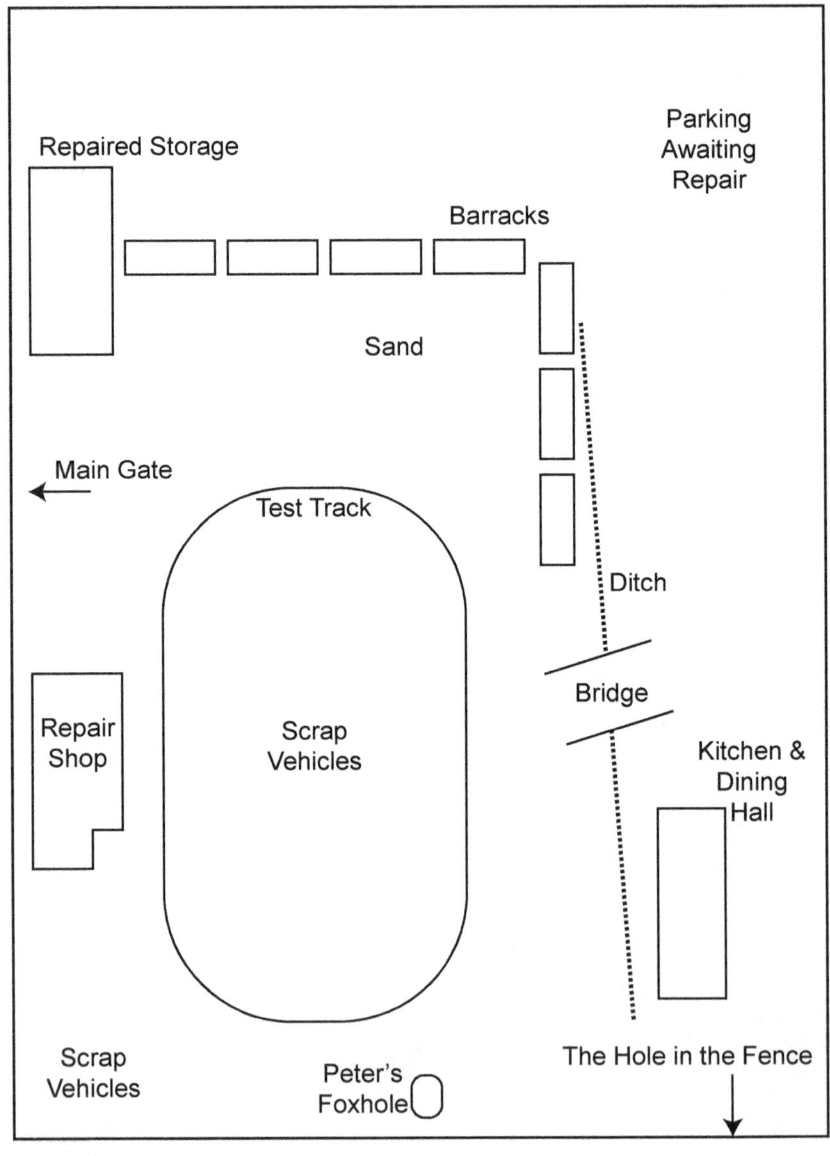

www.ingramcontent.com/pod-product-compliance
Lightning Source LLC
LaVergne TN
LVHW050248310126
830093LV00002B/22

* 9 7 8 1 7 3 9 0 2 3 2 1 8 *